Vernacular Religion

Vernacular Religion

Cultural Politics, Community Belonging, and Personal Practice in the UK's Nepali Diaspora

Edited by

DAVID N. GELLNER

Published 2019 by
Vajra Books and the **Centre for Nepal Studies UK**
with support from the Religion and Society programme
(www.religionandsociety.org.uk)

Distributed by
Vajra Books
Jyatha, Thamel, P.O. Box 21779, Kathmandu, Nepal
Tel.: 977-1-4220562, 4246536
e-mail: vajrabooksktm@gmail.com
www.vajrabooks.com.np

and distributed in the UK by
CNSUK
www.cnsuk.org.uk
email: cnsuk07@gmail.com

ISBN 978-9937-733-04-5

Printed in Nepal

Table of Contents

Tables

List of Plates

Preface

This volume brings together some of the results, previously published in a variety of places, of the three-year project 'Vernacular Religion: Varieties of Religiosity in the Nepali Diaspora' (2009–12; AH/HO15876/1), also referred to as 'VR' below. David Gellner was the Principal Investigator, Sondra Hausner was the Co-Investigator, Bal Gopal Shrestha was the project researcher, Florence Gurung was a funded DPhil student, and both Krishna Adhikari and Chandra Laksamba of the Centre for Nepal Studies UK (CNSUK) were closely involved through carrying out the survey of 300 Nepali households in Britain; another member of CNSUK, Rajubabu Shrestha, also assisted with the household survey. Using SPSS, Krishna Adhikari processed and analysed the survey data that appears, both in tables and in the text, throughout the volume. The collaboration with CNSUK was key to the success of the VR project, as can be seen from the essays collected here, as well as from an article describing CNSUK's engagement with the UK's Nepali diaspora (Adhikari & Laksamba 2018) and from a short film produced by Common Cause (www.youtube.com/watch?v=uaLUDzaEpFI). See also the webpage: www.anthro.ox.ac.uk/vernacular-religion.

The VR project was supported by a Large Grant awarded through the Religion and Society research programme, directed by Linda Woodhead and jointly funded by the UK's social science and arts and humanities funding councils, the ESRC and AHRC (www.religionandsociety.org.uk). In Oxford the grant was administered by the School of Anthropology and Museum Ethnography (SAME). Without the support of all these bodies, as well as that of my college, All Souls, it would not have been possible to see this project through to a successful conclusion. All the participants in the project are well aware that what we have achieved is only to lay the groundwork; far more research remains to be done on many aspects of our subject.

This collection of essays by those associated with the VR project should be read in conjunction with the much larger companion volume, *Global Nepalis: Religion, Culture, and Community in a New and Old Diaspora* (Gellner & Hausner 2018), which was the outcome of a conference, marking the end of the project, held in Oxford on the 9th and 10th July 2012. That conference brought together scholars working on Nepali diaspora populations around the world. While *Global Nepalis* also contains five chapters on the UK (three of them by members of the Vernacular Religion team), its other chapters describe Nepali populations in the USA (three chapters), the Gulf (two chapters), India (two chapters), SE Asia (three chapters), and even Fiji (one chapter). *Global Nepalis* also contains a chapter on the NRN (Non-Resident Nepali) movement and another, by Kathryn March, on the effects of migration on Tamang society back in Nepal (as well as in diaspora), especially on gender relations. In addition to *Global Nepalis*, readers interested in the UK's Nepali diaspora should consult *Nepalis in the United Kingdom: An Overview* edited K.P. Adhikari and published by CNSUK (Adhikari 2012); it is available by emailing cnsuk07@gmail.com.

The essays in this volume focus primarily on the interlocking questions of religious self-definition, the construction of communities, and rituals of everyday practice. The first chapter, an overview of the Nepali diaspora as a whole, appeared also, adapted, as the introduction to *Global Nepalis*. The other chapters all grew directly from the empirical research conducted as part of the Vernacular Religion project. The final chapter, in Nepali, reflects also on the personal experiences of one of the members of the team. Taken together, the articles clearly demonstrate the complexity of Nepali society, a complexity that is reproduced in diaspora as soon as the numbers are sufficient to support it, but which is glossed over and ignored when they are not. The reproduction of divisions and distinctions inherited from Nepal is, of course, an act of re-creation; and, for reasons of diverging contexts, local histories, and changing population make-up, that re-creation is never going to be an exact copy. The different chapters also illustrate the characteristically South Asian, and indeed Asian, tendency towards polytropy at the level of practice, despite all the categorical and political pressures towards unitary religious identity at the level of public performance and community belonging.

Some of the ethnographic observations made in these essays may already be out of date. However, the temptation to update or improve the text of the essays has been resisted (apart from correcting some minor errors, systematizing spellings and references, and other minor adjustments). One term that has been left as in the original publication is 'Kirati/Kirata/Kirat', for which I beg the indulgence of concerned activists; if Ch. 4 were to be written today, the term in the title would be 'Kirat' rather than 'Kirati'. Many population figures are estimates; where estimates vary in different essays, no attempt has been made to disguise the variation.

Some of the summary tables were repeated in different publications in different forms. Rather than repeating them, cross-references have been inserted. In some cases the latest iteration has been substituted (e.g. Table 1.1. includes 2011 census figures, rather than the 2001 census figures originally used). One extra photograph has been added to Chapter 1, which originally appeared in a separate publication not included here; and two photographs taken in 2019 have been added to illustrate Chapter 9.

All members of the Vernacular Religion team deserve thanks for their contributions to all the papers, even where they are not named as authors. In addition, heartfelt thanks are due to both UK-based and other Nepalis, who gave their time and cooperated enthusiastically with research into their religious and community lives.

David N. Gellner
Oxford, April 2019

Contributors

David N. Gellner is Professor of Social Anthropology and a Fellow of All Souls College, University of Oxford.

Sondra L. Hausner is Professor of Anthropology of Religion and a Fellow of St Peter's College, University of Oxford.

Bal Gopal Shrestha is a research affiliate of the School of Anthropology and Museum Ethnography, University of Oxford.

Florence Gurung teaches at the British School, Kathmandu.

Krishna P. Adhikari is a research fellow at the School of Anthropology and Museum Ethnography, University of Oxford.

Chandra Laksamba is a member of the Centre for Nepal Studies UK and affiliated to the Open University Nepal.

Mitra Pariyar is a postdoctoral researcher at Kingston University and a research affiliate of the School of Anthropology and Museum Ethnography, University of Oxford.

Acknowledgements

Grateful acknowledgement is made to the following bodies for permission to republish these essays here: Routledge (chapter 1), *Journal of the American Academy of Religions* (chapter 2), Ashgate (chapters 3 and 4), Toronto University Press (chapter 5), Sage (chapter 6), *Himal* (chapter 7), *Ritual Studies* (chapter 8), Macmillan (chapter 9), and *Diaspora Journalism* (chapter 10).

1

Warriors, Workers, Traders, and Peasants: The Nepali/Gorkhali Diaspora since the Nineteenth Century

David N. Gellner

Defining diaspora

To speak of diaspora implies a scattering of people from a homeland.[1] In the case of the Jews, and other similar cases, this followed a tragic event and expulsion and/or flight. The key event, and the desire for return, were memorialized through rituals. Those rituals become the foundation of collective memory and group identity. In recent decades the term 'diaspora' has been stretched and expanded to refer to any migrant group retaining some memory and some link to their homeland, so that it is no longer possible to insist that diasporas must be born out of suffering and tragedy (Cohen 2008). In this new extended sense,

---

[1] This chapter was published originally in *The Routledge Handbook of the South Asian Diaspora* (Gellner 2013). For helpful comments I would like to thank D.P. Martinez, J. Whelpton, S. Subedi, M. Hutt, C. Laksamba, S. Hausner, T. Subba, M. Sadan, K. Leonard, J. Chatterjee, and C. Stewart.

one can even speak of a British diaspora, since there are still people (in New Zealand, for instance) who idealize the home country and whose identity is grounded in maintaining links to it (ibid.: 69f). There is certainly a Scottish diaspora, encouraged and courted by the devolved Scottish government in Edinburgh. However, it would be an elementary error to assume that everyone with a Scottish surname shares Sean Connery's level of 'diasporic consciousness'.

In the Nepali case, as with the Tibetans—and unlike the paradigmatic Jews, Greeks, or Armenians (all defined by adherence to a distinctive religious tradition)—it would be anachronistic to speak of a diaspora before the modern period and the age of nationalism. Diaspora is not the same as migration *tout court*. There have been continual waves of migration into and along the Himalayas, and this is likely to have been so even in prehistoric times. Within historic times the dominant trend has been for migration to be in a north-west to south-east direction along the Himalayan foothills, so that the Khas people, who are mentioned in textual sources (the Mahabharata among others) as inhabiting Kashmir, are to be found as the 'indigenous' and majority group in western Nepal today. The predominant eastwards direction can be explained by the greater rainfall and greater fertility of the land, the further east one goes (Whelpton 2005: 13). As the Khas moved east they encountered peoples speaking Tibeto-Burman languages who had settled in Nepal (arriving either from the north or the east) much earlier. There have also been plenty of local eddies and counter-currents in population movements alongside the overall macro west-east trend (Dolfuss et al. 2001), with the result that the pattern of ethnic settlement that we have today is thoroughly mixed, not to say Balkanized (Sharma 2008).

For a diaspora to exist there has to be a sense of national or quasi-national (religion-based) identity and the people so concerned must be settled outside the territory with which their identity is bound up. Cultural memories of links to a specific place have to last over the generations (a process much helped if there is continual movement back to that place). Furthermore, there has to be a *boundary*, however conceived. Unless the people are outside that boundary, they can hardly be said to be in diaspora. Where there are no national boundaries—or where the people themselves do not recognize them—they can hardly have a sense of loss at crossing them. The creation of national boundaries in South Asia is still very much a work in progress, a battle that states are waging against ordinary people who are either unaware of them or, if aware, do not much care (van Schendel 2005). It may well be, then, that a 'diasporic consciousness' is more conspicuous or more consistently present in the literary productions of nationalist intellectuals (Hutt 1998) than it is in minds, hearts, and actions of the 'working-class cosmopolitans' who actually move and live abroad. It may also be, as we shall see in the Bhutanese, Darjeeling, and Sikkimese cases, that in order to try and establish themselves in their new host societies people of Nepali cultural background sometimes are obliged to *deny* that they have any diasporic leanings.

Creating Nepal

The modern state of Nepal (though not yet called that) was created in the eighteenth century, largely through the tenacity and strategic vision of one man, Prithvi Narayan Shah (Whelpton 2005). Born in the small hill town of Gorkha in 1722, he became its king in 1743 and immediately travelled to Banaras to buy muskets. Whether or not he anticipated the rise of British power in the subcontinent (as some Nepali historians claim), he was able to create a political unit that dwarfed the tiny kingdom he inherited. At its largest extent, following the conquests of his successors and before the Treaty of Sugauli with the East India Company in 1815, it stretched from the Tista river in the east (now running through Sikkim) to the Satlej river in the west. Thus the Indian divisions of Kumaon and Garhwal (now in Uttarakhand) were under the Gorkhalis for 25 years, a period still remembered for its oppressive rule (Regmi 1999).

The turning point in Prithvi Narayan's career came in 1768-9 with his conquest of the Kathmandu Valley (Stiller 1973; Pradhan 1991; Regmi 1999), which, despite his suspicions of its virility-sapping luxury, he made his capital. It was a wide fertile bowl capable of supporting a higher and denser population than anywhere else in the Himalayas. It was thus an outpost of Indian civilization and a self-constituted sacred centre from at least the third century CE. Its inhabitants were the Newars, an amalgam of local and in-migrating groups ranked in more than twenty castes, with their own language (Newari/Nepal Bhasa) and culture. The new state that Prithvi Narayan created was still quite heavily forested and, by today's standards, thinly populated, but with peace and unification, the population began to grow rapidly. Economically the state was based on extraction of peasant surplus and on taxing trade (Regmi 1984). The main trade routes from India to Tibet ran through the Kathmandu Valley. Some Newar artisans had been invited to move to Gorkha already in the seventeenth century. Others had long travelled to Tibet and were settled, as artisans and traders, in the cities of Shigatse, Gyantse, and Lhasa (some had one wife in Nepal and another in Tibet). The Malla kings of the Kathmandu Valley had provided silver coinage for the Tibetans and gaining control of this contract was one of Prithvi Narayan's motivations for conquest.

No Himalayan migrant peoples thought of themselves as Nepalis before the twentieth century, and for most of the nineteenth century it would have been much more natural to call oneself 'Gorkhali', that is to say, a subject of the Shah dynasty, the 'House of Gorkha' (Whelpton 2008). Their language was also called Gorkhali (an older term was 'Khas Kura' or 'the speech of the Khas'). This was corrupted as 'Gurkha' in British military parlance; often understood as an ethnic term, it is so only in a very weak and extended sense. There is no tribe or caste of 'Gurkhas' in Nepal. In the nineteenth century the name 'Nepal' referred only to the Kathmandu Valley, a usage still current even today in colloquial speech (*(ma) Nepal jane* is the pithiest and simplest way of saying 'I'm off to Kathmandu'). It was not till the 1920s that Prithvi Narayan's descendants followed much earlier British colonial labelling practice and officially extended the term 'Nepal' to all their possessions. This formed part of the first, hesitant steps towards a new nationalist imagining of the Shah dynasty's subjects as 'Nepalis' (Burghart 1984; Whelpton 2005).

Thus, if one were to speak of a Nepali diaspora before 1850, it could only have referred to the Newars, the inhabitants of the Nepal or Kathmandu Valley. In the course of the nineteenth century many Newars became the traders and shopkeepers of the new Gorkhali kingdom and settled outside the Kathmandu Valley in small bazaars and district capitals throughout the middle hills. The Newars are seen by other Nepalis as a trading diaspora, though many are in fact artisans, peasants, and labourers rather than shopkeepers and merchants.

As far as the modern Nepali diaspora is concerned, three distinct waves and types of migration can be distinguished: first, overland, mainly seeking work and land, and mainly towards the east; second, again overland, but more focused on seeking work in Indian cities; and finally, third, travelling by plane to work in the Persian Gulf (or 'arab' as Nepalis refer to it), in Southeast Asia, and beyond, or for education and work in the developed world.

Creating Nepaliness (*nepalipan*) in diaspora

An assertive sense of Nepali national identity first emerged—as has often been the case (the first Greek uprising against the Ottomans took place in what is now Romania)—in the diaspora. Subsequently, in the twentieth century, the ideas and themes of Nepali nationalism—worked out in Banaras and Darjeeling—were taken up by the Nepali state (Onta 1996a; Chalmers 2003). The first writers to think of themselves as Nepalis were scholarly Brahmans in Banaras. There seems to have been a small Nepali quarter in Banaras since at least the eighteenth century and elite Nepalis came on pilgrimage, or stayed in exile there, even before that (Gaenszle 2002b). It was in the 1880s that the movement for

Table 1.1: Ethnic/Caste Breakdown of Nepalese Populations in Different Contexts

<table>
<tr><th>Group</th><th>Nepal, pop'n census 2011</th><th>Proportion of Establishment jobs in Nepal</th><th>Proportion in Gurkha regiments 1894-1913</th><th>Darjeeling 1941</th><th>Sikkim 2005-06</th><th>UK 2009</th><th>Delhi 2000</th></tr>
<tr><td>N=</td><td>26.5m</td><td>1,526</td><td>35,443</td><td>236,434*</td><td>432,198</td><td>18,801+</td><td>402#</td></tr>
<tr><td></td><td></td><td></td><td></td><td></td><td></td><td></td><td></td></tr>
<tr><td>Bahun</td><td>12.2%</td><td rowspan="2">66.3%</td><td></td><td>3.5%</td><td>9.4%</td><td rowspan="2">16–17.7%</td><td rowspan="2">38.3%</td></tr>
<tr><td>Chhetri (incl.Thakuri)</td><td>19%</td><td></td><td>11%</td><td>16.45%</td></tr>
<tr><td>Newar</td><td>5%</td><td>15.2%</td><td></td><td>5.2%</td><td>5%</td><td>3.2–5.2%</td><td>1.2%</td></tr>
<tr><td>Tamang</td><td>5.8%</td><td rowspan="6">7.1%¬</td><td></td><td>18.3%</td><td>9.1%</td><td>2.2–2.4%</td><td rowspan="5">34.3%</td></tr>
<tr><td>Magar</td><td>7.1%</td><td>36.1%</td><td>7.3%</td><td>3.6%</td><td>15.2–17.8%</td></tr>
<tr><td>Gurung</td><td>1.9%</td><td>23.8%</td><td>6.5%</td><td>7.9%</td><td>23.9–24.2%</td></tr>
<tr><td>Rai</td><td>2.3%</td><td>14.1%</td><td>24%</td><td>18%</td><td>11.3–12.5%</td></tr>
<tr><td>Limbu</td><td>1.4%</td><td>13.4%</td><td>7.5%</td><td>13.2%</td><td>13–18%</td></tr>
<tr><td>Tharu</td><td>6.6%</td><td></td><td></td><td></td><td rowspan="2">0.3%^</td><td></td></tr>
<tr><td>Yadav</td><td>4%</td><td rowspan="2">11.1%</td><td></td><td></td><td></td><td rowspan="2">11.9%^</td></tr>
<tr><td>Muslim</td><td>4.4%</td><td></td><td></td><td></td><td>0.01%</td></tr>
<tr><td>Dalit</td><td>13.1%</td><td>0.3%~</td><td></td><td>11.5%</td><td>8.6%</td><td>0.6–1.2%~</td><td>14.1%</td></tr>
<tr><td>Other</td><td>17.2%</td><td></td><td>12.6%</td><td>5.2%</td><td>8.7%</td><td>16.79%</td><td></td></tr>
<tr><td></td><td></td><td></td><td></td><td></td><td></td><td></td><td></td></tr>
<tr><td>Proportion of overall pop'n</td><td>100%</td><td></td><td></td><td>63%</td><td>74.3%</td><td>c. 0.01%</td><td>c. 0.01%</td></tr>
</table>

Categories are not always exactly equivalent. In column one the Dalit figure is controversial; Dalit organizations claim percentages as high as 20% on the grounds that many Dalits are entered as high castes. In column two Bahuns and Chhetris are not distinguished and hill Janajatis are amalgamated, including some 'other' groups. Separate figures for Yadavs and Muslims are not given, but Madheshis as a whole have 11.1% of the top jobs.

Notes
*this was 63% of the total Darjeeling population of 376,369;
¬refers to all Janajatis (except Newars);
~refers to Hill Dalits only;
^refers to all Madheshis;
+number surveyed; total estimated population of Nepalis in the UK in December 2008: 72,173;
#number surveyed, out of a total estimated population of 136,000.

Sources: Nepal census as analysed in Tamang et al. (2014); Neupane (2000) as adapted in Onta (2006); Ragsdale (1990); Pradhan (1982); Tanka Subba (personal communication, based on Govt of Sikkim socio-economic survey, 2005–06); CNSUK survey (see Adhikari & Laksamba 2018); Neupane (2005).

Hindi, led by Harishchandra Bharatendu (Orsini 2002), was getting underway in Banaras, and this clearly stimulated some Banaras-based Nepalis to start producing literature in their own vernacular in order to 'uplift' the language, and to establish it as a worthy vehicle for literature.[2] However, "there remained one overriding limitation of the Nepali literary scene in Banaras: caste and class domination by educated Brahmans who were not reflective of their changing audience" (Chalmers 2002: 90).

In this respect, Darjeeling represented a stark contrast: Bahuns, the priestly and therefore literate caste, were present in much smaller numbers than in Nepal itself (see Table 1.1) but their language became the lingua franca, owned and passionately fought for by Darjeeling Nepalis. One of the key figures was Parasmani Pradhan (1898-1986). His father was a Newar Buddhist (a Shakya) who left home for Banaras and was then sent to sell books in Darjeeling. He adopted the prestigious Hindu surname Pradhan, like most Darjeeling-based Newars. Parasmani was educated in Kalimpong and Darjeeling and became a teacher, schools inspector, writer, publisher, and activist. He wrote quantities of Nepali textbooks, dictionaries, grammars, collections of essays, biographies, translations, and plays. He helped to bring about the standardization of the language and he led the campaign to have Nepali recognized by the Indian state (it was accepted as the teaching language for all primary schools with a Nepali majority in Darjeeling district in 1935, as a national literary language in 1973, and as a national language of India by inclusion in Schedule Eight of the Constitution in 1992).

In Darjeeling migration led to a genuine melting pot—at least when viewed from the perspective of Nepal where caste and ethnic differences were backed by state law until the 1950s. Among those who settled in Darjeeling, tribal languages were lost, many converted to Christianity, and intercaste marriages

---

[2] On the history of Nepali literature (principally poetry and inscriptions) before this period, see Hutt (1988).

were commonplace. Other Nepalis practised circular migration, reinvesting what they had earned in Darjeeling back home in Nepal (Ortner 1990). A strong Nepali consciousness based on the language emerged in Darjeeling (Pradhan 1982, Hutt 2008), although ethnic organizations also existed from the 1920s (Shneiderman 2009: 118, 126-7) and began to assume more importance in the 1990s, as the race to achieve state recognition as an ST (Scheduled Tribe) got under way (Shneiderman & Turin 2006). Thanks to the efforts of Parasmani Pradhan and others like him, "[b]y the late 1930s most of the fundamental questions about Nepaliness had been answered. The Nepali language had adopted a central position in the shared cultural life of Nepalis from different ethnic and linguistic backgrounds. The sense that people from this range of backgrounds could all lay claim to a common identity as 'we Nepalis' had been established and propagated" (Chalmers 2003: 24).

Many Nepalis kept moving, going on to Assam (Russell 2007). As Sinha notes (2009: 15),

> [a] considerable number of high caste Nepalese had moved as herdsmen to the marginal forestlands in Northeast India as graziers. In course of time, they turned out to be the industrious peasant cultivators and pioneering dairymen of the region.

The British made use of the Eighth Gurkha Rifles to put down numerous tribal revolts in north-east India during the course of the nineteenth century (Samaddar 2010: 61), a fact that was not forgotten. With the rise of nativist movements in Assam and the whole of north-east India, Nepalis were

> branded as 'foreigners' and 'migrants'... [and] nicknamed *Dajus* (coolies or porters), *Bahadurs* (chowkidars) and *Kancchas* (household servants). If they raise any demands—literary, political or economic—they are often told to go to Nepal, as the Governor of Assam did recently. (Sinha 2009: 19)

Some Nepalis moved further on to Burma where an estimated 200,000 still live in their own ethnic enclaves as hill farmers among the Kachin and elsewhere, a largely forgotten diaspora (Haaland & Gurung 2007). They are famous as milk-sellers and cowherds in urban areas. When the Japanese invaded in 1942 many fled back to India and Nepal and some even ended up in Kunming in China (Sadan 2007: 237, 239). Some Nepalis migrated even further, whether before the war or because of it, to Thailand, which is said to have up to 100,000 ethnic Nepalis. Today Thai-born Nepalis are increasingly joined by economic and (occasionally) religious migrants coming directly from Nepal, attracted by Bangkok's high level of development (Haaland 2008) and Theravada Buddhist education (Levine & Gellner 2005).

Throughout this period the movement of Nepalis into India, and of Indians into Nepal, was free and unhindered—as it remains to this day, guaranteed in the India-Nepal Friendship Treaty of 1950. (Goods, on the other hand, were and are subject both to state control and systematic smuggling.) Indeed, in the nineteenth century the rulers of Nepal were keen to attract peasants from British India into Nepal in order to open up the Tarai region, just as Bhutan welcomed Nepalis into its southern region. In relation to these southern frontier territories, considerations of lingual or religious nationalism were conspicuous by their absence and were to emerge only in the 1950s in Nepal (Gaige 2009) and in the 1980s in Bhutan (Hutt 2003).

This free movement of people meant that by 1871 Nepalis constituted about a third of the 94,712 population of Darjeeling district. Nepali labour from the adjoining districts had started to be attracted to Darjeeling in the 1850s with the establishment of the tea gardens. By 1941 the population of Darjeeling had grown to 376,369 of whom two thirds were Nepali-speakers. As indicated above and shown in Table 1.1, the ethnic composition of Darjeeling was very different from the Bahun domination of Banaras, and was also significantly different from Nepal as a whole. Whereas in Nepal Bahuns are 13 per cent of the population, in Darjeeling, according to the 1951 census, they were only 5 per cent (Hutt 2008: 114) and according to the 1941 census only 3.5 per cent. By contrast, those now called Janajatis and then known as 'hill tribes'—the Magars, Gurungs, Tamangs, Rais, and Limbus, along with other smaller groups such as the Sunuwar and Thami (Thangmi)—were in the majority (69 per cent or more compared to 40 per cent or less in Nepal). Not surprisingly, given the proximity of east Nepal, Rais and Limbus were present in large numbers. The figures for Sikkim are similar to those for Darjeeling, though Bahuns and Chhetris are more numerous (but still less than their proportion in Nepal). Accurate figures for the ethnic Nepali population of Bhutan are hard to obtain, but it seems that Bahuns and Chhetris were present in considerable numbers, though whether more or less than their proportion in Nepal is impossible to say (Hutt 2003: 94f).

The overwhelming numbers of Nepalis in Sikkim constitute the brute demographic fact lying behind the absorption of Sikkim as the 22nd state of India in 1975 (the combination of democracy and absorption into republican India enabled the majority Nepalis to come to power and sideline the indigenous Bhutiyas and Lepchas). Fear that the same might happen in Bhutan was the key driver leading to increasing ethnic tensions and the expulsion of more than 100,000 ethnic Nepalis after 1990 (Hutt 2003). In this context the Sikkimese and Darjeeling Nepalis have wanted to demonstrate their allegiance to India, and to deflect the charge that they were a fifth column for 'Greater Nepal', so they have wished to downplay their links to Nepal. Some have insisted that they be called Gorkhas, not Nepalis, while others have tried to popularize the label 'Nepamul' ('of Nepali origin').[3]

---

[3] Prem Poddar (2009: 11) comments "I use the term 'Gorkha'... as a self-descriptive term that has gained currency as a marker of difference for Nepalis living in India as opposed to their brethren and sistren in Nepal... While this counters the irredentism of a Greater Nepal thesis, it cannot

Demands for a separate administrative unit for Lepchas, Bhutias, and Nepalis within India go back as far as 1907, but the movement for a separate Gorkhaland state (separate from Bengali domination as part of West Bengal) began in earnest in the 1980s, led by Subhas Ghising and his Gorkha National Liberation Front (GNLF)(Subba 1992). The height of the violence occurred between May 1986 and July 1988 in which over a thousand people are supposed to have died. The bulk of the violence occurred between the GNLF and local cadres of the CPI(M), which opposed the movement, and between the police and the GNLF, but there were also internal clashes within the GNLF (ibid.: ch. 6). In 1988 a Darjeeling Gorkha Hill Council (DGHC) was conceded with powers over primary education, roads, graveyards, irrigation, tourism, and so on; it covered the three hill subdivisions and those parts of Siliguri where Nepalis are in the majority. Subhas Ghising and his GNLF went on to dominate the DGHC until 2008, when Bimal Gurung and his Gorkha Janamukti Morcha (GJM) replaced Ghising. The GJM again raised the demand for a separate state, encouraged by moves elsewhere in India to allow smaller states to be carved out of larger ones.

In 1991 Gorkhaland campaigners destroyed the bust of Bhanubhakta Acharya, the 'adikavi' (founding poet) of the Nepali language, in Darjeeling's Chowrasta, on the grounds that he was a 'foreign poet'. This was a particularly shocking act since it was the Darjeeling Nepalis who had made a hero out of Bhanubhakta in the first place (Hutt 2008: 110; Onta 1996a). Bhanubhakta had been made a Darjeeling hero, Subba writes (2008: 222), because "for every Nepali family in Darjeeling, the Bengalis were a reference group" and the Bengalis had their own national poet in Rabindranath Tagore. In Bhutan the same nationalist and anti-diasporic logic led to Nepali-speakers accepting, to some extent and certain contexts, the official epithet 'Lhotshampa' ('southerner'

completely exorcise the spectres or temptations of an ethnic absolutism for diasporic subjects."

in Bhutanese) and to wearing the Bhutanese national dress while living in refugee camps in south-east Nepal.

The 'brave' and 'suffering' Gurkhas

One of main ways in which Nepalis moved abroad, often deciding to stay there, was through service as Gurkha soldiers. The 1815 Treaty of Sugauli (or Segowli, as the British rendered it) between the British East India Company and Nepal made no explicit mention of the recruitment of Gurkhas, but it was during the war that preceded it that "the British 'discovered' the Gurkhas" (Caplan 1995: 15). The Nepalese regime (for fear of losing its own fighting men) initially discouraged recruitment and would not allow them to be recruited inside Nepal. As they came to trust the British more, and the diplomatic relationship grew closer, the number of Gurkhas expanded.

The British generally recruited from those they (and the Nepalis) considered 'martial races' (Caplan 1995, Streets 2004). In the early years, British and indigenous ideas more or less coincided, so that Kshatriya groups and those allied to them were the main recruits. In the Nepal context, this meant largely Thakuris and Chhetris (as Kshatriyas are called in Nepal) and the associated western tribes, the Magars and Gurungs, who had provided the soldiers of Prithvi Narayan's armies. After 1857 British policy shifted markedly away from north Indian plainsmen, and towards peripheral populations like the Sikhs and the Gurkhas. Within the Gurkhas, this was expressed as a definite preference for Magars and Gurungs. Nepali hill groups began to be seen as 'warrior gentlemen', similar to the British in their hardiness, sense of humour, and not taking religion too seriously—in other words, they were not fanatical like Muslims nor were they ritualistic (and supposedly effeminate) like Hindus. The eastern tribes, Rai and Limbu, were finally accepted as martial towards the end of the nineteenth century. The Tamangs, however, resident principally in the hills around Kathmandu, were not recruited, because the Nepalese elite wished to keep them as their reserve army of labour. Some managed to sneak in by passing as Gurungs (a strategy adopted also by some other ethnic groups not favoured by the recruiters).

From 1908 there were ten Gurkha regiments: the first regiment was based in Dharamsala, the second and ninth in Dehra Doon, the third at Almora, the fourth at Bakloh, the fifth and sixth in Abbotabad, the 7th and 10th at Quetta, and the 8th in Shillong. In all these places Nepali settlements grew up as retired soldiers acquired land or businesses in the areas they knew, preferring to stay on there rather than return to Nepal. More than 200,000 Gurkhas participated in WW1 and over 20,000 died. Of the 11,000 Gurkhas discharged after WW1, only a third chose to return to Nepal, the rest remaining in India (Hutt 2008: 113). It is important to note that in the early and middle years of the twentieth century service in the Gurkhas was not always perceived as the greatly sought-after career that it later became—the pursuit of fame, glory, glamour, and wealth in foreign parts as celebrated in Nepali folk songs. Rather, having one's son sent away by the state was something to be avoided and many sought to hide their extra sons by sending them to the mountains as shepherds or to childless aunts and uncles to pretend to be their only son (Des Chene 1991: 276).

After Indian and Pakistani independence the Gurkhas were split between India and the UK, with the 2nd, 6th, 7th, and 10th regiments going to the UK and being transferred to Singapore and Malaya. It was a shock to Gurkha officers when large numbers of the soldiers in these regiments voted to join the Indian Army rather than continue to be officered by the British (Gurkha histories written by the British tend to explain this by claiming that the men had been 'got at' by agitators, but the real motivation may have been greater opportunity to settle in India at retirement). Des Chene (1991: 207) comments that the British Gurkha regiments had to be reconstructed from scratch in Malaya. A Tripartite Agreement was signed between India, the UK, and Nepal to allow recruitment from Nepal to continue. As the conditions of British Gurkhas gradually improved, and the numbers recruited decreased, it came to be seen as the most attractive option, with intense competition for places. At the same time, there were considerable misgivings from leftist activists, on combined nationalist and socialist internationalist grounds: it was and is felt that Nepali nationals should not be serving in imperialist armies abroad (Hutt 1989). For those, increasingly numerous, who served in the Indian army, there was also the objection that they were serving the regional hegemon, which—to put it at its mildest—could not be trusted to act in Nepal's best interests.

Labour migration to India

Thus far, I have distinguished two waves of Nepali emigration. A first wave occurred, in increasing numbers, throughout the nineteenth and early twentieth centuries. It consisted of Nepalis seeking land and fleeing oppressive tax and labour demands (Pradhan 1991 stresses the latter; cf. Shrestha 1990). They went to Darjeeling, Bhutan, Assam, Arunachal Pradesh, and on to Burma. Mixed in with this diaspora were retired Gurkha soldiers who preferred to stay where they had served rather than return where they would have to face traditional hierarchies of kinship, caste, and clan. Hutt notes that "in this diaspora, as in many others, much of the 'common culture' was constructed after the migrations, not prior to them" (Hutt 2008: 103).

A second wave of migration overlapped with these earlier movements, starting from the 1950s or perhaps even earlier. The distinctive characteristic of this migration was that it was for work in cities rather than in search of land and other agricultural opportunities (work in tea gardens or herding cattle). It started with Nepalis from the far west of Nepali migrating, in a circular fashion, to Indian cities or to nearby Indian districts to work as labourers on roads and building projects. The far west is the poorest and least fertile part of Nepal where seasonal migration for work has long been part of household survival strategies, with those capable of 'eating outside' absenting themselves for six to eight months of the year. They are famous as doormen (*chowkidars*) throughout India (they also work as porters, waiters, and other unskilled labour). Chain migration has meant that specific districts specialize in particular Indian cities: Bajhangis go to Bangalore, for example (Pfaff-Czarnecka 1995). High-altitude populations of Tibetan ethnicity for whom trade between Tibet and the lowlands had been part of their livelihood were also obliged, when the Nepal-Tibet border was closed in 1959, to adapt by spending longer in India, often working as urban peddlers and street traders. Manangis (Nyishangbas), from north central Nepal, were given special permission in the 1960s by King Mahendra to trade in Southeast Asia, though in fact this was a recognition of trading links that were much older (van Spengen 2000, Ratanapruck 2007). Many Nepalis from all over western Nepal have gone to Delhi, Mumbai, and other Indian cities in recent decades (Sharma, 2007, Thieme 2006, Thieme & Müller-Böker 2004). Officially, both India and Nepal insist that one can have only one nationality. Many of their citizens are ahead of them in this, happily holding ration cards and voting in Delhi while also returning to Nepal to vote in general elections there.[4]

The total number of people of Nepali origin in India has often been wildly exaggerated, either by the literary activists seeking official recognition of Nepali under Schedule Eight of the Indian Constitution or by those wishing to legitimate the actions of the Bhutanese state in expelling Lhotshampas. One more sober estimate made in the mid 1990s put the figure at between 1.5 and 2 million (Hutt 2008). Today the NRN organization posts a figure of five million Nepalis in all the SAARC countries (most would be in India).

---

[4] Sijapati (2014) indicates that holding dual nationality in practice without admitting it to the Nepalese state is common among Nepalis in the USA also.

Modern labour and education migration

A distinct third wave of labour migration began in the 1980s and gathered strength in the 1990s, with middlemen and manpower offices in Kathmandu and Nepalganj arranging for men (and a few women) to find work in the Gulf countries (Buslé 2010a, 2010b, 2012a), Thailand, Malaysia, Taiwan, and South Korea. Others managed to migrate on to Europe, Japan (Yamanaka 2000), Australia, New Zealand, and North America, either going to study, or by joining relatives, or by travelling illegally and then claiming asylum. A dark side to this movement of labour migration has been the trafficking of Nepali women to brothels in India, though the extent and the definition of the phenomenon remain controversial (Hausner 2005).

Nepalis are one of the fastest growing ethnic minorities in the UK (Adhikari 2012). A few arrived already in the 1970s and 80s: among them, there are around 300 Nepali doctors working for the National Health Service. Although the 2001 census recorded only 5,943 people born in Nepal, this was certainly an underestimate. The Centre for Nepal Studies UK carried out a detailed survey of 18,801 Nepalis, and a larger more schematic survey of all larger settlements, during 2008 on the basis of which they estimated the total Nepali population in the UK to be 72,173 (the 2011 UK census recorded 60,202 Nepalis in England and Wales). An increasing number of Nepali men serving in the British Army and their families along with a growing number of students, nurses, and other professionals are settling in London, Manchester, Reading, and towns close to army bases (Ashford and Folkestone in Kent, Farnborough and Aldershot in Hampshire—an echo of settlement patterns in India). The first Nepali local councillor (Dhan Gurung, an ex-Gurkha) was elected (for the Liberal Democrats) in 2007 to Folkestone Council. Campaigns for greater UK residency and pension rights have been going on for many years. From 2008 the campaign for all ex-Gurkhas to have the right to settle in the UK was fronted by the actress Joanna Lumley, whose father had been a major in the

6th Gurkha Rifles. In April 2009 the government was defeated in the House of Commons on the issue. The following month it conceded the right for all ex-Gurkhas with four years' service (not just those retiring post 1997 when the brigade's headquarters were moved from Hong Kong to the UK and not just those with 'special personal links') to settle in the UK.

Over 100 Nepali organizations have sprung up. A few are overtly religious, but many more define themselves by ethnicity (e.g. Tamu Dhee [Gurung] Association UK, Thakali Samaj UK, Kirat Rai Yayokkha UK, etc.) or (a more recent trend) in terms of a district or smaller region in Nepal (e.g. Gulmi Zilla Samaj UK, bringing together people from Gulmi district, or the Mauja Bijaypur Samaj UK, based on two villages near Pokhara). Other organizations are simply local community organizations for all Nepalis in a given town or borough of the UK (e.g. Burnt Oak Nepali Samaj, London, Sussex Nepalese Society, or Greater Rushmoor Nepalese Community which brings together Nepalis in the Aldershot and Farnborough area). There are also some professional organizations (e.g. Nepalese Doctors Association, UK, and various ex-Gurkha organizations). In addition there are other organizations that aim to speak for or to all Nepalis in the UK, such as Nepali Samaj UK, Yeti Association UK, NRN-UK, and so on.

Table 1.1 shows that the ethnic/caste make-up of the UK population is subtly different from that in the home country. Dalits, Muslims, and inhabitants of the Tarai are very under-represented; 'high' castes are somewhat under-represented; Magars, Gurungs, Rais, and Limbus—the groups favoured for recruitment to the British Gurkhas—are all over-represented, with the Gurungs' proportion nine times that of their population of Nepal. Ethnic breakdown figures for the USA are not available, but it is likely that there is not the same degree of bias towards Gurungs and other Gurkha groups. It is also very likely that the average levels of education and income is higher among US Nepalis, given that so many middle-class and elite Nepalis go every year to the USA for college study and then stay on to work (the same may apply to Nepalis in Canada, Australia, and New Zealand).

Between them the diaspora in India and the more recent diaspora populations around the world have contributed enormous remittances that have effectively kept Nepal going as an economy through the disastrous lost years of civil war (1996-2006) (Adhikari 2001; Seddon et al. 2002; Graner & Gurung 2003; Singh 2006). This was precisely the time at which export-oriented manufactures (garments, carpets) went into decline, tourism stagnated, and investment in hydro power (for years lauded as the country's future) stalled.

In the 1990s and 2000s a series of diasporas within the diaspora began to emerge, paralleling, and contributing to, the process of ethnicization within the home country (Gellner et al. 2008, Minami 2007). Thus in countries with substantial Nepali populations there emerged organizations speaking for all the major ethnic groups. Since 1990 these ethnic groups are known as Janajatis (the Hindi term that was created to translate the English 'tribe'; Nepali activists prefer to translate the word back into English as 'nationality' following the Chinese nomenclature for minorities). These diasporic ethnic organizations formed international links and networks among themselves (Gurung, Magar, Tamang, Rai, Limbu, Newar, Thakali; latterly Madheshis and Dalits, who are not normally considered Janajatis, have also organized). Alongside these, organizations in which membership was open to all regardless of ethnicity—regional organizations and local organizations (local to the 'host' country), as well as professional and party political organizations, as noted above in the UK example—were very common as well. In all these new associations, the facilitating role of the internet and other new technologies has often been crucial (Bruslé 2012a, 2012b).

Just as the ethnic make-up of the diaspora population is subtly different from that of the homeland, so also religious affiliation is rather different. Nepal was an officially Hindu kingdom from 1962 to 2006, and for long before 1962 Hinduism had formed a central part of the rulers' and the elite's legitimation,

1.1 Gurung Nepalis resident in Britain wait outside the Baptist Chapel next door to Thrangu House in Magdalen Rd, Oxford, on the occasion of the visit of Thrangu Rinpoche on 26 July 2009. (D.N. Gellner)

both in their own eyes and in those of the ruled. Since the late 1980s antibrahmanism has formed a part of the Janajati movement and activists have campaigned for Magars and Tharus (who have no history of Buddhist affiliation) to return themselves as Buddhists in national censuses, rather than as Hindus. Gurungs, who have traditionally had multiple religious affiliations, are now more than ever inclined to return themselves as Buddhists. One consequence of this politicization and ethnicization of religious identity is that while the proportion of Buddhists has risen from a state-encouraged 5.3 per cent in 1981 to 10.7 per cent in 2001, the proportion within the UK population is more like 29.3 per cent, with a further 9.2 per cent saying they are Hindu-Buddhist and 2.3 per cent saying they are Kirant-Buddhist (Chs 2–4, below). Hindus are still the largest single group at 41.4 per cent

1.2 Rais dance as part of the Sakela festival (also known as Ubhauli), held in the grounds of Connaught School, Aldershot, 21 May 2011. (D.N. Gellner)

(roughly half their 80.6 per cent total in the 2001 Nepal census) (figures from CNS-UK survey).

With the blossoming of diverse groups, new coordinating organizations began to appear, both at national and international levels, aiming to bring them all together. A worldwide NRN or Non-Resident Nepali organization was set up at a meeting in London in August 2003 and it was formally launched in Kathmandu the following October. Initial leadership was provided by Upendra Mahato, who had gone to the USSR as a student in the 1980s and is now one of the leading manufacturers of electronics in Russia and Belarus (one of many successful Nepali entrepreneurs in Russia). Thanks to NRN lobbying an NRN Bill was passed in Nepal in August 2007: it defined NRNs as any Nepali living in a non-SAARC country for more than two years, whether holding Nepali or foreign citizenship. By 2009 there were affiliated NRN national associations in 55 countries, including such unexpected locations as Lesotho and Libya. At the Fourth NRN Global Conference in Kathmandu in October 2009 Mahato, having served two three-year terms, stood down and was replaced as President of the Association by Dev Man Hirachan from Japan.

The position of Nepali diasporas varies according to country. The assertiveness and degree of organization on the part of diaspora activists is greater where multiculturalism is favoured, at least in practice if not in official discourse (e.g. in the UK or USA), compared to countries where is more frowned upon (e.g. Japan). The position of Nepalis in India is particularly difficult, because, however many generations they have lived there, they are seen as coming from a foreign country and are vulnerable to vicissitudes in Nepal-India relations (Hutt 2008, Subba 2008). Indra Bahadur Rai, himself an outstanding Nepali Indian poet, writes about another such poet, Agam Singh Giri:

> Giri dealt with the keynote of Nepalese life in India—the search for self-identity. Nepalis are a martial but maligned race; they have all along been fighting other men's battles; it is not at all pleasant to be branded as 'mercenaries of war'. (Rai 2009: 179)

Tanka Subba concludes his autobiographical survey:

> Whether or not to go back to Nepal has never been an issue for consideration of the Indian Nepalis. Most of them are born in India and have no memories—collective or otherwise—of Nepal. They have neither visited Nepal nor do they particularly wish to do so. They may be poor, starving, and living under inhuman conditions in India. They may be harassed and

> humiliated at immigration check-gates or elsewhere in Northeast India. Some rowdy local boys may empty their milk cans or slap them on the street. Yet they cannot think of going back for they have nowhere to go. (Subba 2008: 230–1)

Brubaker (2005: 7) points out that any diaspora worth its name has to last beyond a generation: if second and subsequent generations are wholly assimilated, then it is not a diaspora. Much of the Nepali diaspora in India passed this test long ago. Only time will tell whether the Nepali diaspora elsewhere persists, but the much older diasporas from other parts of South Asia suggest that it will.

2

Category and Practice as Two Aspects of Religion: The Case of Nepalis in Britain

Sondra L. Hausner & David N. Gellner

Introduction: The unitary religion fallacy

In media reports, in state classifications such as census categories, and in most people's ordinary assumptions, faith (a loaded term if ever there was one) is taken to be a singular affair.[1] One is either a Hindu or a Buddhist; a Christian, a Muslim, or a Jew. These accounts have never easily admitted a Newar from the Kathmandu Valley, who, when being asked whether he is a Hindu or a Buddhist replies, "Yes" (Gellner 1992: 41), nor, for that matter, a contemporary London ritualist, who, when asked if he is Christian, shrugs. It would appear to be a defining feature of modernity that, even though censuses have become more sophisticated about ethnic affiliations (allowing multiple and

[1] This chapter was originally published in the *Journal of the American Academy of Religion* (Hausner & Gellner 2012). We are grateful to the UK ESRC-AHRC Religion & Society Large Grants Programme. We would also like to thank the two anonymous JAAR reviewers for helpful suggestions.

mixed responses), both states and citizens subscribe to the popular notion that religious identities must be clear, unitary, and exclusive. No census that we know of allows people to return themselves as Catholic Buddhists or atheist Jews, though it is common knowledge that such people exist.

Social scientists have, if anything, tended to reaffirm the view of one religion per person, one religion per household, or one religion per nationality, focusing research on a particular faith community or adherents of a particular religious tradition in Wales, Leicester, Tower Hamlets, Bradford, or wherever. Political scientists identify entire civilizations with a single religion. Huntington articulates this modernist assumption particularly clearly:

> Even more than ethnicity, religion discriminates sharply and exclusively among people. A person can be half French and half Arab and simultaneously even a citizen of two countries. It is more difficult to be half Catholic and half Muslim (1993: 27).[2]

The West, for Huntington, is that multicultural and secular place dominated neither by ethnicity nor by religion: he admits that Hinduism is the one 'world religion' with which he is not fully acquainted (2002: 14). If he were, he might have understood that religion can be just as blurred as ethnicity.

People in all regions and of all religions have to negotiate multiple and fluid identities. Nepali religion happens to be a particularly good case to make the point: first, it is an exceptionally diverse field, and second, it could be said that religion is integrated into daily life in a more sustained way for a higher percentage of the population than in the West. We use the example of Nepalis in

---

[2] It is possible that Huntington's use of the words 'more difficult' (rather than 'impossible') may indicate some doubt about this claim. But this seems unlikely, given its reassertion—without the question mark—in the book-length version of the argument, *The Clash of Civilizations* (2002).

Britain not because we are advancing any particular thesis about migrant religion *per se* (not here, at any rate), but because migrants must consciously reconstruct their religion in a new environment and thus the tension between category and practice that we describe here is particularly salient for them. But the same processes can be observed in Nepal as well. In short, our main argument about approaches to the study of religion is intended to apply to religion as such, East and West, wherever it appears (or at least wherever there is cultural pluralism).

We see the assumption of singular religion everywhere: the discipline of religious studies, taught in British schools as religious education, combined with a European ethos of pluralist multiculturalism (only recently declared as having failed by both German Chancellor Angela Merkel and UK Prime Minister David Cameron), encourages a segregated (and thereby at least implicitly exclusivist) model of religion. Each 'faith' has its own founder, scriptures, ethics, rituals, or beliefs, each of which fulfils the same requirements in its own way. Singular religions are brought together in inter-faith dialogues, and encouraged to use the same multi-faith spaces. At our own University, staff and faculty of different faith groups were recently invited to participate in a survey, and also to attend focus groups; separate times were scheduled for 'Muslims', 'Atheists and Humanists', 'Christians (all denominations)', 'Hindus and Jains', 'Sikhs', 'Members involved in Inter-faith Work', 'Jewish Members', 'Buddhists', and 'any other interested members'. Promoting wider public understanding of religions is considered a way of more successfully demonstrating inclusiveness, empowering minority communities, and assimilating migrant populations, at all levels of policy and society.

It is time to break up the category 'religion', and to recognize that whenever it is used as if it means only one thing, it is being misused.[3] As Nancy Ammerman remarks, "Paying attention to everyday experience quickly explodes any assumption that religion is always (or ever) one thing, either for individuals or for groups" (2007: 6). As a unitary category, 'religion' is being asked to do too many things in too many discourses, popular and academic. Mark Chaves identifies what he calls the "religious congruence fallacy" (2010: 2), the widespread assumption even in academic study that religious ideas, practices, and values normally all hang together seamlessly. He points out that this is rarely the case, even in the practices of one individual. Hybridity and mixture, blurred boundaries, and a refusal to be either one thing or another—such that one may belong to multiple collectivities simultaneously—is a real, empirical phenomenon, in the spheres of citizenship and ethnicity, where it is well documented, and also, as we argue here, in the sphere of religion.

Thus we cannot refer to religion *tout court* without specifying whether one is referring to religion as a category or religion in practice. Such a distinction is essential (as we will try to show) in order to make sense of two very divergent orders of empirical phenomena: (i) the state's taxonomies or categories of religious identity, and people's subsequent use of them, whether for political or other purposes; and (ii) personal and/or group worship, which usually involves a ritualized practice that may or may not correspond to a putative census or other category. We do not claim that category versus practice is the only distinction

---

[3] Anthropologists have debated the definition of religion since at least the late nineteenth century. More recently, see Southwold (1978) for the argument that religion is in fact a polythetic category: he lists twelve characteristic features, no one of which is present in every case that we would like to designate 'a religion.' In religious studies, Smart (1989) similarly lays out nine dimensions. Other critiques have taken a historicizing approach, examining the genealogy of the modern concept of 'religion' (Asad 1993) and, later, how the discipline of 'religious studies' arose (Fitzgerald 2000, Masuzawa 2005, Stroumsa 2010). For a survey of different disciplinary approaches, see Clarke & Byrne (1993); see also Droogers (2009).

required in our breakdowns of religion, nor that it is sufficient for all purposes.[4] But understanding the difference between category and practice is an essential first step. Religion is such an integral part of so many people's lives—and so remarkably resilient as a feature of human life across time and space—that we need to keep it in sharp theoretical focus, whatever political, cognitive, or social frame we use.

At first inspection, the category of religion may be seen as the religion of the state, or of collective social and organizational structures, while the practice of religion might refer to those activities engaged in by individual people, agents capable of modifying and adjusting exigencies of their daily lives. But collectives, too, engage in practices that may or may not adhere to state categories, and individuals act both to conform to and to evade categories. New religious movements and the charismatic individuals who create them consciously produce new categories that demand new practices. And in some instances new practices that emerge within a religious majority provide fertile ground for mobilizing a breakaway category of practitioners. Taking the category of religion for granted, or assuming it is unitary or easily and unambiguously applied, leads to major distortions and an inability to account for the most basic ethnographic phenomena.

Here we wish to clear the ground for these more complex analyses. Wimmer and Glick Schiller (2003) have labelled the sin of taking *national* boundaries for granted—constructed and recent though they are—as 'methodological nationalism'; in effect, their critique is an updated and specialized version of longstanding and well-established deconstructions of (sociological) essentialism. In a parallel way, what we are attacking here

---

[4] We have written elsewhere on other kinds of distinctions to be drawn. See Gellner (1992; 2001a: chs 3 and 4) for distinctions within the practice of religion, namely those between soteriology, social religion, and instrumental religion. See Hausner (2013a) on distinctions that may be drawn within the category of practice. Experience is arguably a third element of religion that we do not take up here.

could be dubbed 'methodological religionism', i.e. the conceptual error of taking religious boundaries for granted and assuming there is an essence of each religion from which the behaviour and values of its adherents can be deduced. Basing himself on very different kinds of evidence, mainly from north American Christian observance, Chaves has attacked exactly the same mistake. In our terms, Chaves demonstrates that for most people most of the time there is a wide gap between category and practice, notwithstanding the assumptions of academics, politicians, and militant atheists that the two belong together in a consistent whole. Furthermore, he argues—and we would agree—that this disconnect cannot simply be dismissed as inconsistency or hypocrisy. These two fallacies—methodological nationalism and methodological religionism—may be subjected to the same critique, as they both flow from taking the key assumptions of modernity, namely that identity is uniform, universal, and exclusive, for granted. State-based social science instruments to quantify populations (such as censuses and visa records) all tend to view the answers to questions like "Where are you from?" and "What religion are you?" as singular ones. The fact that national and international policies (such as charity status for faith-based organizations or immigration and asylum law) are based upon information derived from such questions may help us understand how it is that assumptions of religious congruence are left unchallenged, despite so much evidence to the contrary.

Thus, members of migrant communities themselves sometimes perpetuate the assumptions of methodological religionism, building new movements around the premise of singular religious belonging.[5] Even as they may be aware of differences between religious practices in 'home' countries and in their new locations, they often actively participate in social processes that reify categories of religious ascription; they

[5] The literature on migration and transnationalism is huge. Basch et al. (1994) and Appadurai (1996) are influential statements. See, e.g., Knott on South Asian diaspora religion in the UK (1991).

Table 2.1: Ethnicity by Religion for Major Categories of Nepali Household Head in the UK (2008), with most Hindu at the left and most Buddhist to the right.

	Ba-Ch (N=418)	Dalit (N=11)	Magar (N=314)	Newar (N=75)	Sunuwar (N=28)	Rai (N=224)	Limbu (N=227)	Gurung (N=437)	Tamang (N=43)	Thakali (N=39)	Sherpa (N=50)
Hindu	92.6	73	58.3	60	39.3	34.8	24.2	12.8	2.3	2.6	
Buddhist	1.9	9	25.2	9.3	10.7	2.2	1.3	64.3	88.4	92.3	98
Hindu + Buddhist	4.9		13.7	9.3	3.6	0.9	1.8	19.5	4.7	5.1	
Kiranti					17.9	34.4	40	0.2	2.3		
Kiranti + Hindu		9	0.32		7.1	15.6	16.3	0.9			
Kiranti + Buddhist			0.32		10.7	6.7	10.1				
Muslim							0.9	1.1			
Christian	0.7	9	1.6		10.7	4.9	4.4		2.3		
Non-religious	0.2		0.32	1.3		0.4	0.9				
Other			0.32					1.1			2
	100%	100%	100%	100%	100%	100%	100%	100%	100%	100%	100%

Note: Ba-Ch = Bahun-Chhetri: the two caste groups were merged in this survey because of the difficulty of distinguishing them by surname.

Source: CNSUK survey, 2008

deliberately and knowingly create and support faith organizations and mobilize around singular religious identities. Expectations and stereotypes about Muslims or Hindus circulate and are reproduced even (and sometimes especially) by Muslims and Hindus themselves in South Asia and in Western Europe, despite the fact that they are fiercely contested within the 'communities' that claim those labels.[6] Even when migrants come from cultural backgrounds that recognize and favour multiple religious allegiances (as in the case of the Nepalis we discuss below), they will likely accept the modernist society's homogenizing and unitary logic of religious belonging and try to work within it.[7]

Nepali Religion in the UK

The importance of the category/practice distinction is best approached by means of a particular example. Nepalis in Britain are a very new ethnic minority. The 2001 UK census recorded only 5,943 Nepal-born people in Britain, a figure which must have been an underestimate. Less than ten years later it is thought that there are approximately 100,000 Nepalis resident in the UK. Nepalis have brought with them an extremely diverse and complex religious history, with very diverse ways of practising religious traditions, some of which can plausibly be labelled 'syncretic' despite the complications inherent in that term.[8]

---

[6] On the parallel and interconnected emergence of modernized versions of Islam and Hinduism in British India, see Van der Veer (1994); for a similar argument in relation to Hinduism, Buddhism, and Jainism, see Brekke (2002).

[7] Processes of creating organizations around categorical identities are by now a transnational phenomenon, but they likely reflect the politics of identity that emerged in the late 1960s (see Taylor 1994 for a much-cited and contested statement on 'the politics of recognition').

[8] On the problems with the category 'syncretic,' see Droogers (1989), Gellner (1997a; 2005), and Hausner (2007b).

Nepali ethnic and religious diversity is illustrated in Table 2.1. Complex though it is, the table is already a considerable simplification for at least four main reasons:

1. only major groups among Nepalis in the UK are included (11 of approximately 68 castes and ethnic groups officially recognized in Nepal are listed here and there are some striking omissions, e.g. Madheshis);[9]
2. there are amalgamations of different caste groups into single categories (Bahun and Chhetri treated as one group; both Dalits and Newars representing agglomerations of several different castes);
3. the different groups are of very different sizes, with the Sherpas, at one extreme, being only 0.68 per cent (154,622 people according to the 2001 census), whereas the Bahun-Chhetri category makes up 28.5 per cent of Nepal's population (more than 6 million people);
4. only a limited number of religious options were open to respondents.

It appears, however, that these simplifications do little to streamline religious designation. In a population of approximately 80,000 people, we have close to 60 cells of religio-ethnic identity, a far cry from the presumed equation of single nationality to singular race or religion.

How are we to approach these diverse kinds of religious identification and the multiple sets of belonging that attach to them? The first thing to note is that ethnic identification, the designations shown across the top of Table 2.1, are a mix of (usually Hindu) caste designations and (often, but not always, Buddhist) ethnic groups. These categories are considered

[9] The relatively new and contested ethnonym 'Madheshi' refers to Nepalis of Indian origin living in the Tarai, the strip of Gangetic plain in the south of the country. For an easily accessible overview of Nepal's castes and ethnic groups, see Gellner (2007).

equivalent identifiers both in Nepali popular discourse and in the census; as with race, they are generally regarded as fixed and inescapable.[10] Until the current generation, most marriages were endogamous and even when they were not, there were rules that ascribed the children to the caste of the father, though often with a loss of status that could be made up after several generations.[11] For most Nepalis the question of which ethnic or caste group they belong to can be stated with precision and without doubt.[12]

The same is not true of religion. Notably in Nepali history, but in other populations as well (in South Asia and elsewhere), religious categories are much more fluid and negotiable than ethnicity. While religious practice is for Nepalis second nature—it was once said of Kathmandu that "there are nearly as many temples as houses and as many idols as inhabitants" (Kirkpatrick 1969 [1811]: 150)—religious categories are not given and obvious; for the majority they must be learned. During the first Nepali census, carried out between 1952 and 1954, the alternatives 'Hindu', 'Buddhist', and 'Muslim' had to be taught both to the people being surveyed and to the census enumerators (Gurung 1998: 94, 2003: 19).[13] Gradually, over the decades, religious

[10] One way—arguably the only way—to viably escape, defy, or transcend these categories is to renounce society by becoming an ascetic (see, for example, Hausner 2007a).

[11] The primary exception here was the tradition that ascribed the children of Bahun fathers and Janajati mothers to the Chhetri caste, from which neither parent had come, a rule which goes part of the way to explain how the Chhetris come to be the largest single caste or ethnic category in Nepal. Many Chhetri men in the past had multiple wives and often only the first was from a Chhetri background; all the children became Chhetris (von Fürer-Haimendorf 1966).

[12] This 'on the ground' reality of social groups is not contradicted by the fact that many of the ethnonyms in use today emerged within recent historical times (on 'Tamang', for example, see Holmberg 1989: 22). In the case of smaller groups not listed here, the process of ethnogenesis is still very much in progress.

[13] Muslims were for the most part already distinct and did not need to be taught that they were not Hindus.

identifications have been internalized and enacted, have bedded down, and have in turn become politically contentious.

On the two poles of the spectrum of ethnic categories shown in Table 2.1, religious affiliation *is* a given: to be Sherpa or Thakali is to be Buddhist; to be Bahun-Chhetri, at the other end, is almost always to be Hindu. For all those who belong neither to the numerically small but strongly Tibetan Buddhist populations found mainly along Nepal's northern fringe and among the Tibetans nor to the dominant Hindu Bahun-Chhetri combine found everywhere all over Nepal, there is considerable leeway and personal choice in religious category. For these Nepalis, the choice of religion has acquired unavoidable overtones of political association. What it means to identify with a particular religious category—'Hindu,' 'Buddhist'—or to enact particular religious practices that are historically associated with those categories—in Nepal, in the diaspora, or in the world at large—has taken on new social and political meanings.

Muslims have settled in Nepal since at least the sixteenth century (Gaborieau 1972) and while there are different, distinct, and endogamous groups within them, they are treated by the Nepali state as if they formed a single ethnic group defined by its religion. Christians are for all intents and purposes a new but rapidly expanding group, drawing converts from all ethnic backgrounds: one could argue that proselytization is a process of introducing new social practices that enable worshippers to cling together through adherence to a single doctrine and a new idea of religious exclusiveness (Gellner 2005). Conversion could be understood as a conscious differentiating of religious practices in order to ground a new category of religious identity, as with the introduction of church attendance, on one hand, and the forgoing of animal sacrifice, on the other.

How Hinduism emerged as a category in India and Nepal

Until May 2008, Nepal was officially designated a Hindu Kingdom—cow slaughter was illegal, the constitution stipulated that the King must be "a descendant of the Great King Prithvi Narayan Shah and an adherent of Aryan culture and the Hindu religion," and ministries were styled 'His Majesty's Government'. All this, however, obscured a tapestry of complex practices—at both national and individual levels—that were not so easily classifiable as Hindu, including shamanism, tribal oral traditions, Buddhism (in different forms), Islam, and a small but growing Christian population. Within the Hindu paradigm itself, the Nepali King sought *tika* or ritual blessing from the child goddess Kumari, who was both a form of the royal tutelary goddess Taleju and the incarnation of the Tantric Buddhist goddess Vajradevi (and who comes from a particular Buddhist Newar caste).[14]

It is true that the word 'Hinduism' as a conglomerate term was a colonial construction, first used no earlier than 1815 and popularized only after 1877, when M. Monier-Williams published his book *Hinduism*. Before 1815, Europeans followed Persian usage: 'Hindus' simply meant 'people living in India'. When religion was in view, they were usually collapsed into the single category of Gentiles, as opposed to 'Moors', or Muslims. Scholars sometimes refer to this early religion as Brahmanism, acknowledging the modal position Brahmans had as religious leaders and exemplars—but more importantly reflecting the fact that we do not actually know much about popular South Asian religiosity for long periods of history.[15]

---

[14] On the Kumari, see Allen (1987 [1975]), Gellner (1992).

[15] See Lorenzen (1999). Also see Lorenzen (1972) on a number of rather more left-wing tantric sects, through which we can clearly see the number and variation of religious practices and categories at work in pre-colonial India. As just two examples, see White (1996) on medieval Nath practices, and Briggs (1973 [1938]) on this particular yogic tradition as observed in the early twentieth century.

With such a long and complex but murky history, it is hardly surprising that many scholars have denied that Hinduism is a religion (von Stietencron 1997) and/or wished to argue that Hinduism was invented by colonialists. As Lorenzen (1999) demonstrates, however, the extreme constructivist position is a mistake: Hinduism clearly did exist and Hindus had a sense of collective identity well before the eighteenth century. They made use of numerous terms that reflected the multiplicity of practices people actually engaged in, including Vaisnava, Saiva, and Sakta ritual traditions (and numerous sub-categories and sects), but they also had an overarching term to refer to all these practices: *dharma*. It is true that was a term shared with 'heterodox' traditions such as Buddhism and Jainism; to specify what we now broadly think of as Hinduism, it was necessary to use the extended but specified term *varnasrama-dharma,* i.e. the religion of *varna* (effectively, caste) and *asrama* (life stages).

That said, it is clear that Hinduism bears little resemblance to religious traditions as usually understood in the West (that Buddhism *did* have such resemblance, and moreover seemed to avoid theistic assumptions, goes far to explain its popularity among Victorians going through crises of faith): Hinduism encompasses many different textual and ritual traditions within itself, with no single founder or text. It is true that many Hindus and Orientalists identified the Vedas as the holiest and most important scriptures or doctrine of Hinduism, but the Vedas were of little or no relevance to what practising self-designated Hindus actually did in the nineteenth century—the enormous gap between what Hindu reform movements wanting to go back to the Vedas (such as the Brahmo Samaj and Arya Samaj) were trying to achieve and the actual practices of everyday nineteenth-century Hindus was a major reason why such movements remained strictly minoritarian. The story of how Hinduism emerged as a category in India has been told in many ways: as a complex intertwined dance of Muslims and Hindus (van der Veer 1994), as the rise of communalism (Chandra 1984, Pandey 1990), as religious revivalism (Brekke 2002), and as the emergence of a new kind of political movement (Jaffrelot 1996).[16]

In Nepal, the growth of 'Hindu' as a politically charged identity category was more a top-down than a bottom-up movement, encouraged and sustained by the palace as a way to legitimate the King's position under the royal regime, and even after its demise (Hausner 2007b). With the fall of the monarchy and the official adoption of republicanism in 2008, and in the absence of a sizeable Muslim minority to serve as the 'internal Other' as in India, it seems less and less likely that Hinduism can form a key criterion of political mobilization across the country as a whole.[17] On the other hand, reactions to 'Hindu' as a census category identified with the dominant elite in Nepal have grounded the ethnic rights movements that have been a powerful force of the Nepali political scene for the past two decades (Hangen 2010).

The politics of religious identification, in Nepal and in the UK

Under an officially Hindu monarch and state, there was subtle—and occasionally not so subtle—pressure to declare oneself as Hindu (rather than Buddhist, for example). During the Panchayat period (1960-90), cases were known of prominent Buddhist scholars entering their religion as 'Hindu' when applying for jobs in the university, on the grounds that only by doing so would they stand a chance of acceptance. Already towards the end of the 1980s Hindu identity began to be vociferously opposed by activists from Janajati groups (particularly Magars and Tharus, who come from groups that are the most deeply Hinduized).

---

[16] While organized Hinduism clearly did have an effect on Congress from an early period, in truth for decades the movement for *Hindutva* was a failure.

[17] Nonetheless, there are places, particularly in the Tarai, where the form of cadre-based organization that is familiar from India may become influential in years to come.

Long instantiated state hierarchy finally provoked a counter-reaction in 1990, and in the new, freer political environment that followed, religious and ethnic activists organized and campaigned for a secular (or religiously non-aligned) constitution.[18] Some ethnic activists also campaigned for 'their' group members to return their religion as 'Buddhism' rather than 'Hinduism,' even where the group had no tradition of being Buddhist and where some members had a strong tradition of affiliation to Hinduism. This newly attested identification was the avowed position of the Nepal Magar Samaj, for example, the national body representing the more than 1.6 million Magars in the Nepal Federation of Indigenous Nationalities. During the 2001 census, Magar activists campaigned for all Magars to return their religion as 'Buddhist' and their language as 'Magar,' regardless of actual practice or knowledge.[19] As part of the intentional production of Magar identity, the Samaj also encouraged the development of new Magar religious specialists who learned how to perform life-cycle rituals in a (Theravada) Buddhist idiom so that Magars would no longer need to call on (Hindu) Brahman priests (Lecomte-Tilouine 2003; Letizia 2005).

Such anti-Brahmanical/anti-Hindu movements of cultural assertion are increasingly popular in Nepal,[20] and also, now, in the UK. Many activists are keen to insist on their group members not being Hindu. Being Buddhist in the UK is an important political stance, given the higher percentage of Janajati groups in

---

[18] These long-stated goals were finally achieved in late 2007 with the declaration that Nepal was no longer a Hindu state but a federal republic, written into an Interim Constitution in 2008. A new Constitution for the Government of Nepal (no longer His Majesty's Government) was originally to have been written by 2010 but is now likely to happen only in 2012) [Note added in 2019: In fact this was achieved only in 2015.].

[19] The likelihood is that there is therefore a bias in the current census figures, the inverse of the bias towards Hinduism found before 1990.

[20] For other examples of pursuing political empowerment in Nepal through cultural means, see Hangen (2005, 2007a, 2007b, 2010), Lecomte-Tilouine (2004, 2009), and Minami (1997) among others.

Table 2.2: Religious Affiliation in Nepal and the UK Compared

Religion	% in Nepal (2001 census) (N= 22.7 million)	% in UK (CNS-UK survey 2008) (N= 7,881)	% in UK (VR survey 2010) (before prompt) (N=1,993)	% in UK (VR survey 2010) (after prompt) (N=1,993)
Hindu	80.6	41.4	48.3	38.9
Hindu + Buddhist	not an option	9.2	5.0	15.5
Buddhist	10.7	29.3	24.6	16.7
Kirat	3.6	10.1	8.7	8.6
Kirat + Hindu	not an option	4.9	4.1	9.1
Kirat + Buddhist	not an option	2.3	0.3	2.0
Muslim	4.2	0.01	n/a	n/a
Christian	0.5	2.2	6.0	6.0

Sources: CNSUK figures: Snowball survey of the whole of the UK carried out by volunteers overseen by trained social scientists; VR figures: administered questionnaire carried out by CNSUK and VR of 300 households chosen from the CNSUK original sample.

Note: See Chapters 3 and 5 for discussions of the 'before prompt' and 'after prompt' distinction.

Great Britain because of the relative ease of obtaining, and therefore higher concentration of, visas for Gurkha and former Gurkha servicemen and their families. The differences of religious affiliation between Nepal and the UK shown in Table 2.2 reflect in part these political considerations. But they derive also from the fact that the Nepali population in Britain does not reflect the demographic makeup of the 'home state.' Nepalis in the UK are drawn disproportionately from those groups with a tradition of recruitment to the Gurkhas. Thus Gurungs are 2.4 per cent in Nepal but form over 22 per cent and are the largest single group in the UK; Limbus are just 1.6 per cent in Nepal but nearly 10 per cent in the UK; and so on. The British Gurkha regiments have long had Brahman (Bahun) pandits to serve as chaplains (Uesugi 2007: 392). Since 2007, they also have Buddhist lamas, one based in Catterick in Yorkshire, another (from 2010) based in Aldershot in Hampshire; it is anticipated that a third will soon be based in Ashford, Kent.

The appointment of Buddhist chaplains alongside the Hindu Brahman pandits came following a steady and active campaign by Buddhist ex-Gurkhas settled in the UK. In other words, the changing balance of demography and religious categorization between Nepal and the UK, as seen in Table 2.2, led to a changing political environment as well. It was no longer the case that Gurkha soldiers from a Buddhist background (many Gurungs, Sherpas, Tamangs) were happy to accept the compromise, described by Uesugi (2007: 396–8), in which Hinduism was accepted as a 'duty religion' and 'national culture,' and therefore followed as military practice (Uesugi points out that Christian officers also participate in Dasain rituals in the regiment in the same spirit), whereas Buddhism was one's personal practice.

Despite the politicization of religious identity and the pressure to be 'not Hindu', there are many groups, particularly Newars and Magars, where over half the group members are quite happy to continue to identify as Hindu, even in the absence of any state encouragement to do so. Among self-designated indigenous ethnic groups, such as Limbu, Sunuwar, and Rai, significant minorities identify as Hindu. Although there is a large drop in the number of Hindus in the UK, as seen in Table 2.2, if the categories 'Hindu', 'Hindu and Buddhist', and 'Kiranti and Hindu' are combined, the total Hindu or part-Hindu population is nearly 56 per cent.

The Buddhist activists who succeeded in getting Buddhist chaplains appointed to the Gurkhas question the ratio of six Hindu chaplains to three Buddhist ones, however (especially because the third has not arrived, detained in Kathmandu because of questions about his level of English). Their successful campaign for the appointment of three Buddhist lamas was accompanied by the appointment of three additional Hindu pandits as well; activists argue that these proportions should be the other way around. The Ministry of Defence defended its practice through a confidential review of its own, which found that the figures within the Gurkhas were as follows: 68 per cent Hindu, 22 per cent Buddhist, 8 per cent Kiranti, and 2 per cent Christian.[21] These figures are actively disputed by ethnic organizations within the UK, however: even in—especially in—a new location, categories determine all.

Three cases of Nepali religion

Religious categories emerge and become salient for people from processes of state action, namely censuses and the politics of representation they provoke. But to what extent do they speak to the entirety of religious identity and experience? We know that religion is a both a set of institutions and a personal orientation towards the world, that is, a category of identity (both asserted and ascribed) and also a mode of practice. To consider the formation and sustenance of social groups is to investigate not only how its members use religion to articulate their cultural norms and boundaries, but also how they practise or articulate religion at a personal level. Interestingly, we are starting to see how mobilization is possible precisely because new practices are taken to be equivalent to a new category, consistent with the rendering of religion as a singular aspect of identity, much as ethnicity has come to be.

Case One: Fluid categories, ongoing practices

Consider the case of Mr. Chhetri and his wife from Wembley.[22] We asked each their religion of identification. Mr. Chhetri said,

---

[21] Letter from Des Browne, Ministry of Defence, to Kaji Sherpa (10 July 2007).

[22] Names and locations have been changed.

"None": he had been born a Hindu, but he did not place much truck in all these religious activities, unlike his wife. Mrs. Chhetri agreed: she was a Hindu. Following these disclosures, we read the list of religions on our questionnaire to them, including the possibility of double or triple identity categories. Upon hearing all these options, Mrs. Chhetri reasserted, quickly, that she was definitely a Hindu. But upon hearing that "Hindu and Buddhist" was an option, her husband pointed out to his wife that her practices included worship to every God (Christian included), and that she was perhaps more ecumenical in her beliefs than the single category indicated. She reflected on this point, and acquiesced: "Hindu and Buddhist."

Mr. Chhetri still maintained he was "none". But just before we left the house, he mentioned that he had been baptized as a Christian during a brief stay in Japan: his friends had gone along to the church one day, and he had joined them. When offered baptismal rites, he followed along with the mood of the moment, and willingly participated. Did he practise now? No, not really. But he did point out the plastic Christmas trees that still lined the dining room sideboard, across from his wife's shrine of Hindu icons, objects, and texts, to indicate an enduring link with the Christian church. A small white paper cross was taped above the fireplace, in a place of honour along with a photograph of his deceased mother. Their daughter felt no self-consciousness at all these religious options: she was happy to identify as both Hindu and Christian. At school she has been participating in the Christmas pageant and finds herself taken with the stories in a book of Biblical tales she had been given. She thought of herself quite easily as part-Hindu and part-Christian.

In this brief interview, we see the fluidity of religious categories, and the ease with which people change their minds about how they and others should identify themselves, in response to other options and to familial pressures. Practices have not shifted, but categories have. Quantitative researchers will know that people's answers to survey questions change in relation to the options and order given. It may come as a surprise, however, that such indeterminacy should surround or be embedded in identifying with religion while ethnic and caste identifications are clear and unambiguous. In the Nepali case, it appears that we have evidence for the malleability of religious identity; interestingly, in an inverse relation, religion—that category widely interpreted in Western scholarship as fixed—is variable, while ethnicity is fixed.

Case Two: One festival, multiple categories

It would be wrong to suppose that with so many religious traditions going on side by side there is nothing that binds all Nepalis together. Until recently, one might have said this was the national Nepali festival, Dasain, in October. The whole of Nepal closes down and people travel long distances to celebrate the festival at home; in many cases this is their one and only annual visit. It is both a festival of the family and household, of patriarchy, of the village or city unit, and of the country as a whole. Until the demise of the monarchy in 2008, the king, or his local representative, was at the centre of the celebrations.[23]

There are notable differences in the ways this national holiday is celebrated in Nepal from the ways it is celebrated in the UK, however. First of all, most British Nepalis do not practise the animal sacrifice that most Nepalis in Nepal perform on the tenth day of the waxing moon, in part because animal sacrifice is not permitted in the UK, and in part because vegetarian and other movements to avoid the killing of animals are on the rise, both in the UK and in Nepal.[24] Second, in Nepal, the rituals of Dasain take place in local temples, where lines of goats led by their

---

[23] There is a considerable literature on the festival, as one might expect: see Bennett (1983), Ramirez (1993), Campbell (1995), Krauskopff & Lecomte-Tilouine (1996), Pfaff-Czarnecka (1996), Hangen (2005, 2010).

[24] See Chapter 6 (= Pariyar, Shrestha, & Gellner 2014), based on Mitra Pariyar's research in Oxford, on the ways in which the inability to perform sacrifice impacts on the older generation of Nepali migrants.

sacrifi(c)ers await their fate. Alternative Dasain traditions exist among minorities, such as Buddhist Newars (Gellner 1992: 219-20), Muslims (Gaborieau 1993), and Tibetan Buddhists, to which may now be added the tradition of boycotting Dasain altogether (Hangen 2005). In the UK, there is not the assertive Dasain boycott found in some parts of Nepal (or rather the moment when that was asserted seems to have passed): Dasain programmes take place in town halls and community schools, and the festivities take the form of cultural performances, speeches, and dancing, with the religious element downplayed so far as to be almost non-existent.

Both in Nepal and in England, most Nepalis celebrate Dasain in some form, no matter which religion they identify themselves by: as the closest thing to a national celebration, Hindu, Buddhists, Kirants, and animists all participate. For strict Hindus, Dasain is about the worship of Durga; but for others it is simply a family festival in which respected elders give *tika* to their juniors and reaffirm ties. To attend a Dasain party is to be Nepali in a religious mode: in East London, as in Kathmandu, there is no contradiction between being Buddhist and fêting Durga in the autumn.

Dasain is also held to be sufficiently Nepali as to be the umbrella festival for other auspicious occasions. On the main day of *tika* giving, two Newar families based in London resolved any hesitation about a cross-religious marriage with an official engagement. Normally opposed to the giving and receiving of *tika*—the iconic Nepali Hindu rite—the Christian bride-to-be did so on the occasion of her betrothal. And indeed, she was selected as a legitimate choice once it was confirmed that she would participate in Hindu marriage rites. In the end, the category of her religious identity was unimportant—or at least could be overlooked—as long as she and her family were willing that she engage in practices that would confirm her role as a legitimate daughter-in-law. She had been introduced as a prospective wife to the family a year earlier, but originally rejected as not Hindu. The groom's family turned their search to Nepal, where they tried to find a suitable Hindu bride, but eventually decided that a Nepali woman's professional aspirations might not be able to be met in London and that the domestic happiness of their son might be threatened. A year later, they returned to the young woman who was a member of a church-going family, and agreed that the marriage should take place.

Case Three: One category, diverse practices

Our first case demonstrates how fluid identification and classification can be, changing from moment to moment depending on context and prompt—all with a fair degree of disconnection from actual practice. The second case illustrates how a shared practice can be explained and understood in very different ways (one practice, multiple classifications)—an old phenomenon in the Nepali context, often labelled multivalent symbolism or 'syncretism' (Gellner 1992: 80–3, 101–2). The third example we put forward indicates how a single shared label, i.e. a common process of classification, covers very diverse practices (one label, multiple practices), and drives home the point that religious categories are sometimes intentionally used by collectives, whatever their religious behaviours may be.

The guru Phalgunanda was born on November 9, 1885, in Ilam district in a poor farming family. His mother died a few days after he was born. At an early age he had spiritual experiences, an angel or *divyapurus* appearing to him and enjoining *ahimsa* (non-violence) and vegetarianism on him. After working as a porter and petty trader, in 1903 he went to work for the British as a coolie building a road to Tibet. While doing this, the same angel appeared to him and called him again to his spiritual path. He spent the whole night of Baisakh full moon reciting the mantras the angel taught him and he left off the coolie work the following day (the academic observer will note that this is the same date that the Buddha achieved enlightenment).

At this point a friend of his older brother, who was serving with the British Gurkhas in Burma, came home to the village and took him back to Burma. According to his biography, he was tricked into putting on army uniform (which was against his principles), but ended up serving three years, continuing his spiritual practice all the while. As time went on he gathered more and more followers, including officers. He eventually left the army and returned to Nepal, spending many years wandering as an ascetic with a Saivite trident, and establishing his tripartite teaching of non-violence, celibacy, and serving others, which became very well established in Panchthar district if less strongly in other parts of east Nepal. There are many stories of his miraculous accomplishments; he died in 1949.

As is evident to his followers, Phalgunanda's path is closely related to Saivite Hinduism, but he put great stress on scriptures in the Limbu language and Limbu script, so that his movement is in many ways a Limbu or Kiranti nativist one. Contemporary followers in Nepal and in the UK tend to be Kiranti activists, and it is a matter of great pride for Limbus and other Kirantis that Phalgunanda was declared a 'national hero' of Nepal in 2009. Practitioners who follow Phalgunanda return their religion as 'Kiranti dharma' in the census.

The term 'Kiranti' or 'Kirata' is in fact an old omnibus ethnic term, understood in contemporary Nepal to refer to Rais, Limbus, Yakhas, and Sunuwars. Thus 'Kiranti *dharma*' has come to apply equally to two very different kinds of religion: (a) the hereditary, traditional religion of these groups passed on by shamanic religious specialists through oral texts known as *muddum* or *mundum*, giving a central place to animal sacrifice and the consumption of alcohol (Gaenszle 2000), and (b) the Phalgunanda sectarian tradition, also known as Satyahangma religion, that, while promoting Limbu language and identity, actively campaigns against the values and practices of traditional Limbu shamanism and animism. At the same time, Phalgunanda followers propagate practices derived from Hinduism (such as fire sacrifice), while firmly asserting the difference between their tradition of Satyahangma and Hinduism. Satyahangma practices, then, appear to adhere to or even conflate Limbu religion and mainstream Hinduism, while insisting on its separateness as a unique religious category.

Limbus in the UK both respect the Satyahangma tradition and their traditional shamanic religion. With animal sacrifice off the agenda, it is easier to gloss over the distinction between them, whereas in Nepal there have been disputes. In Kathmandu the Satyahangma followers have had to set up their own temple, separate from those of other Kirantis, because it was felt that their offerings of fire sacrifices were 'too Hindu.'

Conclusion

We distinguish, then, two key aspects of religion: practice and category. We could also consider the question from the perspective of agent and structure, or individual and collective, or actor and institution, or ascription-by-self and ascription-by-other. Again, there are different analytical models for understanding what is too broadly called religion: being Hindu in the Nepali context comes with a host of assumptions such that people will perform and identify in seemingly contradictory ways if we take religion to be practices, beliefs, and ways of belonging all rolled into one. By breaking apart the definition, we see that people's actions and identifications are not contradictory, but consistent with the way they see themselves and wish to be seen. As we are not the first to argue, it is the official definition of religion that has to adjust (so as to accommodate the many aspects that we have conceptually stacked within it), not the phenomenon it purports to describe.

By Nepali religion, we refer at once to religious identity, religious affiliation—which together may be understood as religious category—and religious practice, in Europe and in Nepal. All of these elements (and places) are encompassed in 'religion', but they may mean very different—even contradictory—things, within one household, possibly within one person, and certainly within what is all too casually called 'one community' or 'ethnic group' or 'minority population'. They will almost certainly change, or at least have different meanings, or be coded differently, in new locations: practices and categories of belonging are thrown into sharp relief against the exigencies of personal and communal dislocation, and the imperatives or attempts to assimilate that may follow.

Like ethnic identities, or the borders of nation-states, what religions are and the parameters of practices, beliefs, and ways of identification are social processes in flux, just like any other. Peggy Levitt (2001) has been careful not to reimpose the nation-state on migrants or travelling populations, and to insist that we recall religion as an important way that diasporas are formed; Vertovec (2000a) suggests that a key object of inquiry will be which elements of religious practice or belief seem to travel well when diasporas take them forward, and which tend to remain more sedentary. And yet the burgeoning ethnographic literature on migrant populations unwittingly plays a part in reifying religion as a singular phenomenon: even careful ethnographers working with migrant populations (never mind censuses and policies) tend to assume that immigrants from a particular place subscribe to one and only one particular religion. These renderings erroneously keep the contours of religious category static across place, even as they consider how religious dynamics—and the larger socio-political contexts in which they operate—shift in each location. Neither religious practice nor the ways particular religions are coded or categorized in a nation's politics, whether in the sending or the receiving context, is static.

Michael Carrithers (2000) has introduced the felicitous term 'polytropy' to refer to "the natural condition of spiritual cosmopolitanism in India": the idea is that there are numerous holy people, sites, and powers, and any rational person will try to remain on good terms with as many as possible, and certainly not restrict themselves arbitrarily to one or other category. Both historical and state contexts will impact the particularities of religious practice and religious identity: what people do, how they worship, what kinds of temples they build, how openly they can gather and organize will depend on their contexts of ascription and the categories they are offered as ways to articulate who they are. We know we can no longer study the religion of a national group within some defined boundary, however, and we are learning that the nature of transnational flows means that a given practice, category, or set of meanings can originate in any location, not necessarily the 'homeland.'

If praxis remains an important element of anthropological thought, after Bourdieu, we cannot relegate religion to the realm of the categorical. Classifications will always exist in human thought—and indeed in collective human practice—and we will engage in practices of identification with one or another of these reified, documented, or legal categories. But what we do may not exactly fit or be coterminous with these categories: they are heuristic devices made real and codified by social structures (and social scientists) as well as by the practices which support them. Religious practices will do more, however, in their soteriological dimension: they will assert personal wishes and desires, encoded in certain worldviews that are produced by particular historical moments. And these may derive and speak to more than one religious code, or none at all.

Our main point is that category and practice must be analysed as separate and separately malleable elements of religion. Sometimes they are very separate indeed, and the discourses of categorization appear to operate in a universe that has little to do with the polytropic and ecumenical environment in which real life goes on. At other times there may be a closer link, either because people do not always find themselves in between traditions in the way that so many Nepalis do, or because there has been a conscious attempt to shift practice towards some more modal categorization (as when Muslims respond to the call of the Tablighi Jamaat to live 'as good Muslims'), or to claim historical practices that confirm the legitimacy of a category.

We see therefore that categorization is a particular kind of practice, one that is particularly associated with governments and nation-states, but that also may be advocated by individuals—political or charismatic—who wish to make certain claims for difference or empowerment. Either we can either take those categories for granted, as the methodological nationalists and religionists do, or, in realizing that such an alignment may be falsely applied (or consciously manipulated), we can try to bring to light the processes by which particular categories come to appear natural, necessary, and even universal. In interrogating its construction among Nepalis in Britain, and the way in which religion appears to encompass a multiplicity of presumed acts, beliefs, and identities under an ostensibly singular term, we might find that the differentiation between category and practice usefully speaks to the origins or designations of other religions at other moments in history. But more importantly, they may break apart religion as a solid and knowable entity, in scholarly and popular circles alike.

nation state, but that also may be adumbrated by individuals — political or charismatic — who wish to make certain claims for [illegible]

[illegible]

3

Multiple versus Unitary Belonging: How Nepalis in Britain Deal with 'Religion'

David N. Gellner & Sondra L. Hausner

Introduction

The rise of identity politics generates a tension between those who want to make particular identities the central and determining aspect of their social being and people who do not wish to do so or who refrain from doing so.[1] The latter group, arguably the majority, mobilize such identifications either only strategically (or tactically) or not at all.[2] Formal identities, once accepted by the state, provide the basis for the politically implicated process of regular counting, i.e. censuses, and (eventually) the distribution of resources. Such identities are,

[1] This paper was originally published in an edited volume coming out of the Religion and Society research programme (Gellner & Hausner 2013).

[2] On strategy and tactics in religious practice, see Linda Woodhead's keynote speech at the Sacred Practices of Everyday Life conference: http://www.religionandsociety.org.uk/events/programme_events/show/sacred_practices_of_everyday_life.

therefore, the focus of much detailed attention from sociologists and other social scientists. This focus in the academic study of religion (or ethnicity) can easily give rise to a well-known fallacy of misplaced concreteness: the fact that a category can be counted is wrongly taken to mean that a self-conscious group exists.[3] Reality, however, rarely corresponds perfectly to academic theory and indeed often confounds expectations: for example, for many Nepalis with whom we have worked, the religious category into which they fall is by no means obvious and may depend on context. Furthermore, since the mobilization of categories is a process with status and political implications, in many cases there is a rather large gap between what people actually do in the privacy of their own shrine room and their declared identities when responding to census-takers or when participating in public meetings. Reflecting on this gap, we have argued elsewhere that a fundamental distinction is required for any adequate understanding of religious phenomena, namely that between *category* (census label) and *practice* (what people actually do) (Ch. 2 above). South Asian data bring out very clearly how very fluid religious categories are and how fallacious it can be to assume that they correspond to distinct, homogeneous, and mutually exclusive social groups.

Other scholars have independently and in different (mainly Christian/Western) contexts come to rather similar conclusions. Mark Chaves, for example, castigates what he calls the 'religious congruence fallacy': "attitudes and behavior correlate only weakly, and collections of apparently related ideas and practices rarely cohere into logically unified, mutually reinforcing, seamless webs … This is true of culture in general, and it is true of religious culture in particular" (Chaves 2010: 2). This incongruence is manifold and can appear (i) among beliefs, (ii) between beliefs and actions, and (iii) between different contexts; such incongruity

---

[3] For an attack on this fallacy in the study of ethnicity, see Brubaker (2004).

is, within the social science of religion, "an established uncontroversial fact" (Chaves 2010: 5). Yet, both in society in general and in the sociology and anthropology of religion in particular, it is a truism that we all too often forget. People are surprised at 'non-congruent' behaviour, when in fact it is the attainment of 'congruence' that is unusual and in need of explanation. Chaves allows that congruence is occasionally achieved, but argues that the default presumption in the study of religion ought rather to be that it is unlikely to obtain; the onus should be on the observer of religion who claims to have found congruence (believers who are entirely consistent in their beliefs and between their beliefs and their actions) to prove that it is there, not the other way around.

Starting from an empirical study of ordinary 'mainstream' people in Yorkshire, Abby Day (2011) likewise found a gap between formal census categories and what people actually believed or did. She notes a moment of epiphany in her research when a 14-year-old boy asserted, quite emphatically, that he believed in nothing and was a Christian (Day 2011: 29). That her research was carried out in Yorkshire, where there are towns like Bradford with prominent Muslim minorities, is no doubt relevant here. Her explorations of religious belief, which avoided direct questioning about religious affiliation, revealed that it was far too simple to see people as either Christian or not, as either religious or secular. What she found was a largely performative anthropocentrism that mostly rejected conventional religion and religious categories, and yet had plenty of space for belief in ghosts.

In the vernacular practice of most people in South Asia, such varied belief and practice according to context is very much the norm, and arguably always has been. Michael Carrithers (2000) has coined the term 'polytropic' for this situation.[4] In South Asia it is taken for granted that the world contains numerous spiritual

[4] See Gellner (2005) for its applications to Nepali religious history.

powers and that ordinary people should respect and propitiate them, without concerning themselves about the particular religious traditions or labels (categories) applied to them. Deities belong to more than one religious tradition, or are thought to be incarnations of each other (Gellner 1992: 74–80). Polytropy is not quite the same thing as ecumenicism, in that the former refers to an attitude that simply ignores the differences between religious traditions or teachings, whereas the latter acknowledges different and separate traditions and seeks a unity behind or between them. If ecumenicism looks to an equality of religious traditions or religious categories, polytropy is simply uninterested in the question of category. In practice, these two stances—though analytically distinguishable—often blur or blend in to one another.

The phenomenon of multiple religious belonging, if we may call it that, is so widespread in Indic religions—multiplicity in paths, teachings, teachers, healers, local practices, and traditions—that ultimately the problem is less to explain how something Westerners view as singular became or becomes multiple, but, on the contrary, via what route we might have arrived at expressions of singularity. The very practice of placing oneself in a single religious category was not something ordinary South Asians were expected to do until the British started to carry out censuses. Or rather, it was something that was characteristic only of religious virtuosi and those who imitated them. Most lay people would not have dreamt of doing so. It is probably a social universal for religious specialists to regard the practice of lay people as imperfect, if not downright impure; in the South Asian context it was equally normal for lay people themselves to be ignorant of or to disregard such views, even if they deeply respected those very virtuosi and sought their blessings and instrumental assistance.

In short, multiple belonging is a frequent and attested position for South Asians. It is no longer a majority position—the modernist assumption of singularity has by now taken deep root—but, as we hope to demonstrate, multiple belonging remains a viable mode of identification in the Nepali cultural world.

Changing religious categories in Nepal and in the diaspora

In Nepal the practice of classifying people into discrete religious boxes started only in the 1950s, when people—or at the least the census-enumerators—had to be taught how to apply the categories. 'What is your religion?' was not then a meaningful question to many people; by contrast, 'what is your caste?' was unavoidable, and in most contexts permitted only one exclusive answer. Prior to 1951 people needed to know what *jat* (caste or ethnic group) they belonged to ('Muslim' was treated as a kind of *jat*): this knowledge was essential for all kinds of rights and duties, as well as for everyday interactions, not to mention marriage. Thus one's caste was the first and most important sociological fact any Nepali needed to know about any other whom they encountered (and is arguably still so today, even though the consequences that follow from it are vastly attenuated when compared to a century ago). Until it was replaced in 1963, the law code of the country differentiated punishments and rights according to one's caste (Höfer 1979). By contrast, although people practised religion, and although some of them were certainly aware, for example, that their tradition was Buddhist and therefore different from the Shaivite (Hindu) majority, it was not necessary for ordinary Nepalis to affirm belonging to one and only one religious category.

During Nepal's modernizing Panchayat regime (1960-90), state classification by *jat* (caste or ethnicity) was replaced by classification by religion (the exact opposite of what happened in the transition from the Ottoman Empire to post-Ottoman Balkan states, where religious *millets* became translated into 'nations' or 'national minorities'). As a modern educational system gradually expanded throughout the country, children were taught at school that Nepal was 'the world's only Hindu kingdom'. Hindu high-caste modes of being dominated the nationalist developmentalist imaginary and school textbooks (Pigg 1992); high castes also dominated the apparatus of the state. But explicit reference to caste and ethnicity was kept out of the public sphere. It was considered important that the decennial censuses should show an overwhelming majority of Hindus in the country (see Table 3.1).

In the post-1990 era, with a return to party politics and the rise of ethnic activism, Nepal moved from an era of nation-building to one of ethnicity-building (Hachhethu & Gellner 2010); arguably it has now become one of religion-building. In the new multiculturalist environment, it again became possible and required to count ethnic groups. Furthermore, there was the sudden introduction of the new global discourse of indigeneity, which entered Nepal in 1993 on the back of UN initiatives (Gellner 2001b). Conflict over which groups should be considered indigenous and what rights should follow from that recognition intensified in the period that was supposed to lead up to the promulgation of a new secular and republican constitution (2008–12).[5]

Over the last 25 years the dual dominance of Hinduism and of Bahun-Chhetris (Brahmans and Kshatriyas, the two highest castes) has been increasingly contested, both by religious activists and by ethnic activists.[6] In this context of increased political activism around ethnicity and identity, religion has become a way for ethnic groups to claim a unique, and often non-Hindu,

---

[5] In the end the Constituent Assembly was unable to come up with a workable constitution, even after four years. The most difficult stumbling block was the role of ethnicity in defining federal units and what, if any, differential rights there should be (Thapa 2012; Adhikari & Gellner 2016a).

[6] See Gellner, Pfaff-Czarnecka, & Whelpton (2008), Hangen (2010), and Lawoti (2005) for introductions to the ethnic issue. LeVine & Gellner (2005) describes the Theravada Buddhist movement, which saw itself as resisting Hinduism and Hinduization, and aimed to reform the traditional Vajrayana Buddhism of the Kathmandu Valley.

Table 3.1: The Religious Breakdown of Nepal according to the Decennial Censuses

Religion	1952/4	%	1961	%	1971	%	1981	%	1991	%	2001	%	2011	%
	Number		Number		Number		Number		Number		Number		Number	
Hinduism	7,318,392	88.9	8,254,403	87.7	10,330,009	89.4	13,445,787	89.5	15,996,953	86.5	18,330,121	80.6	21,551,492	81.3
Buddhism	707,104	8.6	807,991	9.3	866,411	7.5	799,081	5.3	1,439,142	7.8	2,442,520	10.7	2,396,099	9.0
Islam	208,899	2.5	280,597	3.0	351,186	3.0	399,197	2.7	653,218	3.5	954,023	4.2	1,162,370	4.4
Kirati									318,389	1.7	818,106	3.6	807,169	3.0
Christianity			458		2,541		3,891	<0.1	31,280	0.2	101,976	0.5	375,699	1.4
Jainism			831		5,836		9,430	0.1	7,561	<0.1	4,108	<0.1	3,214	<0.1
Nature													121,982	0.5
Bon													13,006	<0.1
Others	684								26,416	0.1	86,095	0.4		
Unstated			5,716	0.1			365,445	2.4	18,138	0.1				
Total	8,235,079	100	9,412,996	100	11,555,983	100	15,022,831	100	18,491,097	100	22,736,934	100	26,630,809	100

Sources: H. Gurung (1998: 95), Dahal (2003), and 2011 census; percentages do not always add up to 100 because of rounding; the last digit of the total for 1981 has been corrected from '9' to '1'; the total for 2001 is left as reported in the 2001 census even though it is 15 too few.

identity. The modernist assumptions that each group should have one religion and that everyone belonging to a given ethnic group should share the same singular religious identity have become deeply embedded, if also contested. But multiplicity is never far from the surface; everyone is aware that it is in fact a pervasive feature of Nepali religious practice and as such is frequently praised as 'religious tolerance' or even 'secularism' (Letizia 2011).

Official Hindu dominance came to an end with the fall of the monarchy in 2006. In January 2007 the new Interim Constitution removed all mention of Hinduism and by 2008 the country had formally become a secular republic, with the king reduced to the status of private citizen and his main palace converted into a museum. The relationship between the state and religion, and between the state and its premier Hindu shrine, Pashupatinath, became ever more problematic and controversial (Hausner 2007b; Letizia 2011). After the fall of the Panchayat regime in 1990 the number of Hindus recorded in the census began to drop off, as Table 3.1 shows. Buddhists who had previously been returned as Hindu started to assert themselves and certain ethnic activists (particularly Magars and Tharus) began to advocate for their co-ethnics to return themselves as Buddhists rather than as Hindus (Letizia 2014). Despite this campaign, Hindus still comprised over 80 per cent of the population in 2001.

An even more striking change post 1990 is the emergence of a new category: 'Kirati' (often written 'Kiranti'). This is an ethnic 'super-category', which brings together several small groups in the far east of the country (namely the Sunuwars, Rais, and Limbus, who make up 0.42 per cent, 2.79 per cent, and 1.58 per cent respectively of the population as a whole; other small groups in the plains in the south of the country also count as Kirati.)[7] The term was first adopted to provide a home for the followers of a new religious movement known as Satyahangma, based on the

---

[7] See Gaenszle (2000) for a detailed discussion of the term 'Kirati/Kiranti/Kirata' and its modern use.

teachings of the reformist and nativist Limbu religious leader, Phalgunanda (1885-1949). In earlier ages Satyahangma would have been classified as a Hindu sect, despite its use of Limbu writing for its scriptures, thanks to its adoption of Hindu symbols (the sacred syllable Om, the fire sacrifice, the conch shell), its avoidance of alcohol and animal sacrifice, and its teachings of vegetarianism, purity, and service to others. And indeed many Limbus who follow the traditionalist religion, which is based on the very things Satyahangma rejects, namely oral scriptures, the consumption of alcohol, animal sacrifice, and shamanic practice, do regard Satyahangma as being a form of Hinduism. Nonetheless, Satyahangma acquired its own separate category in the census as 'Kirati religion'. Subsequently, whatever their actual practices may be, it appears that most ethnic Kiratis have begun to adopt the same label: the proportion returning themselves as adherents of the 'Kirati religion' in the Nepal census more than doubled, from 1.7 per cent to 3.5 per cent of the total population, between 1991 and 2001.[8]

Moving to the UK (Table 2.2, above, p. 20), we find some remarkable contrasts. Hinduism is still the largest category, but it is no longer so dominant. This is partly because recruitment to the British Gurkhas is skewed (whatever the Ministry of Defence may claim) towards particular ethnic groups (and in fact became more so after 1947, when the regiments that traditionally recruited Chhetris were assigned to India).[9] Those ethnic groups include the Gurungs, who happen to be the largest ethnic group among Nepalis in the UK (over 20%) even though they are relatively small in Nepal (2.4%). Many Gurungs have a strong, and increasing, identification with Buddhism. Tamangs, Thakalis, and Sherpas—all strongly Buddhist groups—also have significant representation among Nepalis based in Britain. The number of Christians also increases considerably; whether that is as much of

---

[8] We explore further the diverse practices falling under the single 'Kirati' label in a separate paper (see Ch. 4).

[9] On Gurkha recruitment, see Caplan (1995) and Ragsdale (1990).

a contrast between Nepal and the UK as appears at first sight will only be known once the Nepal 2011 census figures for religion are released.

Importantly, our data for religion in the UK permit and record multiple religious belonging. Despite the dominant census ideology, both in the UK and in Nepal, that allows only singular religious identities, 10 per cent of Nepalis in the UK opt outright for dual religious belonging when asked what their religion (*dharma*) is. Moreover, once read out a list of possibilities, including dual (and triple) affiliations, a further 16 per cent of Nepalis in Britain choose multiple identifications. Before being prompted in this way, they assume (correctly, in this cultural context and popular paradigm) that they must select only one religious identity. Once they are given permission to be multiple, they seize the opportunity, sometimes enthusiastically.[10] The multiple identities they chose are shown in Table 3.2.

Table 3.2: Religious Affiliation, Before and After Prompts

Before/ After	Hindu	Buddhist	H+ Bt	Kirat	K+H	K+B	Non-r	Other	Total
Hindu	461 (79.6%)	4	43	10	53	4	3	1	579
Buddhist	0	196 (67.6%)	83	0	0	11	0	0	290
Kirat	0	0	0	92 (88.5%)	7	5	0	0	104

Note: the figure in the final column is the number who answered 'Hindu', 'Buddhist', or 'Kirat' before prompt; the other columns show how those figures were distributed after prompt.
Source: VR survey.

[10] Our quantitative data on Nepali religion in the UK comes from two different surveys. The first, conducted by the Centre for Nepal Studies UK, in 2008 (Adhikari 2012), was a comprehensive effort to capture the demographics of the Nepali population in Great Britain. The 300 households surveyed for the Vernacular Religion project in 2010-11 were selected as a randomized sample of CNSUK's list. Thus the VR survey was not a totally independent sample; that similar figures were returned two years apart provides some grounds for confidence in the broad outlines of the results.

Parsing the figures further gives us some sense of what is at stake in variable religious identifications. For example, unsurprisingly, no one, having answered 'Buddhist' in the first instance, changed their mind to become 'Hindu' once the list of options was read out: the politics of religious identification in Nepal mean precisely that being Buddhist is, in the current day and age, at least in some way understood as meaning not Hindu, or in opposition to the religion that was the dominant identity of the state. But close to 100 people—nearly a third—of those who originally identified as Buddhist did choose a category that included another religion when given the option: 83 opted for Hindu/Buddhist, and 11 for Kirati/Buddhist. And nearly 10 per cent of those who were originally just Hindu also chose the Hindu-Buddhist option.

Practice, rather than categories

So far, we have concentrated on categories which people subscribe to or acquiesce in being allocated to. Let us now turn to the question of the relation of those categories to what people actually do. Those who opt for multiple religious labels do so, presumably, in the spirit that multiple belonging reflects better what they actually do and (in some cases) how they actually feel. There is, of course, also the widespread Hindu attitude that Hinduism includes everything, so that Buddhism (as well as other South Asian paths, and indeed all religious wisdom) is just a branch or part of it; some Christian ecumenical attitudes might be seen as taking up a similar position. This inclusivist Hindu discourse was encouraged by the state during the Panchayat period, as a way of encapsulating Buddhism within a wider nationalist Hindu identity, and is bolstered by the tradition that the Buddha is one of the ten incarnations of the deity Vishnu. Interestingly, some old-fashioned Buddhists did not find this encompassment objectionable and were quite capable of playing the contextual Hindu card themselves when they might gain some benefit from it (a government job, for example). Well before 1990, however, younger Buddhist activists found this 'domination by subordinate inclusion' utterly infuriating, and protested against it. Nowadays (since the People's Movement of 1990, which precisely allowed the assertion of variable identities in public space), Hindus, though still tempted by the inclusivist line of argument, know that they must accept Buddhism as an equal partner or interlocutor.

Despite the emergence of a multiculturalist discourse ostensibly treating all religions equally, the traditional inclusivist attitude or stance of Hinduism remains a deep part of Hindu practice. There can hardly be said to be any kind of problem (Chaves's incongruity) if a declared Hindu keeps a Buddhist image in his home shrine space. He would not on that account feel that he should shift himself into the Hindu-Buddhist category. It is probably less true the other way around. Buddhists who keep Hindu images in their shrine are more likely to feel that this evidence of multiplicity ought not to be done from a strictly Buddhist point of view and that they should therefore accept the Hindu-Buddhist label. This stance accords with traditional ways of thinking too, in which 'true' (or 'truer') Buddhism was identified with the more exclusively Buddhist practices of monastic or clerical virtuosi. These differences between Hinduism and Buddhism probably account for the significantly larger proportion of Buddhists than Hindus shifting to the Hindu-Buddhist category (Table 3.2), once given permission to opt for multiplicity.

We have outlined different ways in which people's practices may be related to the category or categories they place themselves in: sometimes their practice is highly congruent (as when they claim to be Buddhist and all their practice takes place in a Buddhist idiom, for example); sometimes their practice is mixed and they decide to claim the requisite label. But there is another possibility, namely that the religious label and the actual practice vary, such that they are nearly independent of each other. This seeming incongruity may happen because the husband is very concerned to claim a particular label for political reasons, but the wife wishes to continue worshipping in the way she knows and believes in, and simply gets on with it. It may also happen because the whole family is agreed on the need to claim a particular unitary religious identity (for socio-political reasons, for example), and at the same time is quite happy to practise in a multiple manner.[11]

Multiple belonging as the outcome of particular ethnic histories

Multiple belonging, although arguably very much a part of Nepali history across the board, now appeals to some groups more than others (Table 3.3). The various ethnic groups of Nepal may be categorized on a spectrum from Hindu to Buddhist. At one end of the spectrum are the most Hindu groups, the high-caste Bahuns and Chhetris. At the other end are the exclusively Buddhist Sherpas. Among these groups at either end of the continuum the tension between category and practice is least; history and identity are—from the religious point of view at least—less complex than for others. Among the other groups, both practice and category (as can be seen from Table 3.3) are much more mixed. A large part of the explanation of this variation is to be found in particular histories.[12]

---

[11] There are also contexts in which the vast majority of people are far less concerned with the label than with efficacy; the paradigm here is healing or magical contexts. In these cases, the religious affiliation(s) of the healer, medium, or Tantric priest are of little relevance to the supplicant, who wishes to get better, to get rid of bad luck, or to avoid an evil influence. In an analysis of Punjabi religion, Ballard (1996) calls this level of religion kismetic (from *kismet*, fate). We call it instrumental. These religious practices tend to fall into those areas of life where people are least concerned with labels or particular forms of belonging or social identity; they aim rather to solve life problems and we do not explore it further here.

[12] There is probably little significance in the relatively high percentage of Newars choosing the 'non-religious' option in Table 5.4 (15.1 per cent as

Table 3.3: Religious Affiliation in the UK by Ethnicity (2010)

	Bahun (N=154)	Chhetri (N=72)	Dalit (N=29)	Magar (N=205)	Newar (N=53)	Sunuwar (N=48)	Rai (N=135)	Limbu (N=146)	Gurung (N=203)	Tamang (N=37)	Thakali (N=29)	Sherpa (N=33)
Hindu	91.6	93.1	86.2	52.2	47.2	18.8	26.7	8.2	7.4	2.7		
Buddhist				16.6	13.2	2.1	0.7		37.4	70.3	55.2	100
Hindu + Buddhist	1.9	2.8		20.5	24.5	8.3	2.2		47.3	13.5	31	
Kirati							23.7	48.6				
Kirati + Hindu						43.8	26.7	29.5				
Kirati + Buddhist							9.6	6.8	0.5			
Kirat + Hindu + Bt						10.4						
Bon									3			
Bon Buddhist											13.8	
Christian	4.5		13.8	10.7		16.7	6.7	6.2	3.9	13.5		
Non-religious	1.9				15.1			0.7	0.5			
Other		4.2					3.7					

Source: VR survey, 2010, percentages: religion as given after reading out a list of prompts.

If we start with the three Kirati groups, Sunuwar, Rai and Limbu, we note that among the Sunuwars, a clear majority (nearly two thirds) opt for one or other multiple religious affiliation. Among the Rais this falls to 38.5 per cent and among the Limbus, 36.3 per cent. Among the Rais, over a quarter are happy to call themselves straight Hindus, even when multiple affiliations are on option. Among the Limbus nearly half choose the label Kirati (though, as we have discussed, this category may cover, as with 'Hindu', a considerable variety of practices). All these variations reflect the fact that Rais, Sunuwars, and Limbus have their own indigenous oral traditions but have been subject to a whole range of Hinduizing influences for at least a couple of centuries, some of them explicit and encouraged by the state, others hardly perceptible (Allen 2008; Gaenszle 2011).

Similar histories explain why over half the Magars surveyed were happy to be classified as Hindus (see Table 3.3), even though their national organization, the Nepal Magar Sangh, has campaigned in Nepal for Magars to return their religion as 'Buddhist' (and their language as 'Magar'; see Lecomte-Tilouine 2003). Even in the UK, as far as public affiliation is concerned, the UK Magar Association aligns itself with Buddhism and organizes its biggest annual gathering on Buddha Purnima (the full moon when the Buddha is believed to have obtained enlightenment). The Buddhist content of the celebration, however, is minimal. Of all the various Janajati groups, the Magars have spent the longest time in close association with the Bahun-Chhetri high castes and were very much a part of the original 'unification' or conquest of

---

opposed to zero for many groups, with Bahuns at 1.9 per cent as the second-highest group). Due to the small numbers involved, this 15.1 per cent amounts to just eight individuals in three households. In two households the response 'non-religious' was evidently taken to mean 'not much involved in religious practice': in one household the teenage children were so designated, in the other the male members of the household. In only one household did all four members of the household return themselves as 'non-religious'.

Nepal and the creation of the state of Nepal in the eighteenth century. The Magars are also the group most assimilated to the Nepali language (Whelpton 2008: 58-9). The daily religious practice of many, if not most, Magars in the UK is deeply Hindu—and many are happy to categorize themselves as such.

From the eighteenth century the Gurungs were associated with the ruling group almost as much as the Magars, but, unlike the Magars, they have always had a strong link to Buddhism. One of their leading clans is named 'Lama', and they practise a form of Tibetan Buddhism (considered 'low' and 'unorthodox' by Tibetan teachers, but nonetheless accepted as related). Thus, though many Gurungs worship Hindu gods, many of them also consider themselves firm Buddhists. Meanwhile a strong activist group, the Tamu Pye Lhu Sangh (literally 'Gurung oral scripture association') argues that both Hinduism and Buddhism are foreign and recently introduced to Gurung culture, and that the true Gurung religion is actually the shamanic, animist religion of the traditional Gurung priests, the Paju and Khlibri (or Pachyu and Gyabre; see tamu-pyelhu.org). They argue therefore that all Gurungs should record their religion as 'Bon' or 'Bonism' (showing up as 3 per cent in the VR survey, though their strength, as demonstrated by the numbers who turn up for the events they organize, is certainly more than this figure would indicate, at least within the UK diaspora). In all these cases, different activists argue over what is the true religion of the group.

In other instances, members of the group feel themselves pulled in different directions, but are often quite happy to affirm that they belong to, or practise, several traditions at once. Here is Chandra Laksamba, ex-Gurkha, Limbu, and PhD from the University of Surrey, responding to the question 'Are you still able to practise your religion?' in a video at the exhibition 'Nepali Connections' at Surrey Heath Museum:[13]

---

[13] 'Nepali Connections: An exhibition celebrating the local Nepalese population, Nepalese culture, Nepal, the Gurkha background and how Surrey Heath has become home', 21 April to 30 June 2012.

> Nepalese people do not strongly stick with one religion, they are always with at least two or three. I do believe and practise in three religions: Hindu; I go the Pashupati temple in Kathmandu, a very famous Hindu temple, when I go to Nepal. I go to Swayambhu, and the birthplace of Lord Buddha, that is the Buddhist religion. And I do practise my Kirat religion. Even though I practise Hinduism and Buddhism in my day-to-day life, I have a small *puja* place [shrine] in my house. I have Hindu and Buddhist statues. On top of that, at the time of birth and death, death rituals mainly, when you do wedding ceremony or naming ceremony, we have to follow Kirat religion. Especially when we die, death ritual is based on Kirat religion. We don't use Hindu priests or Buddhist lamas. I practise, directly or indirectly, three religions. But we are not very hardcore fundamentalist type of thing. When I was in the army I used to go to church. We do celebrate Christmas as well, we Gorkhas [sic] celebrate all (laughs).

In this case, we may see a primary sense of belonging to an ancestral religion (Kirati religion) but the full acceptance that alternative, scriptural religions are also practised.

An alternative response to the challenge of singular religious identity is to affirm a single belonging, while in practice going ahead and worshipping in more than one idiom. Thus one Gurung respondent said, "In fact I am both Hindu and Buddhist, but I tell people I am Buddhist." Another, a Rai, born a Hindu, said:

> There are no restrictions on religion in my family. They can become Buddhist, Muslim, Kirat, and so on. I want to see their happiness just like me. I am a happier person since I became a Christian. I would not stop my son becoming Muslim if he believed that it was for him. In my opinion, we do religious practice to feel happy. My wife feels happy when she does Saibaba *bhajan* [hymn-singing to Sai Baba]. So, I do not stop her doing this and

> I do not like to take away her happiness. This is my philosophy (*darshan*) of life. I believe in democracy and I want to see democracy in religion as well.

Here we see the tension between singular and multiple belonging played out within one family in the diaspora, and across the Abrahamic/Indic divide. We should not be surprised (just as Chaves advises) if there are disparities between the ways people represent their religious belonging publicly or in censuses (see Table 3.2) and what they say they do in their everyday religious practice.

It would be wrong to generalize from this one case and assume that Nepali families do not value unity or shared practice—most families do not in fact have different members going off in different religious directions. The sentiment that religious practice is about obtaining psychological happiness and peace is widely shared, however, whatever the different means of achieving it. It is also the case that there are more spiritual choices facing people today, whether in urban Nepal or in the diaspora: it has always been possible to combine adherence to one's family's traditional forms of religion with following a personally chosen guru and/or spiritual path; but with the new connectivity of different parts of globe and Indian TV channels with Hindu programming now easily accessible in most Nepali diaspora homes, it is possible that multiple belonging may be about to stage a significant comeback.

Conclusion

Discourses of ecumenicism and practices of polytropy are particularly attractive for non-dominant groups who find themselves in between competing hegemonic traditions. Today there is the additional pressure of singular or homogenizing activist agendas. Ecumenical attitudes may be increasingly prevalent throughout the world; polytropic practices, with their long history in South Asia, appear to be resilient even in the diaspora. Some activist groups have had success in their appeals to singular religious belonging, but even in these cases, a not insignificant number of individuals still opt for multiple identities. This trend should be of no surprise in the South Asian case, as it closely adheres to long-held religious histories and practices. Furthermore, it is clear that many lay people in China (Chau 2011), Japan (Reader 1991), and doubtless many other parts of Asia share the same relaxed attitudes to questions of religious belonging.

In the UK there is a striking contrast in the ways officialdom treats religion and national identity. In the census of 2011, when responding to the question on national identity, people were encouraged to tick as many as they thought applied, but in the questions on religion and ethnicity, answers were discounted if more than one was selected. The significant difference between religion and ethnicity was that there was a whole section under ethnicity for 'Mixed/multiple ethnic groups', whereas there was no such option under 'Religion'. Thus, in the UK's 2011 census, multiple belonging in nationality was encouraged; in ethnicity, it was permitted; but in religion, it was disallowed.

What we hope to have shown is that multiple religious belonging, although by no means normative or universal for South Asian or Nepali religions, is a viable and coherent stance, with deep historic roots, taken up by many Nepalis in Britain. They do so in full consciousness of what they are doing; they are usually aware how such a position relates to Nepali history and how it counters British public discourse. Religiosity is a central aspect of their identity, and they deal with the modern cultural expectation that people should have a singular religious identity by quite deliberately choosing to adhere to more than one.

4

Buddhist, Hindu, Kirati, or Something Else? Nepali Strategies of Religious Belonging in the UK and Belgium

DAVID N. GELLNER, SONDRA L. HAUSNER,
& BAL GOPAL SHRESTHA

Introduction

National diasporas have a tendency to break up into multiple sub-diasporas, when there are sufficient numbers to support fragmentation and where there is sufficient cultural difference on which to base organizational separation.[1] Characterized as Nepal is by great ethnic and religious heterogeneity, it is hardly surprising that there are hundreds of different community, professional, and religious organizations that have emerged in the UK and in Belgium. This chapter compares the processes of community formation in the UK with those in Belgium, where there are many fewer Nepalis, but where there is an even higher per capita

---

[1] This chapter was originally published in a volume edited by Ester Gallo, *Migration and Religion in Europe* (Gellner, Hausner, & Shrestha 2014). We thank Ester Gallo and Martin Gaenszle for helpful comments.

number of organizations. We suggest that a higher degree of religious mixing in Belgium may derive from a greater focus on political identity groups, reflecting both a likely political orientation prior to migration to Belgium, and also a necessary politicization of the migration process, insofar as claiming asylum depends on the assertion of a political identity.

It is a question often raised in the study of migration how far the backgrounds and the motivations of migrants play an important role—alongside the social, political, and economic contexts to which they migrate and the conditions under which they migrate—in determining the degree to which a migrant community flourishes, once established in a new environment.[2] With this in mind it is interesting to compare Nepali migrants in the UK and Belgium, especially migrants from the Gurung and Limbu ethnic groups, as a pair of contrasting, yet in many particulars similar, cases. Both Gurungs and Limbus count as 'Janajatis', what before 1990 would have been called 'hill tribes' and are today often colloquially referred to as 'ethnic groups' (as opposed to 'castes'); in India the equivalent designation would be 'Scheduled Tribe'.[3] The UK is now home to a large number of retired Gurkha soldiers and their families, who make up approximately 60 per cent of the UK's Nepali population. Many of them are Gurungs and Limbus: if current estimates are right there are over 20,000 Gurungs and nearly 10,000 Limbus in the UK.[4]

---

[2] Watson (1977: 13), while discussing Marxist approaches that view migrants as no more than recruits to the working class, states that "it is a fallacy to argue that the migrants' own cultural predispositions and personal attitudes are irrelevant."

[3] Whether or not Janajatis, who make up between 35 and 45 per cent of Nepal's population, should have the sole right to be considered indigenous is a highly controversial question in Nepali politics (for an early discussion, see Gellner 2001b; see also Hangen 2010).

[4] Britain began recruiting soldiers from the Himalayan foothills in the early 19th century. These Gurkhas, as they were called, amounted to ten regiments at Indian independence in 1947; six regiments went to the Indian army and four to the British army. While India continues to

The particular cultural and religious histories of these two groups, the Gurungs coming originally from west Nepal and the Limbus from the far east of Nepal, mean that similar debates about religion and ethnic identity play out differently in the three contexts—UK, Belgium, Nepal—that we examine here. Throughout the chapter, we make links between the religious and political dynamics taking place in Europe with those in Nepal: these transnational conversations appear to be more salient in the lives of Nepalis in the European diaspora than are the debates about religion (about secularization or sacred symbols and the public sphere, for example) taking place in Europe, in their so-called 'host countries'.

In some ways, Britain and Belgium represent contrasting examples: the UK has longstanding ties with Nepal so that a few ex-Gurkhas and doctors from Nepal have been settled in the UK from the 1980s or even earlier, whereas Nepali migration to Belgium began only in the 1990s. The Centre for Nepal Studies UK produced an estimate of 72,173 Nepalis in the UK for 2008; it is often asserted that the number must now have surpassed 100,000. The biggest area of settlement is Greater Rushmoor (including Aldershot and Farnborough), the second biggest Ashford in Kent, and after that west London (Wembley, Southall) and east London (Plumstead). Nepal has long been an area of out-migration, due to landlessness and poverty; in the past migration was always overland and to different parts of India (to the north-east, westwards to Uttarakhand and beyond, and to the big cities). It was only in the 1990s that migration, for work and education, to countries outside South Asia began in earnest.[5] It is

---

recruit in large numbers, the UK has repeatedly cut back, so that only very few Nepalis join the British army's Gurkha Brigade today (176 in each of 2009 and 2010). For a summary of sociological information about Nepalis in the UK, see Adhikari (2012); on the ex-Gurkhas and their campaigns for equal treatment, see Laksamba (2012).

[5] On Nepali migration to India, see Hutt (2008), Sinha and Subba (eds) (2003), Thieme (2006), Sharma (2007); on the diaspora generally,

Table 4.1: Estimated Population Breakdown in the UK and Belgium Compared

<table>
<tr><th>Group</th><th>Nepal, pop'n census 2001</th><th>UK 2009</th><th>Belgium 2011</th></tr>
<tr><td>N=</td><td>22,736,934</td><td>18,801+</td><td>5,900</td></tr>
<tr><td></td><td></td><td></td><td></td></tr>
<tr><td>Bahun</td><td>12.7%</td><td rowspan="2">19.3%</td><td rowspan="2">16.9%</td></tr>
<tr><td>Chhetri (incl.Thakuri)</td><td>17.3%</td></tr>
<tr><td>Newar</td><td>5.5%</td><td>6.9%</td><td>8.5%</td></tr>
<tr><td>Tamang</td><td>5.6%</td><td>1.4%</td><td>1.7%</td></tr>
<tr><td>Magar</td><td>7.1%</td><td>13.9%</td><td>20.3%</td></tr>
<tr><td>Gurung</td><td>2.4%</td><td>22.2%</td><td>25.4%</td></tr>
<tr><td>Rai</td><td>2.8%</td><td>8.3%</td><td rowspan="2">5.1%</td></tr>
<tr><td>Limbu</td><td>1.6%</td><td>9.6%</td></tr>
<tr><td>Tharu</td><td>6.7%</td><td rowspan="2">0.3%^</td><td>?</td></tr>
<tr><td>Yadav</td><td>3.9%</td><td>?</td></tr>
<tr><td>Muslim</td><td>4.3%</td><td>0.01%</td><td>?</td></tr>
<tr><td>Dalit</td><td>12.8%</td><td>1.3%</td><td>1.7%</td></tr>
<tr><td>Sherpa</td><td>0.68%</td><td>1.56%</td><td>16.9%</td></tr>
<tr><td>Other</td><td>16.62%</td><td>16.79%</td><td>?</td></tr>
<tr><td></td><td></td><td></td><td></td></tr>
<tr><td>Proportion of overall pop'n</td><td>100%</td><td>c. 0.01%</td><td><0.001%</td></tr>
</table>

Notes
+number surveyed; total estimated population of Nepalis in the UK in December 2008: 72,173.
^refers to all Madheshis.

Sources: Nepal census; CNS-UK survey (*Nepali Sandesh* 8/9/09, pp. 1,3); fieldwork: informant estimates

Note: the UK figures are estimates but probably not far out, given the number surveyed; the Belgium figures are informed estimates only

now estimated that there are approaching a million Nepalis working in the Gulf, roughly half a million in Southeast Asia and South Korea (not including older diaspora populations in Burma and Thailand), 150,000 in the USA, and easily over 100,000 in Europe. In Belgium sober estimates put the total number of Nepalis at around 7,000 (see Table 4.1), so it is a small community in comparison with some other countries. Of course, Nepalis' citizenship status (or lack of it) varies considerably between these diverse contexts; in some of them (for example, the Gulf, Malaysia) there is little or no chance of ever gaining long-term rights to settle.

While most Nepalis come to the UK either as ex-Gurkhas or as students or professionals of some kind (doctors, nurses, chefs, computer programmers), the overwhelming majority of Nepalis came to Belgium as asylum-seekers. Nepalis knew that Belgium in the 1990s was relatively welcoming to political refugees, allowing them to claim citizenship after five years if they could show they had been disenfranchised in their home country. Our claims in this chapter are based on ethnographic work not with the political authorities of either the UK or Belgium, but rather with the Nepalis who have migrated to these two European countries. From our on-the-ground observations of associational life of Nepalis in Britain, community organizations (based on ethnic group, religious affiliation, Nepali district of origin, or British place of settlement) are the most common and salient in the UK, whereas in Belgium organizations with Nepali political party affiliation loom larger. This difference may stem from different macro-level European policies regarding religion and its categorization, or, as we suggest here, it may equally be the result of different groups choosing to migrate in different ways, that is, to different places, depending on existing networks and professional—as well as political—affiliation, or by maintaining a

---

see Chapter 1 above and Gellner & Hausner (2018); on migration to SE Asia, see Haaland (2008), Haaland & Gurung (2007); on labour migrants in the Gulf, Buslé (2010a, 2010b).

focus upon different aspects of Nepali identity. Whatever the ultimate mix of causal factors, the effects of different kinds of migrants 'ending up' in different European countries via different migration trajectories appear to affect the way religion is variably practised and mobilized around in new contexts.

The relative importance for Nepalis in Belgium of politics in the narrow sense, and the relative salience of a markedly 'polytropic' (the term is Michael Carrithers', 2000) and irenic attitude towards religion—or at least neutrality as to which religion one explicitly identifies with—are the main differences with the UK that we hope to explain. We distinguish here between *ecumenical* attitudes, which start from the notion that religions are distinct, separate, and equal, and should engage in tolerant dialogue with each other, from the characteristically Asian *polytropic* approach that presupposes the existence of numerous spiritual powers in the universe, many or all of which should be respected, religious labels being irrelevant and unnecessary in doing so. In South Asia, discourses that stress the ultimate unity of divinity and the ultimate oneness of truth behind a surface religious diversity are very widely known, to the point of being clichés, but such discourses are mobilized very differently in different contexts. In Belgium, it is our impression, they are far more salient and far more commonly heard, whereas in the UK considerable effort is being expended on defining and creating different, separate, and distinct religious traditions.

To be sure, the difference between Britain and Belgium is one of degree: committees and organizations affiliated to Nepali political parties certainly exist in the UK, and there are at least thirteen ethnic organizations in Belgium. Nonetheless, the relative prominence of political affiliation in Belgium when compared to the UK is striking.[6] The group with the largest following in Belgium is agreed to be the Congress Party, but it is

[6] The Nepali community in Australia is also said to be organized largely around political affiliation.

widely perceived as fissile and rarely capable of united action (split, in other words, into factions following the major leaders back in Nepal). The pro-Maoist organizations comprise the second biggest group: they are both more committed, people say, and more united, with considerable organizational strength. One of their greatest campaigning successes, on their own account, came in 2003 when, in alliance with Belgian leftists and Greens, they persuaded the Belgian government not to continue exporting machine guns to Nepal during the civil war, thereby gaining an advantage for their own party in Nepal and substantially increasing the pressure on the then Prime Minister, Sher Bahadur Deuba.

Whereas politics are more salient in Belgium (at least, so far), religious difference is more stressed in the UK. There certainly are Buddhist Nepalis in Belgium, and many Nepalis in Belgium participate in Buddhist events regardless of their primary religious identity. This pattern applies particularly to the celebration of Buddha Jayanti at the monastery of Huy in the east of the country (as many as five or six coachloads of Nepalis go each year). However, there is no specifically Nepali Buddhist organization in Belgium and most Nepalis in Belgium seem happy not to draw religious boundaries in any exclusive way, as will be discussed further below. Belgium's reputation as relatively liberal in its attitudes towards asylum-seekers encouraged politicized Nepalis to come, in the hope that, in light of their political affiliations and the vulnerabilities those implied in a Nepali context, they would be given the right to stay in Belgium. It may be that, even if they were not politically involved before leaving their home countries, Nepalis ending up in Belgium found themselves obliged—or inclined—to develop political attachments, because these were the most prominent and active organizations there.

The UK and Belgium, despite these differences, represent not wholly dissimilar contexts of migration, especially when contrasted with places like Malaysia or the Gulf on the one hand, or India on the other—which are the most common destinations for Nepali migration. In both European contexts there is the prospect of obtaining citizenship, or beginning the path to obtaining it, after five years of continuous residence. In both countries the number of those who have failed asylum claims and found themselves deported is low; most do in the end manage to stay. In both countries, within a relatively short time of settlement, a rich associational life has grown up and a few individuals have even stood in local elections (and some have won office as Labour or Liberal Democrat councillors in the UK).[7] The Gurkha connection is of course unique to the UK. The successful campaign to win the right of settlement for all retired Gurkhas with at least four years' service (for which the actress Joanna Lumley was the most public figurehead) created a new route to citizenship and a new kind of migration not found elsewhere.

The similarity between Nepali migrant communities in the two countries is even stronger in that the same groups seem to be represented in both places (see Table 4.1): in both the UK and in Belgium, the Gurungs (just 2.4 per cent of the population of Nepal) are the largest ethnic group; in both countries, Madheshi, Muslim, and Tharu groups from the Nepalese Tarai (the southern strip of Gangetic plain) are relatively under-represented. Dalits and Muslims are the poorest groups in Nepal and it is no surprise that few of them have succeeded in migrating to Europe. The proportionately large number of Sherpas in Belgium is also worthy of note: in absolute terms there are more Sherpas in the UK, but as a percentage they form a much bigger part of the Belgian Nepali diaspora.

---

[7] For overviews of the literature on immigrant organizations, see Schrover and Vermeulen (2005) and Moya (2005).

Gurungs in Nepal and in the UK: Difference and contestation[8]

In the past, in Nepal, competition between different religious streams within Gurung society certainly existed. Mumford (1989) has described in great detail how the 'dialogue' between the shaman and the Tibetan lama played out in a northern Gurung village when Tibetan refugees settled nearby. Much of this debate centred on whether animal sacrifice is a sin (the Buddhist view) or rather is essential to appease the gods (the shamanic view, and one incidentally shared by many Hindus)—still a live issue among Janajati groups and more widely in Nepali society today.[9] Elsewhere, in more southern villages, Gurungs also made considerable use of Bahun (Brahman) priests, and of course Gurungs in the British army had—on the official level—recourse to Brahman pandits as religious chaplains. Uesugi (2007) describes how Gurkha soldiers adapted very well to the official Hinduism of the Gurkha brigade whatever their preferences when back home.

After 1990 in Nepal, in the new freer political atmosphere of multi-party Nepal, the Janajati movement encouraged many groups to seek a non-Hindu identity. The Nepal Magar Samaj, for example, encouraged Magars to return their religion as Buddhist in the census of 2001; there was a movement to train Magar religious specialists in Buddhist ritual so that Magar villagers would no longer need Brahman priests to perform them (Letizia 2005, 2014). There was, likewise, a meeting in Kathmandu in the mid-1990s that decided that the Gurung religion was Buddhism.

---

[8] It is necessary to deal with Nepal and the UK together because, as Moya (2005: 837) puts it, "[t]o focus only on [immigrants'] experiences in the new land is to miss half the story."

[9] Ortner (1990, 1998, 1999) has described how reformed monastic Buddhism carried all before it among the Sherpas during the 20th century, and the concomitant disappearance of shamanism among them. See also Hangen (2005), Adhikari & Gellner (2016b), and Michaels (2016).

But this verdict never commanded full assent, and the Tamu Pye Lhu Sangh (TPLS) was founded to promote the claims of the traditional shamanic priests, allowing for the inclusion of the 'Bon lama': the lama priest from the Gurung Lama clan, rather than the more 'cleaned up' Lamaism more directly tied in to the institutions of Tibetan Buddhism.

This religious and associational ferment in Nepal after 1990 was reflected in the UK: members of the Nepali diaspora created numerous professional, literary, district, and ethnic organizations (see Table 4.3), and also a variety of different Hindu and Buddhist organizations. To a considerable extent the types of organization created reflected processes to be found equally in Nepal. The growth of the discourse of indigeneity in Nepal, for example, with the concomitant redefinition of religious identities, is certainly matched and supported in the diaspora.[10] But it would seem that, even beyond this, there is a separate effect of the very Western notion of separable and separate religious identities. In the UK a far greater proportion of Nepalis identify as Buddhist than in Nepal. This difference is partly to do with the balance of ethnic population (the larger proportion of Gurungs, for example, most of whom now identify as Buddhist), but it is also reinforced by the absence of the wider Hindu context of Nepal.[11]

In these different circumstances, many Gurungs in the UK, whose parents would have been happy to be classified as Hindu in the census in Nepal, now claim assertively that they are Buddhist. For instance, a London-based Gurung attending a religious

---

[10] On the concept of indigeneity in the Nepalese context, see Fisher (1993), Pradhan (1994), Gellner (2001b, 2009), Onta (2006), Whelpton, Gellner, & Pfaff-Czarnecka (2008), Hangen (2010), Adhikari & Gellner (2016a), and the websites of NEFIN (www.nefin.org.np) and NFDIN (www.nfdin.gov.np).

[11] For more on singular religious identity as a modern Western concept and its influence on the rise of religious groups among Nepalis in the UK, see Chapters 1 and 2 above.

service by Thrangu Rinpoche in Oxford in July 2009 explained to Gellner:

> We have no Hindu gods in our prayer room; we are pure Buddhist. You see, we Gurungs came from the mountains. Then we mixed with Bahuns. They were educated and we were not. So we adopted a lot of Hinduism. In my father's generation people were very mixed up. There was chaos (*anyol*). But now we know. Now we don't observe [the Hindu festivals] Dasain and Tihar.[12]

Other Gurungs argue on the contrary that the Gurungs' original religion was neither Buddhism nor Hinduism, but the shamanic oral tradition of the Paju and Khlibri shamans, which is a kind of 'nature religion' (*prakritivad*), or 'animism' (*jiv-vad*).[13] Insofar as there was a Buddhist element, it was adapted to these indigenous shamanic traditions and, it is claimed, is better labelled as 'Bon' (referring to the pre-Buddhist religion of Tibet). These fierce debates over what is the true Gurung religion assume that every ethnic group should have a single religion, ideally one that distinguishes it from its neighbours, just as it should have its own language. It is also often assumed that paradigmatically a people should have their own script (two Nepali ethnic groups, the Newars and the Limbus, do indeed have their own distinct scripts, and Tamangs and other similar groups make use of the Tibetan script; in nearby Sikkim, where this form of scriptophilic multiculturalism has gone the furthest, the *Sikkim Herald* newspaper appears in as many as ten different scripts).

[12] As a matter of fact, most Gurungs do continue to observe Dasain, at least to the extent of participating in Dasain parties. Practice within people's homes is very diverse, but many who claim publicly to be Buddhist or Bon continue to worship Hindu deities at home. See Chapter 5 below.

[13] For an examination of activists' discourses of 'naturism', see Lecomte-Tilouine (2010).

In the Gurung case, arguments over religion, in the UK as much as in Nepal, are given considerable emotional force and political bite by the fact that there are two sub-groups (defined by clan membership). In the past one of the two Gurung sub-groups claimed a higher status than the other—a view vehemently and passionately contested today and denounced as the result of a Brahmanical plot to divide Gurungs among themselves (Macfarlane 2008). Nowadays there is no hierarchy of Gurung clans, and in fact marriages happen fairly often between the two sub-groups, but the memory of the hierarchies that were asserted well within living memory has made the whole issue of religion far more sensitive than it otherwise would have been.

As a consequence, though many Gurungs are happy to patronize the religious services of different specialists in the UK, there is an undeniable polarization, which is felt by all Gurungs (even those who would prefer to resist a clear-cut, one-identity-for-all-contexts form of religiosity). On the one side are those Gurungs who favour Mahayana Buddhism and increasingly take recourse to Tibetan and Tibetan-trained teachers, most of whom are members of the organization Tamu Dhee. On the other are the supporters of the Tamu Pye Lhu Sangh (TPLS), who reject Buddhism entirely and seek to create written versions of the oral liturgies and scriptures of traditional Gurung shamans. They argue that what all Gurungs actually follow has always been, and should now again be recognized as being, the Bon tradition.[14] One aspect of the polarization is that the two groups, one led by the Tamu Dhee, the other by the TPLS, observe their own separate Lhosar (New Year) celebrations, sometimes on the very same day. When competing festival occasions coincide in this way, most people have to choose which one to attend, though a few high-profile individuals feel obliged to show equal loyalty to both groups, and may go first to one and then the other event.

---

[14] See the Tamu Pye Lhu Sangh website, for further details: www.tamu-pyelhu.org.

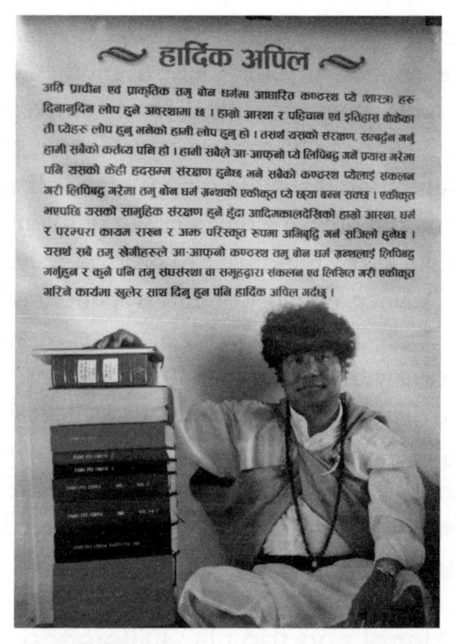

4.1 A poster showing Paju (shaman) Yarjung Kromchhen Tamu posing with the oral scriptures that he has redacted. The poster is an appeal (in Nepali) for supporters to help preserve the scriptures which are said to be essential for Tamu (Gurung) identity. The poster was on display, along with many others, as well as ritual implements, during the annual TPLS Lhosar (New Year) celebration in December 2010 held in Aldershot. (D.N. Gellner)

Even as we chart religious change between adult Nepalis in the UK and their elderly parents in Nepal, one point to note about the Nepali community in Europe is that religious difference is not a question of the younger generation mobilizing to reject and/or reform the traditional practices of their elders. Young Nepalis most certainly do organize separately—for sporting, musical, and social service events. But in religion—so far—they generally follow the preferences of their parents. If they express any contrary view at all, it is to complain about the divisions within their parents' generation, which may mean that they find themselves obliged to attend different events from their friends.

The religious pluralism practised by so many in Nepal—following one religion in one context, another in a different context, without it being conceptualized as 'different religions'—has increasingly come to be seen as a problem in the face of the modernist assumption that all individuals, and all ethnic groups, should have one and only one religion.[15] In this context, there has been a campaign, led by Buddhist ex-Gurkhas, to have the British Ministry of Defence employ Buddhist pundits alongside the Bahun ones. There is now provision for three such Buddhist chaplains to serve with the Gurkhas, in comparison to six Hindus. Buddhist activists continue to fight for greater Buddhist representation. They argue that Buddhists are actually in a majority among serving Gurkhas, and reject the Ministry of Defence's position that the six to three ratio correctly reflects the religious balance within the brigade.

Limbus in Nepal and the UK: Difference and accommodation

The Limbus of the far east are a slightly smaller proportion of Nepal's population than the Gurungs. A considerable number are found over the border with India in Sikkim and Darjeeling as well. They came under the rule of the Shah dynasty later than the Gurungs and are proud that they were incorporated into the kingdom of Nepal by means of a treaty in 1774, which guaranteed them the continuation of their traditional form of collective land tenure, *kipat* (although this right was to all intents and purposes revoked by the land reforms of the 1960s [Caplan 2000: Postscript]).

Unlike the Gurungs, many of whom, as we have seen, identify as Buddhists, the Limbus, like others in eastern Nepal, have undergone very little influence from Buddhist populations to

---

[15] Fisher has described the same issue among the Thakalis. He was present at a five-day meeting, held in Pokhara in 1983, when it was discussed at length by Thakali leaders (Fisher 2001: 3–4, 143f).

their north and east. Limbus, Rais, Sunuwars, and Yakkhas, although all listed as separate ethnic groups by the Nepalese state, recognize kinship among themselves: all count as Kiratis (or Kirantis), a very old ethnic category designation for Himalayan mountaineers found in the Mahabharata and other ancient texts.[16] They all have oral traditions, known variously as *mundhum*, *muntum*, *muddum*, or *diula*, which contain myths about the ancestors and details of the rituals to be performed in their memory.[17] There are several types of traditional priest, some more shamanic than others, among the Limbus, as among other Kiratis.[18] They are all associated with animal sacrifice and with the use of alcohol as an offering and as part of ritual occasions.

A very different reformist tradition was established by the Limbu guru Phalgunanda (1885-1949), who established the Satyahangma sect (often abbreviated to 'Satyahang'). His teachings stressed non-violence, celibacy, and serving others. The Satyahangma movement became well established in Panchthar district if less strongly in other parts of east Nepal. There are many stories of the miraculous accomplishments of Phalgunanda. The leader of the sect today is Atmananda, who is held in no less respect.[19]

As is evident to at least some of his followers, Phalgunanda's path, with its ritual use of the conch shell and fire sacrifice, is closely related to Saivite Hinduism (though also taking inspiration, via the Josmani sect, from the Sant movement). However,

[16] See Gaenszle (2000) for a detailed scholarly discussion of the term 'Kirata/Kiranta' and its modern uses. There are some Tarai populations (Danuwar, Meche, Rajvamshi) which also self-identify as Kiratis. On Kiratis generally, Iman Singh Chemjong wrote an influential history, the original version of which was published in 1948 (Chemjong 2003); see also Subba (1999).

[17] These Kirati oral texts are distantly related to the Gurung *pye* (part of the TPLS's name) (Gaenszle 2002a: ch. 1).

[18] See the papers by Jones, Sagant, Fournier, and Allen in Hitchcock and Jones (1976).

[19] For more on the movement, see Gaenszle (2011).

Phalgunanda also put great stress on scriptures in the Limbu language and Limbu script, so that his movement is simultaneously a Limbu or Kirati nativist one. Contemporary followers in Nepal and in the UK tend to be Kirati activists, insofar as they lay claim to an original or indigenous religious tradition of Nepal; it is a matter of great pride for Limbus and other Kiratis that Phalgunanda was declared a 'national hero' of Nepal in 2009. Practitioners who follow Phalgunanda return their religion as 'Kirati dharma' in the census, but so, increasingly, do other Limbus who are not followers of the Satyahangma tradition. Consequently the label encompasses radically different practices, some of which are defined by their rejection of those of their co-ethnics who claim the very same identity.

Among Limbus in the UK, whether activists or not, there seems to be no desire to use the strong religious difference between the two practised forms of religion as the basis for any kind of social separation. Yet, in practice, two distinct groups, one followers of Satyahangma, the other traditionalists, are working separately to raise funds for a Kirati dharma temple or *manghem* in Ashford, Kent (the biggest centre of Limbu settlement). It is not clear if they will be able to accommodate both kinds of religion equally. In Kathmandu, although they started together in a site in Hattiban shared with other Kirati groups, the followers of Phalgunanda were expelled in 2006, following a severe disagreement, on the grounds that their practice was 'too Hindu' (especially the performance of fire sacrifice) and they had to found their own temple elsewhere (Gaenszle 2016; Shrestha & Gellner 2018).

In the UK, one ex-Gurkha Limbu, Ram Kumar Thebe, has taught himself the rituals and become a *sabdi guru* or Satyahangma priest so that he can carry out prayers and rituals for Phalgunanda followers. He, his wife, and like-minded Limbus do their best to spread the thoughts of Phalgunanda in the UK. Similarly, those who practise traditional Limbu religion now have at least two priests to call on: both are ex-Gurkhas who arrived in 2010 and

4.2 A *mangseva* ritual performed in Coate Water Country Park, Swindon, in June 2012 by followers of the Satyahangma religious movement. Led by sabdi guru Ram Kumar Thebe, participants offer worship to the fire sacrifice pit. (B.G. Shrestha)

2011 respectively. Both claim that the knowledge of the *mundhum* or oral scriptures came to them suddenly in a trance many years ago, and that they had no choice but to take up and continue the tradition. One of them told Shrestha, "I had never read anything about the *mundhum* before. Trance caught me from time to time but I did not practise reciting the *mundhum* as a professional priest (*samba*). It was only from 1985/6 that I began to chant regularly. I could not prevent either the trance or the chanting. If I had not taken up practising [as a priest], it [the divine power] would have harmed me."

Compared to the Gurungs, Limbus in the UK are less well organized, at least as far as religion goes. This is partly because their majority practice is the shamanically based traditionalist religion, with few practitioners, no scriptural learning, and no formal history of organization; some priests are self-chosen and others have gurus, but these are personal lineages, not organizational structures. The reformist tradition founded by Phalgunanda has the rudiments of such an organizational framework, but it has yet to institutionalize itself in any substantial way outside of Nepal. By contrast the Gurungs have been tied in to pan-Asian and global Buddhist networks for some time. Their shamanic tradition is also in a healthy state in the UK, where there is one charismatic teacher, Paju Yarjung Kromchhen Tamu (see Plate 4.1), with many disciples and considerable support. This in turn has generated an effective transnational organization, the Tamu Pye Lhu Sangh, active in the UK, Nepal, and Hong Kong. The TPLS is working hard to establish a new religious identity, namely Bon, which it hopes to persuade all Gurungs to adopt in due course. It is, however, noticeably absent in Belgium.

Religious developments in Belgium

As noted above, Belgium has a much smaller population of Nepalis than the UK, even though the proportions of different ethnic groups are for the most part strikingly similar. The largest number of Nepalis in Belgium is found in Antwerpen (Antwerp), followed (in order) by Leuven, Brugge (Bruges), Sint Truiden, Brussels, and Ostend. What is immediately noticeable, when listing the various Belgian Nepali associations, is that, unlike in the UK where there are at least two specifically Buddhist groups, there are no groups for Buddhist worship there (see Table 4.2). Nepalis join with Belgian Buddhists, who are on the path to becoming an officially recognized religion (see Roos 2014), but have not attempted to organize as Nepali Buddhists. As one would expect, because the total population is small, there are many fewer regional associations, whether based on Nepali districts or based on localities in the country of settlement.

The numbers of Gurungs in Belgium are insufficient to support separate Gurung organizations. And in any case there are no Paju and Khlibri priests as there are in the UK, or facilities to train them, as there are in Nepal and in the UK. So Gurungs are Buddhist both by default (their own shamans are absent in Belgium) and as an assertion (as Janajatis who are no longer content to be identified as Hindus). A further factor is said to be the different, much less balanced, internal clan structure in

Belgium (contrasting with Britain where the two macro groups are more or less equal in size). Gurungs in Belgium recalled the fact that a conference in Kathmandu in the 1990s had decided that the Gurung religion was and should be Buddhism, and insisted that the Gurung organization in Belgium had consciously set out to be inclusive.

For Limbus in Belgium, the case is similar. There are no Satyahangma priests in Belgium. Although people have heard of the sect there, the movement is regarded as something distant and exotic, 'good for society', but not something they themselves practise. In Belgium, rather than organizing separately, Limbus join with other Kirati groups (Rai, Sunuwar, Yakha, Danuwar) to form the Samyukta Kirant Samaj (United Kirant Society). However, though they maintain the 'traditional' religion, rather than Satyahangma reformism, there is general agreement that in the new context of Belgium it would not be acceptable to perform animal sacrifice, and so, by force of circumstance, they have come closer to the Satyahangma ideal without adopting its liturgies or rituals.

Both in the UK and in Nepal, there is a certain amount of anti-Dasain discourse: boycotting the principal Hindu festival, which is the foremost annual festival of the country, is a mark of distinction for Janajati activists.[20] Many Janajati individuals in the UK do now observe it (and most probably never stopped doing so); but they observe it merely as a social festival, an annual pan-Nepali event. Specifically Janajati *organizations* do not observe it. In Belgium the same is true, though all seem to participate equally and to a greater extent than in the UK. The classical South Asian discourse, mentioned above and familiar from the Panchayat period in Nepal and within India since the 19th century at least, that all religions are effectively equivalent, that labels do not matter, that one can be a Hindu, a Kirati, a Christian, and a Muslim all at once, and that it does not matter where one prays

---

[20] See Hangen (2005, 2010).

Table 4.2: Complete List of Nepali Organizations in Belgium (as of 2011), with year of foundation where known

General	Belgium regional	Nepali regional	Political	Ethnic	Religious	Professional	Cultural and social
Non-Resident Nepali Belgium (2004)	Nepali Samaj Ostend (2010)	Baglung Samaj (2010)	Janasampark Samiti [NC] (2006)	World Magar Federation (2002)	Sanatan Dharma Seva Parisad (2008)	Nepalese Businessman's Association (2006)	Nepali Youth Club (2009)
Belgian Nepalese Tibetan and Bhutanese	Everest Nepali Society (Brugge) (2010)	Sikles Parche Kalyan Kosh (2003)	Nepali Janapragatisil Manch [Maoist] (2000)	Samyukta Kirat Samaj (2010)	Jayatu Samskritam (2008)	Euro Nepal Kalakar (artists) Sangh (2009)	International Nepali Literary Society (2007)
	Shangrila Society (Leuven) (2005)	Chitwan Aid Trust (2006)	NDF Belgium [UML] (2006)	Tamu Samaj [Gurung] (2000)			Nepali Sanskritik (Cultural) Samaj (1998)
	Himalayan Society (Sint Truiden) (2003) [formerly Nepali Bhutani Pariwar (2001)]	Myagdi Overseas Nepalese Association (2007)	RPP Nepal (2000)	Sherpa Samaj (2005)			Indra Dhanus Club (2002)

		Parbat Samaj	Nepali Progressive Women's Forum [Maoist]	Pasa Pucha [Newar] (2004)			
				Kshetri Samaj (2010)			
				Tharu Samaj			
				Tamang Samaj (2009)			
				Thakali Samaj			
				Dalit Samaj			
				Nepal Janajati Sarokar Manch			
				Tamuwan Mukti Morcha (liberation front) [Gurung, Maoist] (2009)			
				Magarat Mukti Morcha (liberation front) [Magar, Maoist] (2008)			

Table 4.3: Selected Nepali Organizations in the UK (as of 2011) with year of foundation

General	UK regional	Nepali regional	Political	Ethnic	Religious	Professional	Cultural and social
Non-Resident Nepali UK (2003)	Bracknell Nepalese Society (2006)	Baglung Samaj UK (2008)	Nepalese Democratic Forum [UML] (2004)	Association of Nepalese Madhesis in UK (2008)	Buddhist Community Centre, Surrey (2005)	British Gurkha Welfare Society (2004)	Nepalese Youth UK (2006)
Help Nepal Network (1999)	Burnt Oak Nepalese Society (2004)	Barpaki Samaj UK (2005)	Pragatishil Nepali Samaj UK [Maoist] (2004)	Bishwakarma Welfare Society (2006)	Lumbini Nepalese Buddha Dharma Society (1997)	British Nepal Lawyer Association (2009)	Pravasi Nepali Sahitya Samaj (Nepali Diaspora Literature Society) (2001)
Himalayan Yeti Nepalese Association in the UK, Manchester (1992)	Colchester Nepalese Society	Bhojpur Welfare Society UK (2009)	Tarai Madhesh Democratic Party (UK) (?2008)	Chhetri Samaj UK (2010)	Nepali Hindu Mandir Construction Committee UK (2005)	Gurkha Army Ex-Serviceman's Association (GAESO) (1990)	Nepali Sahitya Bikash Parishad UK (1985)
Yeti Nepali Association (1960)	Folkestone Gurkha Nepalese Community (2003)	Chitwan Aid Trust UK (2003)	Nepali Janasampark Samiti UK [NC] (2003)	Kirat Rai Yayokkha (UK) (2004)	Osho Sagar Dhyan Kendra, Worthing	Nepalese Caterers Association (2002)	Koseli Cultural Fusion (1986)
Nepal Support Society (1997)	Greater Reading Nepalese Community Association (2001)	Dharan Samaj UK (2007)		Kirat Sunuwar Welfare Society (2007)	Shiva Culture UK (2006)	Nepalese Doctors' Association (1985)	
Friends of Britain and Nepal: Nepal Tourism Organization (1999)	Greater Rushmoor Nepalese Community (2001)	Gorkha Zilla Gurung Samaj (2008)		Kirat Yakthung Chumlung UK [Limbu] (2003)	Tamu Pye Lhu Sangh (2005)	Ex-Nepal Police Family Forum (2004)	

	Hays and Harlington Nepalese Association (2002)	Gulmi Jilla Samaj UK (2007)		Lila Phung (Ghale Samaj) (2009)	United Nepalese Christian Fellowship (?2008)	Nepalese Nurse Association (2008)	
	Nepal Forum UK, Greenwich (2002)	Hyalmo Samaj UK (2009)		Magar Association UK (2002)	World Hindu Federation, UK (2003)	Nepalese Artists Association (1996)	
	Nepalese Community of Oxfordshire (2006)	Lamjung Samaj UK (2007)		Pasa Pucha Guthi UK [Newar] (2000)		Worldwide Nepalese Students Org UK (2000)	
	Nuneaton Nepalese Community (2005)	Myagdi Overseas Nepalese Association UK (2006)		UK Sherpa Kidug (2003)		Sagarmatha Gurkha Community (2004)	
	Sussex Nepali Samaj (2010)	Sankhuwasabha Samaj UK (2007)		UK Tamang Society (2006)			
	Wales Nepalese Community, Cardiff (2009)	Taplejung Samaj UK (2007)		Tamu Dhee UK [Gurung] (2000)			
		Terhathum Samaj UK (2009)		Pun Samaj UK (2007)			
				Thakali Welfare Society UK (2000)			

Source: *Directory 2011 of Nepali (Individuals, Businesses and Organizations) in the UK*. Reading: Centre for Nepal Studies UK.

Note: This is only a selection of the many organizations operating in the UK. In particular, some aid and charitable organizations are not represented; there are also many clan or sub-caste organizations, as well as many functionally independent branches of the ethnic and ex-Gurkha organizations. In addition the many organizations of particular intakes of Gurkha soldiers (e.g. 1970 intake, 1984 intake, etc.) are also omitted.

4.3 Traditional Limbu priest (*phedangma*) Padma Prasad Sambahamphe worships nine jungle deities in a private garden in Ashford, Kent, as a prelude to the public celebration of Chasok Tongnam, a Limbu harvest festival, in December 2011. (B.G. Shrestha)

since God is ultimately one, appears to be much stronger in Belgium than it is in the UK. This 'polytropic' discourse seems to fit well with the smaller numbers of Nepalis and the more fluid relations between them. Thus, when emphasizing their distinctiveness as Kiratis, informants stressed that their religion, unlike Hinduism, consists in the worship of nature; in other contexts, they were equally happy to be seen as part of traditional Nepali culture, even while asserting the antiquity of Kirati identity.

Furthermore, worship of and reverence for Sai Baba seems to cut across all ethnic and religious lines in Belgium as it does in the UK. The followers of Sai Baba encourage this South Asian disregard for religious labels. The several hundred people attending the celebration of Sai Baba's birthday in Southall in 2009 were exhorted with the following sayings of the guru:

- You can be Hindu, you can be Muslim or Buddhist or Christian, but follow the path of truth (*satya*). Sai has no dharma but *manava* [human] *dharma*. Service (*seva*) is the highest dharma…
- Make love the centre of everything…
- Start your day with love and end your day with love (*prem*).

Nepalis in Belgium are very prone to the same discourses about religion more generally:

- We started [the] Sanatan Dharma [association], but we also attend Buddha Jayanti. Anyway, Krishna, Shiva, Vishnu, Buddha—there's no real difference. (Newar businessman, Brussels)
- We don't take *tika*, but we do often participate [in Nepali festivals]. Teej is our favourite festival. [Rather than the Moroccans with whom we pray] Bahuns and Chhetris are among our closest friends. (Nepali Muslim family, Leuven)
- I have sought holy places and found equanimity and peace in a church, in a mosque, anywhere; if I'm there I feel *santi* (peace): ISCKON temple, Huy *gompa*—there is peace everywhere. Yes, I belong to the various Nepali organizations [for religion] but that's not the focus. (Bahun businessman, Brussels)
- SH: "How come you [a Gurung] are at a Sherpa event?" We are of the same culture—mostly Buddhist... "So what is your religion?" He writes on a piece of paper (in English): PEACE. (Gurung man, Leuven)
- SH (on seeing pictures of Sai Baba and Shiva upstairs, whereas downstairs the restaurant is full of Buddhas): "Aren't you a Buddhist?" I don't care, I can go to church, no problem; I'm Nepali. (Gurung businesswoman, Leuven)

What these quotations illustrate is that Nepalis in Belgium are not at all concerned to distinguish separate religious categories, or even to mark out particular deities and/or locations as

4.4 A memorial meeting for the late Krishna Prasad Bhattarai, held by the Congress-aligned Jan Sampark Samiti (Public Relations Committee) in Leuven, Belgium, on 14 March 2011. The banner reads 'nationalism, democracy, socialism; Nepali Jan Sampark Samiti; Belgium estd 2000'. (B.G. Shrestha)

legitimate or illegitimate objects or places of worship. They are comfortable with the assertion of particular ethnic identities, but they are not taken with the religious purification strategy (implying a one-to-one correlation of religion and ethnicity) that many activists, both in the UK and in Nepal, are increasingly insisting upon. By contrast, Nepalis in Belgium *do* generally make a point of insisting on their party-political affiliation. Religion is a context in which they insist on commonalities. Even when they organize on ethnic lines (which by definition divides Nepalis from each other), other non-member Nepalis are always welcome to participate. Religious differences, as we have seen, are downplayed in Belgium to the point of being denied altogether.

Another factor may well work in the same direction for Nepalis in Belgium: namely the relative importance of religion and language in Belgian politics. While the idea of separate religious identities certainly comes into play in Belgium (Roos 2014), it is possible that, because communal and political conflict in the country focuses much more on language than on religion, this is another reason why religious difference is relatively less stressed among Nepalis in Belgium than it is among Nepalis in the UK.

Conclusion

Implicit in this brief survey are four paired comparisons: between Nepalis in the UK and Nepalis in Belgium, between Gurungs in the UK and Gurungs in Belgium, between Limbus in the UK and Limbus in Belgium, and between Gurungs and Limbus in Europe. In the background there has also been the contrast with processes in Nepal itself. As we have seen, Gurungs in the UK (though not in Belgium) tend to split on the question of religion, whereas Limbus, while recognizing religious differences, are inclined to assert a collective identity regardless (and indeed in Belgium do so in shared organizations with both other Kiratis and other Nepalis). Thus, the smaller numbers of Nepalis in Belgium mean that religious splits found both in the UK and in Nepal are not reproduced there; however, as we have seen, political divisions are salient in Belgium, despite the small numbers involved, and do faithfully reflect political conflict back in Nepal.

One immediately obvious conclusion is to acknowledge the influence of scale: without minimum numbers no organization and no movement can get off the ground (a point also made by Moya, 2005: 852, on the basis of a global comparison of migrants). Although the numbers are not certain or reliable, it would seem that on a per capita basis the Nepalis in Belgium manage to have more organizations than in the UK (compare Tables 4.2 and 4.3). But, because of the much lower overall population in Belgium, certain cultural identities cannot or choose not to find expression in organizational form. This explains the separation of religious identities within both Gurung and Limbu groups in Britain:

movements that flourish in the UK (TPLS, Satyahangma) do not exist in Belgium.

Second, it is instructive to see that the same argument about the appropriateness or otherwise of animal sacrifice (denounced as it is by Satyahangma adherents among the Limbus and the Buddhists among the Gurungs) is taking place among both Limbus and Gurungs everywhere (as indeed more widely in Nepal). However, the religious difference has only led to publicly articulated social distinction among the Gurungs. The probable reason for this is that only among the Gurungs does such a religious difference correlate with previous, and now fiercely resisted, social hierarchies. It seems that this social division does not occur among the Gurungs in Belgium because only in the UK are Gurungs present in sufficient numbers to support separate organizations.

A third conclusion is that the greater degree of politicization in Belgium (relatively speaking) is likely to be connected to the manner in which most Nepalis arrived there. One sophisticated informant ascribed the salience of politics in Belgium to the fact that the majority of Nepalis there are between 30 and 45. In other words, they belong to the generation that came of age in the newly and highly politicized period in Nepal, 1990–2006. Several Belgian Nepalis noted the parallels between Belgian and Nepali politics (no government for long periods, the politicization of ethnicity and language, and so on). Even if an individual was not politically minded in Nepal prior to migration, the process of moving to Belgium, whether for existing networks or the possibility of asylum, could lead to a politicization—or a retrospective politicization—of the migration process. We have tentatively suggested that migration to Belgium has in many cases been linked to political commitments. This pattern has led in turn to the predominance of political identity rather than religious grouping, though, to be sure, the fact of smaller overall numbers and the need to find cohesion rather than difference in such a context are also important influences. The Belgian context in which Hinduism and Jainism are not officially recognized as religions may also play a role here.

For a number of reasons a 'polytropic' attitude to religion—though common in Nepal and the UK—is even more pervasive and dominant in Belgium. The polytropic attitude—that religious identification is unimportant—can easily merge into an ecumenical one: the idea that religious identification is important but there is good in all religions and that all religions are equivalent in a significant way. No doubt Nepalis in Belgium do not consciously distinguish the two stances and stress them differently according to context. For Nepalis in Belgium religion is an important sphere in which they can come together and emphasize unity; for Nepalis in the UK that is all but impossible.

5

Shrines and Identities in Britain's Nepali Diaspora

David N. Gellner, Sondra L. Hausner, Chandra Laksamba, & Krishna P. Adhikari

Introduction

Migration often (though not always) gives rise to diaspora populations.[1] Where there are diaspora populations, there are often (but not always) public conflicts over culture and religion. In the study of such conflicts, Vertovec (2011) suggests, social anthropologists are in a good position to question the homogenizing and totalizing views of culture that are often invoked. In particular, anthropologists are able to examine how

[1] This chapter appeared originally in the journal *Diaspora* in 2016 (though with a cover date of 2010). In this paper all quotations from research participants are taken from interviews with Chandra Laksamba and all photographs (except Plates 5.1 and 5.2 by Bal Gopal Shrestha and 5.11 by K.B. Rai) are also by him. We thank all those who so graciously agreed to be interviewed and photographed. They have all given permission for the photographs of them and their shrines to be used.

far the conspicuous ritual and political statements made in the public sphere reflect what people actually do in the rest of their lives. In other words, they (and anyone who shares their commitment to ethnographic fieldwork) are well placed to ask and analyse in what ways Baumann's 'official discourse' is in tension with 'demotic discourses' (Baumann 1996). The issues raised by this tension are perhaps nowhere more salient than in contexts of changing identity such as religion in diaspora.

In this article we ask what kinds of relationship there are between the actual practices of private shrine-making by Nepali migrants to the UK (most of whom arrived after 2004) and the complex and contested processes of public religious identification, which are perhaps easier to track and generalize about (though, as will be seen, they are very far from being straightforward). The Vernacular Religion (VR) project brought together anthropologists from the University of Oxford (Gellner, Hausner), with Nepali social scientists based in the UK, who had set up their own research organization, the Centre for Nepali Studies UK (CNSUK), including the two co-authors (Laksamba, Adhikari) and Rajubabu Shrestha, as well as one full-time researcher (Bal Gopal Shrestha). As part of the project, in 2010–2011, Adhikari, Laksamba, R. Shrestha, and B.G. Shrestha surveyed 300 households. The households were selected randomly (but with care to have representation from all sub-groups) from a larger non-random sample of 2,151 households (7,842 individuals) put together by CNSUK two years earlier (see Adhikari 2012 for details). Along with information about age, education, and employment, the VR survey of 300 households collected detailed data on levels and kinds of religious practice. After every interview, the respondents were asked permission to photograph their shrine, if they had one.

Our focus on ordinary shrines in people's homes may seem unusual. Historians of art have, not surprisingly, tended to focus on outstanding images and objects of veneration, on objects of great ritual significance, or on objects that might be of interest to

Western art dealers because of their visual or practical uniqueness—although there are notable exceptions (see Garnett & Rosser 2013). Anthropologists of material culture have naturally reacted against this trend and concentrated on mundane or popular art (e.g. Pinney 2004), but religious art, or that used in devotional contexts, tends to be considered the domain of the specialist. Here we focus on the vernacular ritual objects that are used by Nepalis for everyday worship in their homes and in order to create private sacred spaces in a new country. We suggest that diaspora Nepalis[2] use various material strategies to express their relationship (or lack of relationship) to different religious currents (Buddhist, Hindu, shamanist, and other, including a blended religiosity), but also that particular patterns of expression are difficult to ascertain: like other modes of visual self-representation, personal preferences or circumstances may determine the configurations of a shrine as much as religious identifications do. Sometimes shrines are fully aligned with explicitly asserted political or ethnic affiliations, while at other times they seem to be entirely independent of or even at odds with them.[3]

The emergence of Nepali national identity

The stretch of hills and adjoining plains and mountains on the southern flanks of the Himalayas that we know today as Nepal was united under a single ruler, Prithvi Narayan Shah, for the first time in the 1760s. His descendants continued their conquests both west and east in the decades that followed, but with the Treaty of Sugauli signed with the East India Company in 1816, Nepal was restricted, more or less, to its present boundaries (four

---

[2] We are aware that many diaspora scholars would question whether Nepalis constitute a diaspora given how young the community is (Tölölyan 2012). However, Nepalis in the UK and elsewhere frequently refer to themselves as a diaspora and there is even a Nepali magazine based in London called *Diaspora*.

[3] This tension is examined in Chapters 1 and 2 above. On the themes of this paper, see also Chapters 3 and 4.

districts in the mid and far west Tarai were added as a reward for backing the British in the 1857 Indian rebellion). The idea of uniting all the diverse subjects of the Shah dynasty within one state system was expressed by the Muluki Ain or National Legal Code of 1854. It was supposedly modelled on the Code Napoléon, which the then Prime Minister Jang Bahadur Rana had learned about on his visit to Paris (Whelpton 1991). But a legal code less like the Code Napoléon it would be hard to imagine, since it was built on the principles of traditional Hindu law, and therefore sought to maintain and reinforce caste differences: Brahmans (in line with the Hindu idea that killing Brahmans, women, children, or cows were great sins) were not subject to capital punishment, and in fact many punishments varied with the caste of the offender.

The notions of Nepal as a nation, Nepali as a national language, and the country as a cultural unit, began to be promoted, and then very tentatively, only in the first half of the twentieth century while the country was still under the dictatorial rule of the hereditary Rana Prime Ministers (Burghart 1984). The nation-building period par excellence came only with the introduction of King Mahendra's non-party Panchayat regime (an authoritarian and modernizing guided democracy under the leadership of the king).[4] This configuration lasted thirty years, from 1960 to 1990, when it was overthrown by a revolution known as 'the People's Movement' (*jan andolan*). Favourite slogans of the Panchayat regime—alongside those emphasizing the leadership of the King and the role of the monarchy in bringing democracy, and advancing development, and

---

[4] For an introduction to the political history of Nepal in this period, see Hachhethu & Gellner (2010). For more detailed treatments, see Joshi & Rose (1966), Hoftun, Raeper, & Whelpton (1999), and Whelpton (2005). For introductions to the tumultuous events of the Maoist insurgency/civil war (1996-2006), see Hutt (2004), Thapa (2004), Pettigrew (2013), and Adhikari (2014). As well as describing the Maoist insurgency, Jha (2014) is a key introduction to the Madheshi issue.

guaranteeing national integration—were variations on 'unity in diversity' and 'religious tolerance' as hallmarks of Nepal. Political parties were banned: it was claimed that they encouraged sectional (or 'communal' as it is known in South Asia) interests. Organizations representing particular ethnic groups were not permitted. There was no positive discrimination for 'tribals' or 'untouchables' (Dalits) as established in India from 1947. The dominant ideology was that all Nepalis, whatever their background, were now equal (an official position that—as figures collected later and presented in the third column of Table 1.1 (above, p. 6) prove—hid considerable advantage for high castes). Foreigners who asked about caste occasionally found themselves rebuked for bringing up something that no longer existed.

These dynamics all changed with the collapse of the Panchayat regime in 1990 and the reintroduction of party politics. The new constitution still banned parties based on communal interests, but increasingly ethnic parties were formed anyway. There was an enormous efflorescence of ethnic activism (Lawoti 2005; Gellner et al. 2008; Hangen 2010); a decade later the ethnic issue was pushed still further up the political agenda because of the support it received from the Maoists (Hutt 2004; Lawoti & Pahari 2010; Adhikari 2014; Jha 2014). The election of a Constituent Assembly in 2008, where the Maoists were the largest party, was followed rapidly by the removal of the king, and declarations that federalism, republicanism, and secularism would be foundational principles of the new constitution. This first Constituent Assembly collapsed in May 2012 without being able to produce a constitution (Adhikari & Gellner 2016a). New elections were held in November 2013 (Gellner 2014b), which resulted in a very different balance of power: the Maoists were reduced to third place and the role official opposition. Following the devastating earthquakes of April and May 2015, a new constitution was declared in September 2015. However, the country immediately became mired in controversy and ethnic conflict, as the Tharus and Madheshis in the plains protested against what they saw as discriminatory provisions.

The years of increasing political turmoil, starting just before 1990, were also the years in which migration from Nepal took off. Nepalis have long migrated, usually in search of land, and latterly in search of jobs and other forms of livelihood. Thus, there are millions of Nepalis in India, particularly in northeast India, where they are famous as cattle herders. Many of these migrants continued onwards into Burma and others went still further into Thailand in the first half of the twentieth century. A second type and wave of Nepali migration began even before Indian independence in 1947, but accelerated after it: here Nepalis, rather than migrating east in search of land, went south and west looking for jobs as coolies, porters, waiters, and watchmen in the towns and cities of India. A third wave of migration began in the late 1980s as Nepalis started to go further afield: to the Gulf, to Southeast Asia, to Korea, Taiwan, and Japan. Others began to arrive in Europe, particularly Britain, and in North America and Australasia: many came as students, many others were economic migrants, at both low income levels and higher ones, in 'highly skilled migrant' or 'skilled work' visa categories. In Britain there was the special link with the Gurkha brigade of the British army: in 2004, post-1997 retirees were given the right to settle in Britain; following a public lobbying campaign and the defeat of Gordon Brown's government on the issue in 2009, pre-1997 retirees with at least four years' service were finally granted the same right.[5]

The more settled and better-off of these diaspora populations were and are in increasingly close touch with events in Nepal and often provide support for particular movements and parties within Nepal. They also support philanthropic efforts in Nepal and increasingly in their new locations in Britain. Although far removed from their homeland, they tend to recreate, or create in a new form, the cultural and religious practices of Nepal. Indeed,

[5] Nepali/Gorkhali migration history is summarized in Chapter 1 above. On labour migrants to Delhi, see Thieme (2006), and to Qatar, Bruslé (2010b, 2014). On Nepalis in the UK, see Adhikari (2012) including Laksamba (2012).

new forms of religious practice and identity found in the diaspora are also, interestingly, found in Nepal: the links across space appear much stronger than the fact of displacement in this regard, although it may well be that moving countries in the first place enables some known forms of religious activity to change in certain ways. Sometimes, however, the shifts in Nepali political culture have produced changes in religious practice, and these new forms move equally quickly to the diaspora.

Changing religious and cultural identities

Given the fact that Nepal encompasses terrain stretching from the Tibetan plateau and high Himalayas in the north to the flat Gangetic plains in the south, taking in foothills (which would count as mountains anywhere else) in between, it is hardly surprising that Nepal is culturally extremely diverse. It could well be argued that it is even more diverse than mere geographical determinism would predict, exemplifying a sociological pleasure in luxuriant diversity for its own sake, packing in as much linguistic, cultural, and religious difference as is humanly possible within short distances from valley to valley and village to village, divided as they are by ridges, rivers, and forest. Certainly Nepalis are proud of this range of cultural practice and language, although it is not easy to govern such a diversity of communities.

One illustration of this diversity can be seen in the official recognition of fifty-nine Janajati groups ('nationalities') as well as numerous caste groups making a total of 125 castes and Janajati groups registered in the census of 2011. Before 1990 Janajati groups were usually referred to as 'hill tribes' (or just 'tribes'—some of them, like the Tharus, are in fact found in the plains), Since 1990, they have often been, loosely, called 'ethnic groups'; they correspond to what in India are called Scheduled Tribes (but their proportion of the population in Nepal is much higher than it is in India). A still unpublished 2011 government field survey by Professor Om Gurung, an anthropologist at Tribhuvan University, suggested that a further twenty-five groups should be recognized (it also found that two of the fifty-nine officially listed groups did not exist). Several of these fifty-nine groups are tiny, with some having fewer than 100 members. The main ones are large: e.g., Magar (1.8 million), Tharu (1.7 million), Tamang (1.5 million), Newar (1.3 million), Rai (0.6 million), and Gurung (0.5 million). These sizeable populations have, over the last two decades, become major players in Nepal's ethnic politics, in Nepal and sometimes in the diaspora.

The major macro-categories—Khas-Arya, Dalit, Janajati, Madheshi ('people of the plains')—and their referents are shown in Table 5.1. Membership in the macro-categories is disputed and fluid. For people in the plains, everyone in the hills is a Pahadi: Khas-Arya, Dalit, and Janajati alike. Who exactly should belong in the Madheshi category is a highly political and contentious subject. Some Tharus (in the east of the country) are happy to be included in Madheshi political movements; others (more in the west) are vociferously opposed to being clubbed together with Madheshis. The term *Janajati* was fixed, for a time, by government recognition granted in the late 1990s. In 1994, Janajati intellectuals declared 'Janajati' to be equivalent to 'Adivasi' (indigenous). But as the political advantages of indigeneity became clearer, the category expanded, so that in the dying days of the Constituent Assembly's tenure, in May 2012, the government even conceded indigenous people's status to the Bahuns and Chhetris—the highest Hindu castes—thereby approximating Nepal to the Northeast of India where almost 100 per cent of the population is indigenous.[6]

In the diaspora these larger macro-categories (Dalit, Janajati, Madheshi, and Khas-Arya, as shown in Table 5.1) continue to be important but to a lesser extent than in Nepal (where, since 2008,

---

[6] Five days later the government reversed this decision under pressure from the Nepal Federation of Indigenous Nationalities (NEFIN). On the whole history of this Bahun-Chhetri mobilization, debate over the category 'indigenous', and the collapse of the first Constituent Assembly, see Adhikari & Gellner (2016a).

Table 5.1: Major Castes and Ethnic Groups of Nepal

Parbatiyas ('hill people')		Hill minorities (Janajatis)		Language loss among hill minorities	Taraians/Madheshis ('plains people')		Others	
Bahun	12.2%	Magar	7.1%	68%	Tharu	6.6%	Muslims	4.4%
Chhetri (incl. Thakuri)	19%	Newar	5%	34%	Yadav	4%		
Dalit (hill)	8.1%	Tamang	5.8%	11%	Dalits	4.4%		
		Rai	2.3%	16%	(+ many small castes incl. Tarai Dalits and Janajatis)			
		Gurung	1.9%	50%				
		Limbu	1.4%	14.5%				
Totals	**39.2%**		**+ c.27.2%**			**+ c. 28%**		**+ 5% = 100%**

Sources: Nepal Census 2011 census (total: 26,494,504) and Tamang, Chapagain, & Ghimire (2014: 6-9), with figures for hill minority language loss from 1991 census.

Notes: Dalits = former Untouchables; Janajatis, underlined, are mainly those who were formerly called hill tribes. Estimated figures for language loss are taken from Whelpton (2008: 59). All figures and some labels are likely to be disputed. The total of all Janajatis, when Tarai Janajatis are also included, is 37.2% according to the 2001 census. The label 'Madheshi' is particularly disputed. Bahun and Chhetri Parbatiyas have recently (at the time of the 2013 election) come to be labelled 'Khas Arya'.

Calculating language loss figures from 2001 and 2011 censuses is less reliable because many ethnic organizations campaigned for people of group of X to return 'mother tongue' as X, regardless of whether it was spoken or not.

proportional reservations for political seats and quotas for jobs in public service depend on them). Exactly how diaspora ethnic politics play out depends very much on the size of the population. Where Nepalis are few (as in Scotland or in Belgium), distinctions between different castes and ethnic groups are downplayed. Where the population is larger, internal differences begin to loom larger as well (Ch. 4 above).

Ex-Gurkha identity is particularly important in Britain. The salient caste and ethnic groups, and how their balance changes between different contexts, are shown in Table 1.1 (above, p. 6). The most striking differences between Nepal and Britain are that the Gurungs, who constitute only 2.4 per cent of the population of Nepal (according to the 2001 Census of Nepal), make up more than 20 per cent of the Nepali population in Britain, and the Limbus, who constitute just 1.6 per cent in Nepal, make up between 13 and 18 per cent in Britain (Adhikari 2012: 44). These differences are due to the fact that the British Army's Gurkha brigade historically recruited young men mainly from hill Janajati backgrounds, especially Magars, Gurungs, Rais, and Limbus. Other groups (e.g. Tamangs) often managed to get themselves recruited by passing as Gurungs.

The figures for religion in Nepal are shown in Table 3.1 (above, p. 59). They show that Hindus constitute the vast majority in Nepal, but the number of people reporting themselves as Hindus has decreased since 1990, following the fall of the Panchayat regime. Some Magar and Tharu activists have campaigned for 'their' people to return their religion as Buddhist—another major religion that is, significantly, not Hindu. Many Limbus and some Rais have been increasingly inclined to adopt the label 'Kirat' (or 'Kirata'), an indigenous category that was first introduced in 1991.[7] The ways in which the

---

[7] See Gaenszle (2000) for detailed discussion of the term 'Kirati/ Kiranti'. We prefer the form 'Kirata/Kirati' because Kirat groups themselves argue that the nasal sound is absent in their own languages.

various categories have shifted with the move to Britain are shown in Table 2.2 (above, p. 40).

A major shift between Nepal and Britain is evident in the much lower proportion of Hindus in the latter. Nonetheless, if one adds up the various dual identities (allowed in our surveys, but not in national censuses), Hindus still account for 55 per cent of the UK's Nepali population. Buddhists certainly make up a much larger proportion in Britain (more like 40 per cent as opposed to around 10 per cent in Nepal). The reason for this is the changed ethnic balance, with a much higher proportion of Gurungs, Thakalis, and Sherpas than in Nepal. Only Tamangs seem to be present in Britain in smaller numbers than in Nepal, which can be understood as the result of both the historical ban on their being recruited into the Gurkha forces and, relatedly their relative poverty and disadvantage compared to the Janajati groups that were regularly recruited, which very likely makes it harder for them to migrate to desirable destinations.

Table 3.2 (above, p. 62) has two different columns with figures from the VR survey. One shows the breakdown of religious identification when people were simply asked their religion ('before prompt'). The second column shows the response after they were read out a list of possibilities ('after prompt'), which included multiple responses (e.g. 'Hindu and Buddhist'). A comparison of the two columns shows that about 15 per cent of people, once made aware that they are allowed to have multiple religious affiliations, opted for two or more religions. Many people (especially Gurungs) shift from being simply 'Buddhist' to the 'Hindu and Buddhist' category.

Multiple religious belonging is much more common among some Nepali groups than among others (Table 3.3, above, p. 66). To the far right of the table are the Sherpas, the most strongly and unequivocally Buddhist group: they remain 100 per cent Buddhist, even when made aware that a dual religious identity was possible and allowed in the survey. At the other end of the spectrum are the Bahuns (Brahmans) among whom 91.6 per cent reported themselves as Hindu. In between, there are many different options, with the Gurungs and the various Kirat groups (Limbu, Rai, Sunuwar) particularly divided between the various options.

Which shrines for which religions?

Religious identification for Nepalis is clearly not a straightforward issue. Both in Nepal and Britain, religion rather seems a fluid and, for some, an explicitly political category. But do these various categorical distinctions, which are of so much interest to activists and religious specialists seeking to firm up their support base, matter to 'ordinary' lay people? In their daily practice do they observe any of the boundaries that census-takers and surveyors seek to describe? Can shrines help us to answer the question about affiliation as far as people's daily practice is concerned?

Fifteen per cent of the 300 households surveyed had no shrine. This total figure obscures the fact that, for most of the categories, the figures were lower (under 10 per cent)—meaning that more than 90 per cent of Nepalis in Britain had household shrines—with three notable categorical exceptions: of those who classified themselves as Kirat, 32.1 per cent had no shrine; of Christians, 65 per cent had no shrine; and, of those who identified as 'non-religious', 50 per cent (three out of six respondents) had no shrine. That Nepali Christians would put more emphasis on the Bible than on a visible altar and that 'non-religious' Nepalis would lack a shrine is hardly surprising. More interesting are the three cases of 'non-religious' household heads who nonetheless reported a shrine in their house. This seeming paradox may be the result of frequently gendered distinction—globally—between public affiliation (which in this case would be the domain of the male household head), and actual daily practice in the home (which would here fall into the sphere of the woman of the house).

That a significant number of Rais, Limbus, and Sunuwars (the Kirat groups) did not have a shrine at home reflects the fact that they have a distinctly different attitude to shrines and icons.

As the traditional Kirat tribal religion is based on oral scriptures, self-conscious adherents are aware that historically the Kirat tradition is aniconic. As one informant put it:

> Kirat people just need three water pots and some Titepati leaves to worship [the deities] Him Mang, Yuma, Theba, and Tagera Ningwaphumang. Once worship is over, these will be cleaned [and put away]... We Kirat do not have photos of our gods and goddesses. No one has seen the true likeness of God. Statues and pictures of God and Goddess are all imaginary. (Limbu, Kirati religion, Plate 5.10)

Thus, those who chose the 'Kirat' identity were much more likely not to have statues in their shrines. Only 40 per cent of Kirati-identified households had statues, whereas the figure for all other categories (Christians excepted) was 68 per cent or more.

It may be that what we are seeing here is the fluidity of the 'Kirat' religious label and a clear demonstration that one cannot read off any particular practice from a given census category. It could also be that the 40 per cent of those who identified as Kirat who did possess statues were making a political point by claiming their religion as Kirati, when in fact their practice was a mixture of Hindu and Kirat (often Hinduism for daily worship, Kirat tradition at birth and death). A Gurung, active in the Gurung cultural organization, Tamu Dhee, admitted a parallel kind of self-conscious slippage: "In fact I am both Buddhist and Hindu. I practise both religions in the real situation. But I tell people that I am Buddhist because we perform birth and death rites in the Buddhist way" (see Ch. 9 below). Indeed, this informant had a main silver shrine containing images of Hindu holy men and statues and images of Hindu divinities, with Buddhist images (clearly actively worshipped) placed right next to it (see Plates 5.15–5.17).

The simplest shrines are made on a shelf in the sitting room or bedroom, or a cupboard shelf in the kitchen or storeroom.[8] Sometimes even a small corner shelf on the staircase or landing may serve the purpose of creating an altar. A few posters or small framed pictures with a space to put offerings in front of them are all that is necessary; a bell and vessels for water and coloured powder may also be added. Sometimes a box with a door (such a bread bin) may be used to provide a complete enclosure.

Much more elaborate shrines are of course possible, when a whole room, or, as in one case, an entire garden shed, is devoted to creating a sacred space. These more elaborate (and relatively rare) cases tend to be found where the person concerned is wholly committed to one or other religion, usually Hinduism or Buddhism. Some committed Nepali Christians turn the whole home into a sacred space in the same way. Whether or not one does this depends partly on religious inclination, but it is also determined by constraints such as how long they have been settled in the UK and whether or not they own their own house.

Divine images were by far the most predominant icons on household shrines: 79 per cent of the 300 households surveyed had photos or posters of gods, 78 per cent holy objects (excluding photos, statues, and texts), 64 per cent had statues, and 33 per cent had holy texts.[9] Of total posters in the shrines of all responding households, 81 per cent were Hindu, 14 per cent Buddhist, and 5 per cent 'other'. That Nepal was historically a Hindu kingdom—meaning that Hindu-inflected practices run deep even among

---

[8] One young couple in Scotland dispensed with the need for any material object or space: they had a picture of the god Ganesh saved on their laptop and called it up to worship whenever they wanted to; which they justified as more environmentally friendly, as well as politic, since their landlord might not like them burning incense. Sometimes they also participated via Skype in rituals back home.

[9] The average number per household of all holy items kept in the shrine was 11; that of posters was 3.34; of statues, 2.14; of religious texts, 1.03; and of other holy objects (such as flasks, bells, or oil lamps), 4.98.

ethnic groups promoting alternative religious identities—is apparent through an analysis of these images. In Bahun household shrines, 99 per cent of posters were Hindu and only 1 per cent were Buddhist. Among households who identified as Buddhist, however, 42 per cent of the posters in their shrines were Hindu. Likewise, in the shrines of those who identified as both Hindu and Buddhist, 82 per cent of the posters were of Hindu gods. The equivalent figures for those identifying as Kirat, Kirat and Hindu, and Kirat and Buddhist were 84 per cent, 88 per cent, and 67 per cent respectively. By contrast, the position of Sherpas as strictly Tibetan Buddhist was clear: not a single Sherpa household had a Hindu poster, whereas 96.4 per cent had Buddhist posters.

A similar pattern is found with statues: Hindus are much less likely to have Buddhist statues than Buddhists are to have Hindu ones. Thus, only 10 per cent of statues in all Hindus households were related to Buddhism, but 36 per cent of the statues in Buddhist households and 71 per cent of the statues in 'Hindu and Buddhist' households were Hindu. A similar pattern was also found among Kirat dharma followers: 77 per cent of statues in the shrines of Kirat followers were related to Hinduism, as were 78 per cent of those who were both Kirat and Hindu, and 64 per cent of those who were both Kirat and Buddhist.

Taking all this variation into account, we propose a model as shown in Table 5.2. We borrow the term 'congruence' from Mark Chaves (2010), who argued, quite rightly, that "attitudes and behavior correlate only weakly, and collections of apparently related ideas and practices rarely cohere into logically unified, mutually reinforcing, seamless webs ... This is true of culture in general, and it is true of religious culture in particular" (Chaves 2010: 2).[10] It is naïve of scholars to expect that people will always hold consistent beliefs, that their actions and their beliefs will always be consistent with one another, or that what they do across

[10] The ideas here—the distinction between (census) category and (everyday) practice; and the difference between being multiple vs. being unitary in one's religious identity—are examined in Chapters 1 and 2 above.

Table 5.2: Kinds of Relationship between Religious Identification and Shrine Practice

Congruence (either specialist or lay)	**Incongruence** (usually laypeople)
Specialists: with elaborate shrines by the standards of their co-religionists	Claims to unitary identity combined with multiple practice (the identity claim can be to Hinduism, Buddhism, Kirati religion, or Bon)
	Claims to multiple identity combined with multiple practice (can be combined with a claim to ecumenical congruence)
Laypeople: simple Hindu, Buddhist, Satyahang, Kirati, or Bon shrines or places of worship	Claims to multiple identity, but where the practice would appear to be fairly uniform (rare)
	Multiple practice with claims to be unsure of 'true' religious identity

different contexts will always be entirely consistent. Consistency in beliefs and between beliefs and practices may occur, but inconsistency is far more predominant. In particular, the idea that everyone should have one and only religious identity is relatively new in the South Asian context and its arrival there has to do with the introduction of modernity, however mediated (see Chapter 2). Many Nepalis are starting to assume that each individual should have one and only one religious identity, and this modernist position has translated into the widely held stance that ethnic groups should share a singular religious identity that is authentically and originally theirs.[11]

Thus, there are many Nepalis in the UK who do try and sometimes succeed in being 'congruent'. On the whole, religious specialists tend to be purists who try hard to be consistent in their practice, and it is no surprise to find them being so (Plates 5.1–2). Some examples of lay people who are also congruent in this

[11] For a brief description of the ideas and writings of one Newar intellectual, Baldev Juju, who has tried to argue for a single 'Newar religion' underlying the apparent division into Hinduism and Buddhism, see Gellner (2011).

5.1 The elaborate Tibetan Buddhist shrine of Tirtha Ghale, Buddhist priest. (B.G. Shrestha)

5.2 The domestic shrine of Sabdi Guru (Satyahang priest), Ram Kumar Thebe, which is elaborate by the standards of Kirati religion. (B.G. Shrestha)

5.3 Simple Hindu shrine owned by Khon Bahadur and Chet Kumari Rana Magar and family (Hindu), shown in Plate 5.4. (C. Laksamba)

5.4 Khon Bahadur and Chet Kumari Rana Magar and family. (C. Laksamba)

5.5 Simple Hindu shrine in the house of Dinesh Khadka (a Chhetri). (C. Laksamba)

5.6 A simple Sherpa Buddhist shrine belonging to Phurlamu and Nim Tenzing Sherpa. (C. Laksamba)

5.7 Phurlamu and Nim Tenzing Sherpa and family. (C. Laksamba)

5.8 A Bon 'shrine' belonging Amar Tamu (Gurung). (C. Laksamba)

5.9 A simple Satyahang shrine with photographs of Guru Phalgunanda and the parents of the owner, Jamin Limbu. (C. Laksamba)

5.10 A Limbu couple, Subarna and Nanda Shobha Limbu, with no shrine: he is a traditionalist Kirati religion adherent. (C. Laksamba)

5.11 The home shrine of Karna Bahadur and Krishna Kumari Rai (see Plate 5.12). (K.B. Rai)

5.12 Karna Bahadur and Krishna Kumari Rai, who claim Kirati religion but evidently practise in a Hindu mode. (C. Laksamba)

5.13 Home shrine of Dharma Raj and Savitri Sunuwar. (Note the more minimalist style of the shrine.) (C. Laksamba)

5.14 Dharma Raj and Savitri Sunuwar, who also claimed a triple identity as Kirat-Buddhist-Hindu. (C. Laksamba)

5.15 and 5.16 The shrine and Buddhist images next to it of Surje and Pavitra Gurung. (C. Laksamba)

5.17: Surje and Pavitra Gurung; Surje claims Buddhism as his census category, but accepts that his practice is Hindu-Buddhist. (C. Laksamba)

5.18 and 5.19: The shrine and pictures of Nepaldhan Rai (a Roman Catholic), whose wife Bhagawati is a Hindu devotee of Sai Baba. (C. Laksamba)

manner are shown in Plates 5.3–10. We have already noted that there are many Nepalis who claim a unitary identity, usually for reasons of ethnic, cultural, and/or religious politics, while their practice remains multiple (e.g. Plates 5.11–12, 5.15–16).

There are also those diaspora Nepalis who accept a multiple identity and practise multiply (though the descriptor may be contested: Hinduism is usually a happy label for such inclusivist attitudes, although some claimed a dual or triple identity category when given the option: see Plates 5.13–14). Others accept the dominant unitary identity expectation, and realize that their own practice contravenes it. One man, a Magar and a Hindu, with no shrine in his house, but a Hindu shrine in his shop, said:

> Actually I am in 'confusion' as to which dharma I observe. In my opinion perhaps I follow two religions: Buddhism and Hinduism. Because I observe all the Hindu festivals like Dasain and Tihar. And I go for *darshan* [sacred vision of deities] to both [Hindu] temples and [Buddhist] *gompas*. But when we die, we have to make use of Lamas. I myself do not do any scripture recitation, nor do my wife or sons.

Here we have a self-conscious exploration of what it means to identify multiply, and to practise multiply, in the context of a modernity that assumes singularity and congruence. There are also those who solve the problem by giving each individual a free choice. Nepaldhan Rai, a Roman Catholic, whose wife is Hindu (see Plates 5.18–19 above), explained the situation as follows:

> There are no restrictions on religion in my family. They can become Buddhist, Muslim, Kirat, and so on. I want to see their happiness just like me. I am a happier person since I became a Christian. I would not stop my son becoming Muslim if he believed that it was for him. In my opinion, we do religious practice to feel happy. My wife feels happy when she does Saibaba *bhajan* [hymn-singing to Sai Baba]. So, I do not stop her doing this and I do not like to take away her happiness. This is my philosophy (*darshan*) of life. I do believe in democracy and I want to see democracy in religion as well.

Conclusion: The display of religion

To what extent are individual lay shrines congruent with people's categorically asserted religious identities? As we have shown, sometimes they are and sometimes they are not. Geertz would appear to have been uncharacteristically naïve here: "Religious symbols formulate a basic congruence between a particular style of life and a specific (if, most often, implicit) metaphysic, and in so doing, sustain each with the borrowed authority of the other" (1973: 90). He had, perhaps, forgotten internally pluralist or highly diverse societies, where the politics of religious identification will likely mean that one cannot simply read identity from symbol. The presence of the goddess Sarasvati or Durga on someone's shrine does not necessarily mean that that person is Hindu: he or she could be Buddhist, Bon, Kirati, or some combination of all these categories.

Sometimes, it turns out, religious images are just that: symbols that evoke religiosity writ large. The content of what they convey—their standard identifying category (Sarasvati and Durga as 'Hindu' goddesses, for example)—is less important than that they symbolize devotion and divinity in general. Having a shrine is more important in these instances than the specific objects or images that are displayed on that shrine. A religious category may be asserted, but equally, multiplicity may be the underlying semantic message of these collage-like altars. Still others may be 'cabinets' or collections of religiosity. Simply being a holy symbol—from any so-called world religion—is sufficient to constitute an object's worth in an altar. Conversely, in some cases, as we have seen, refusing to display or use icons may also be a statement of religious intent.

Shrines are a different way in to the problem of religious identity and practice: they may reflect a person's articulated religious identification, or they may demonstrate a different leaning. They are an articulation or assertion of religious practice, a means through which to express devotion to a particular deity or multiple deities. What we have stressed here is that they are private religious spaces in one's own home as compared to a public showing or attendance at a collective event, and as such speak to personal or soteriological religion rather than to collective religion, or religious affiliation as demonstrated through group identification.

When an individual or a family is publicly associated with a given religious organization or an activist movement that depends on religious identity, shrines at home may go further to confirm that identity. But this congruence is not always found: some activist members of religious organizations who might be thought to position themselves in opposition to mainstream religiosity have personal shrines that actually reflect a dominant soteriology. Shrines may reflect a spoken category or resist it. They may be consonant with a category, or they may constitute a practice—whatever worship, prayer, or thought that emerges from its owner's encounter with the icon or holy object—that is at odds with the articulation of the owner's category. That incongruity may remain unresolved, or a new more encompassing category may emerge. What had seemed incongruent is no longer so, from the new more encompassing point of view. Multiplicity is not aberrant in South Asian religions: a new form, a new adaptation, a new divergence works just as well as attempts to consolidate or unify in the name of purity and reform. It is a different mode of religious change, one where proliferation is not anathema to the very tenets of religiosity.

The point here is that personal religion is capable of evading the sharp lines and clear articulations of public or collective religion, since there is no one questioning the category. Shrines are a way—or better, a place—to be religious without being obliged to narrate religiosity. There is thus a striking contrast between the ecumenism of many personal shrines, on the hand, and the public campaigns to establish new temples in the name of particular religions in Britain, on the other. Although some Nepalis had thought that it might be possible to have a Hindu temple with a Buddhist *caitya* (small stupa or monument) attached, as is frequently found in Nepal, in practice this goal has so far proved impossible, and separate religious sites are now planned for Hindu and Buddhist organizations.[12] Likewise, plans for a temple in Ashford, Kent (the largest of Limbu settlement in the UK), which was originally envisaged as a shared space for both the reformist Satyahangma movement and the traditionalist Kirat religion, had to be abandoned.

A final remark is in order about the possible pitfalls of a focus on diaspora: as far as personal shrines are concerned, no clear differences between what people do in diaspora and what they do in Nepal are apparent (with the sole difference that some people in the UK are constrained by the premises in which they live to have smaller, less elaborate shrines). Nothing we have found stands in opposition to religious trends in Nepal. 'Diaspora' in

---

[12] The planned Non-Resident Nepali house in London is intended to have a Swayambhu and a Pashupati shrine side by side. In this more political and less religious context, this may prove acceptable.

this instance is a red herring, except to indicate that people's religious views and practices inside the home remain remarkably consistent across space.[13]

Where a diasporic lens may become useful, however, is in assessing the distinction between public and private in different parts of the world: arguably there is a sharper distinction between public and private for Nepalis in Britain than for Nepalis in Nepal. In Britain, the tensions we see in building public religious spaces appear to reflect a more consistent—or congruent—unitary religious positioning, while multiplicity remains a frequent symbolic discourse within people's homes.[14] This possibility, if borne out by further research, would confirm what South Asianists have long suspected: the analytical distinction between the public and the private domains that is seen as natural in the West does not have the same weight in South Asia. But that distinction clearly emerges in the diaspora: for Nepalis in Britain, personal shrines may remain a place of multiple and sometimes incongruent religious practice, while public spaces have started to become places of unitary categorical assertions, in keeping with modernist views of religion and the position of the national census that one may have one and only one religious affiliation.

---

[13] More than half of those surveyed did, however, say that they did less religious practice than in Nepal (one third said they did the same amount as in Nepal).

[14] This difference, at least, would be consistent with the trends for greater compartmentalization and more self-conscious alignment with global or world-religious models in the diaspora, as summarized by Vertovec (2000b).

6

Rights and a Sense of Belonging: Two Contrasting Nepali Diaspora Communities

Mitra Pariyar, Bal Gopal Shrestha, & David N. Gellner

Introduction

Whether or not a particular group of people feel that they belong in a given place depends, it need hardly be stressed, on a number of factors.[1] Age, generation, and the simple passage of time all play important roles. A group that has barely arrived, however favourable the circumstances, is unlikely to feel fully integrated and is bound to feel the pressures of an unfamiliar cultural and legal environment, as the Oxford UK case discussed here will illustrate. On its own, the simple passage of time is not enough to

[1] This paper was originally published in Toffin & Pfaff-Czarnecka (2014). It is based on the MPhil dissertation research of Mitra Pariyar carried out in Oxford in 2009–10 and the postdoctoral research of Bal Gopal Shrestha in Sikkim carried out mainly in 2004. It is also informed by the VR project. Thanks are due to Joanna Pfaff-Czarnecka for constructive feedback on earlier drafts.

engender a sense of belonging. Groups that experience systematic and ongoing exclusion from the host society may feel like the paradigmatic stranger in a strange land even if they have been settled for many generations (for example, South Asians who have been working in the Gulf states for several generations—though one should be careful not to take it for granted that such populations must necessarily be wholly alienated from the place where they live, just because they lack full citizenship rights). The role of succeeding generations, as is well known, is crucial: by the third generation they may even feel so at home in the new environment as to take up cultural and linguistic revival as a conscious choice.

The notion of belonging has recently begun to receive considerable attention as a sociological concept.[2] The notion of belonging manages to combine within it both ideas about ownership, rights (legal and moral), relationships to particular places and people, and subjective senses of well-being. These manifold links to diverse social fields and the very fluidity and processual nature of the concept perhaps explain why it appears preferable (or at least more promising) to some than the overused philosophical notion of identity, with its (on the face of it) de-socializing, homogenizing, and mathematical overtones.

One factor that seems to play a key role both in symbolizing people's sense of belonging, and in creating it in the first place, is ritual. One of us has explored this in relation to Newar people in Nepal (Gellner 2011): how rites make rights, so to say. It is interesting to see that in diaspora too ritual (whether one can freely perform it or not; how one performs it) becomes a crucial part of generating belonging (or failing to do so).

The second case to be considered in this chapter, that of Sikkim, illustrates a complex situation where all are citizens, but some have greater rights than others, which gives rise,

---

[2] See the introductions to Pfaff-Czarnecka & Toffin (2011) and Toffin & Pfaff-Czarnecka (2014) for overviews. For an introduction to the Nepali diaspora in general, see Chapter 1 above.

unsurprisingly, to complex and graded senses of belonging. The South Asian context is one in which different and graded senses of belonging have always existed. These subtle, complex, and overlapping forms of belonging are now, in the modern world, confronted with the pervasive assumption that everyone should have the same rights and that these should be articulated in clear, articulable, and legally enforceable ways. There are therefore sometimes uncomfortable clashes between older ways of articulating identity and the newer ones; and, however these are resolved or held in tension, the stage is set for multiple belongings: as a member of various nested 'ethnic' or otherwise defined groups; as a citizen of one or more nation-states; as members of professional groupings (e.g. ex-British soldier), and so on.

The ex-Gurkhas of Oxford

On 29 April 2009 UK Prime Minister Gordon Brown suffered a famous defeat, when an opposition motion was passed allowing all ex-Gurkha soldiers with more than four years' service in the British Army to settle in the UK.[3] Until that time Gurkhas retiring after 1997 (when Hong Kong was handed back to China) had the right to settle, but pre-97 retirees, who, the Ministry of Defence argued, had not formed any lasting attachment to the UK, did not. A high-profile campaign, with actress Joanna Lumley, the daughter of a Gurkha officer, as its very vocal and effective figurehead, had successfully enlisted the backing of the Liberal Democratic Party, some Conservatives, and much of the conservative British press and general public not normally known for supporting anything that would encourage greater immigration. The argument that soldiers willing to die for the UK should at the very least have the right to live there had become, in

[3] The term 'Gurkha', derives from the hill town of Gorkha, the origin of the Shah dynasty that ruled Nepal until the declaration of a republic in May 2008. It is used to refer to soldiers from Nepal serving in the British and Indian armies, in the Sultanate of Brunei, and in the Singapore police. This chapter concerns only British ex-Gurkhas.

a world more closely globalized than ever before, politically unanswerable.

The post-97 retirees, by definition a younger group, had already started arriving in the UK in large numbers following the 2004 decision to allow them to settle in the UK. The biggest years for arrivals were 2005-07. Today the largest Nepali communities are to be found in the Farnborough-Aldershot area (Greater Rushmoor Borough Council), in Ashford, Kent, and in Plumstead (east London). The total number of Nepalis in the UK may be between 100,000 and 150,000. About two thirds are either ex-Gurkhas or their dependants; the remainder are mainly divided between highly skilled migrants, students, nurses, restaurant workers, and asylum seekers. A few Nepalis (particularly doctors) had already come in the 1980s or 1990s, but the number of people born in Nepal and recorded in the 2001 census was only 5,943. By 2008 a survey by the Centre for Nepal Studies UK estimated that there were 72,173 Nepalis in Britain.

According to the Nepalese Community in Oxford (NCO, founded 2006), approximately 100 Nepali families live in Oxfordshire. Some Nepali students had been in Oxford beforehand, but ex-Gurkhas started arriving in Oxford in 2004. Pariyar's survey of twenty families revealed that the largest number of arrivals—45 per cent—occurred in 2006, 25 per cent came in 2007, and only 15 per cent came in 2008. The declining figures for new arrivals over recent years are in line with falling UK arrivals from Nepal generally (CNSUK 2011: 7-8).

Ninety per cent of Pariyar's sample are permanent residents (holding ILR or 'indefinite leave to remain') and the other 10 per cent have already become British citizens. Of those who had not yet become British, 33 per cent said that they wanted to become British citizens but 39 per cent did not wish to do so. The remaining 28 per cent were undecided. Many of them found themselves in a real dilemma. On the one hand, they did not wish to deprive themselves of facilities, such as free healthcare, free education for children, and help with care for the elderly, which were not available back home. More importantly, they saw no prospects for their children in Nepal. But they were not sure whether they would always be welcome in Britain. They were very nostalgic about their much easier and happier life in Nepal: the savings from Gurkha service and from second jobs overseas, coupled with a regular Gurkha pension, meant that in Nepal they did not need to work hard for subsistence, unlike in the UK. Many of them also did not like the idea of sundering their official link with their homeland. As one of them remarked, "How could we visit our own country on a tourist visa?" Many would be very willing to become British citizens if the Nepal government assured them that they could keep both passports. (Despite a strong campaign by non-resident Nepalis, the government of Nepal does not yet recognize dual citizenship.)

Many Oxford-based ex-Gurkhas intended to return to Nepal after seeing their children settled in Britain. Chandra Limbu's wife, for example, looked forward to going back because she had grown tired of working as a hotel cleaner.[4] Similarly, Shakti Limbu wanted to return once his only son, currently at school, went to university. However, everyone reckoned that their return would ultimately depend not only on their personal circumstances at the time but also on the situations in Nepal and in the UK. They would be more inclined to return, for instance, if Nepal acquired a degree of political stability, effectively tackled the problem of insecurity, developed its infrastructure, improved the delivery of public services, and so on. There were a few who explicitly stated that they had made up their minds to stay permanently in the UK, and again the reasons for this were a mix of personal interests and the situation in both nations. Part of the reason why Kus Bishwakarma was not looking forward to going back to his hometown in Lamjung (in the central hills) was that, as a member of a 'low' caste, he felt that he would still be socially ostracized in

[4] All names are pseudonyms.

Nepal, despite being wealthier than many others in the town.[5] Some thought they would probably have to remain in the UK because by the time they were ready to return to Nepal their parents there would have died and most, if not all, of their children would be in the UK.

It was interesting to tease out, beneath the slogans of Gurkha politics, what actually inspired them to emigrate in the first place. Most answers contained a mixture of personal and national issues. As indicated above, the most popular reason for moving to the UK was the pursuit of better prospects for their children. One ex-Gurkha remarked: "It would be foolish if a Lahure [soldier in a foreign army] did not have any children and yet came here to toil for survival." Many of them had significant savings from Gurkha service and other jobs overseas; some of them were actually working in Hong Kong, Taiwan, and other places before moving to the UK. Some blamed Nepal's political problems as well.

Shakti Limbu used to run two small factories in the town of Bhaktapur. However, he had to suffer regular extortion by the Maoists and other groups. On a number of occasions, although his life was in danger, he could never rely on the Nepal police. Moreover, the problem of frequent strikes organized by political parties and other groups meant that his factories suffered disruption and profits were inevitably low. Unfortunately, he ran into trouble with his job in the UK as well. As the financial crisis deepened, a few Gurkhas working as private security officers locally, including him, were made redundant. He struggled to find a job for several months. This shocked him and his friends in Oxford, who had now learned the hard way that it was never safe to assume all would go well in the UK.

Most ex-servicemen in Oxford work as private security officers and a few are bus drivers. About 5 per cent were

---

[5] However, it would be wrong to assume that caste discrimination is entirely absent within the Nepalese diaspora in the UK: see Pariyar (2011, 2018).

unemployed at the time of the interviews. The average annual income of those working was £25,000, which is roughly the same as the UK national average. Bus drivers are the highest earners; they could make more than £30,000. Most Gurkha spouses work, most of them as cleaners in hotels or colleges, on the minimum wage.

Migration has brought a profound change in the lives of Gurkha wives. As Subba shows, describing Gurkha families in the town of Dharan, the children are habituated to an easy life; so long as they get support from parents working abroad, they prefer not to work (Subba 2007: 299). Money earned overseas is rarely invested in income-generating activities. Although she does not refer to Gurkha spouses directly, the same observation is true for them as well. A Gurkha wife in Nepal epitomizes the life of luxury, of extravagance, and of prosperity without hard work—a lifestyle impossible for them to achieve once they are in the UK. The husband's income is generally not sufficient to meet the costs of the household, which means wives were forced to start working outside the home for the first time. Although a few wives managed to evade work on different pretexts, the majority of them were working.

The lack of work experience coupled with the problem of English language skills means that most of the wives end up working as cleaners—the work that their maids used to do at home. There was a well-known case of a group of about eight women who worked for a hotel in north Oxford. The payment of about £6.50 per hour was made not on the basis of the actual number of hours worked but according to the number of rooms cleaned. The expectation was that they should complete 18 rooms in six hours, but most women could not finish this within the stipulated time. Therefore, they worked an average of two hours extra per day to finish the rooms allocated to them, which was not paid. The women and their husbands were fully aware that the system was exploitative, but they dared not complain for fear of losing the job and not finding another one.

Gurkha spouses' attitudes to work differed quite significantly from person to person. Some of them hated having to work so hard to make a living and therefore lamented their migration. But others quite enjoyed the experience of working, despite the physical hardship, because they found it empowering in the sense that they no longer needed to depend fully on their husbands for money. Furthermore, work also gave them an opportunity to come out of the house, explore the world, meet new people, and learn the local language. When asked if they would contemplate working as cleaners in hotels in Nepal, none said they would do it. The reason was that in Nepal such work is categorized as polluting and is therefore bad for their family honour. The same work in Britain was apparently not seen as deleterious to family prestige.

As with many other migrants, remittances are an important link between ex-Gurkhas and relatives back home. Sixty per cent of the sample regularly sent money to Nepal; the average among those who sent was £1500 p.a. They reckoned it had to be much higher than this for those whose families had not joined them in the UK. Part of the reason why some of them had stopped sending money to Nepal was that all of their dependants had shifted to Britain. Many respondents eagerly supported small development schemes such as drinking water taps for schools, building or repairing temples for local deities, and so forth, usually in their villages of origin. They also gave small sums of cash to their relatives every time they visited Nepal. Dev Limbu visited his home for two weeks in January 2009 and distributed a total of £2,000 to his numerous affinal and consanguineal kin.

Forty per cent of respondents were home-owners, and the figure was likely to rise as many others were in the process of selling a part of their property in Nepal and investing the proceeds in UK houses. A few older Gurkhas, like Subash Rai, struggled to purchase houses as they were denied mortgages because of their age. For economic reasons they tended to share a house or flat between two families (often not relatives).

The Limbus, from the eastern hills of Nepal, are the predominant ethnic group in Oxford, and most of them live in Rose Hill; Rais, also from east Nepal, live in this area in significant numbers. A few Magars, Gurungs, and low-caste ex-Gurkhas are settled in different parts of Oxford. There are also Nepalis from other backgrounds not normally recruited to the Gurkhas (Newars, Bahuns).

Dasain and the construction of community in Oxford

The Dasain festival is the biggest single celebration of the Nepalese religious calendar (corresponding to Durga Puja/Dassera in India). Government offices close for days (as at Christmas/New Year in the West) and everyone who can do so returns home to celebrate the festival with their kin. In recent years (particularly since 1990) it has come to be contested by many from a Janajati ('tribal') background because it is strongly associated with Hinduism (and the now defunct monarchy). However, it remains the premier festival and is accepted by almost all Nepalis, even Buddhists, Christians, and Muslims, as a cultural and national holiday.[6]

The former soldiers in Oxford were indeed influenced, to a certain degree, by ethnic politics in general and by the movement for boycotting Dasain in particular. Although most of them had not stopped celebrating the festival altogether, they had nonetheless given up using traditional red *tika* (vermilion spot on the forehead) and replaced it with a white one. They did this because they trusted their ethnic activists' claims that not wearing *tika* at all or at least not using the traditional red colour was a powerful way of symbolizing their rejection of the hegemonic

---

[6] There is by now a considerable literature on the Dasain festival, including on activists' attempts to persuade people to boycott it. See Ramirez (1993), Campbell (1995), Krauskopff & Lecomte-Tilouine (1996), Pfaff-Czarnecka (1996), Gellner (1999), and Hangen (2005, 2010).

Hindu order that placed them in a debased position. A counter-myth created by ethnic activists says that the demons slain by Hindu gods and goddesses in the mythical stories were the ancestors of ethnic and indigenous people. For them, therefore, wearing red *tika* would be celebrating the blood of their own forefathers. Not everybody in Oxford took the story to be true, but they were, nevertheless, keen to maintain the distinction between the colours of *tika*, and through this, to fight their subordination to Hindu 'high' castes, although this does not mean much in British society. Moreover, some Gurkhas told me that their families and kin back home had stopped celebrating Dasain altogether. Upon further examination, it became clear that what they actually meant was that their families had stopped observing the festival as a religious affair but had continued with the usual feasting and socializing.

Interestingly, Oxford Gurkhas do not seem to hold a similarly negative attitude to blood sacrifice, although it is the very re-enactment of the slaying of the demons. In fact, many of them had a strong propensity for performing sacrifice not just at Dasain but also in their tribe-specific rituals. There were in fact some who did not like the sacrifice as an offering to deities and spirits, but even they missed slaughtering goats, pigs, and chickens at home particularly on special occasions like Dasain. On the basis of his fieldwork in a Limbu village in east Nepal in the 1970s, Philippe Sagant observed: "One morning the festival opens to the sound of Damai horns. From then on it is one endless round of slaughtering goats and chickens, buffalo and pigs, and going from house to house drinking" (1996: 265).

Every year the executive committee of the Nepalese Community in Oxford (NCO) takes a decision on which festivals of the Nepali calendar to celebrate, when and how. Normally it organizes at least three events annually, including the Nepali New Year and Dasain party (sometimes a combined Dasain–Tihar party), the latter being the most popular. In 2009 there was extended discussion about who should be included as official guests that year and finally it was agreed that the Labour MP for east Oxford, Andrew Smith, should be the chief guest. Other guests included officials from Oxford County Council and representatives of a few private organizations that had contributed small sums of money to run this or other events.

Interestingly all non-Nepali guests were members of the native British population; there was nobody from other communities, such as the British Pakistanis who have a large presence in east Oxford. Much of the 'social field' of the Gurkhas was exclusively within the Nepalis, and often indeed with members of the same tribe or caste. All of them had been commanded by British officers while in military service and most of them still worked with White British people. Though they admitted there had been generally no problem working with them, there was hardly any evidence of them socializing with anybody from a non-Nepali group. A change of attitude could be observed, however, among a few Gurkha children. For instance, Chandra Limbu's younger daughter lived with her Irish boyfriend in her parents' house in Rose Hill. Despite the overt unhappiness of some other Limbus, he and his wife apparently had no problem with the situation. They considered him to be their daughter's *de facto* husband. They happily included him in Nepali functions such as the Dasain festival and introduced him to other Nepalis as their *juwaĩ* (son-in-law).

The NCO committee set certain rules about the conduct of the Dasain festival, which everyone was expected to follow. Food had to be explicitly Nepali. An ex-Gurkha was ridiculed at one meeting when he suggested including pasta in the menu. Perhaps it might have been acceptable for some other occasion such as the summer barbecue, but it was almost a sin to think about having Western food as part of a Dasain feast. Despite their prolonged work overseas, most Gurkhas remained strictly Nepali in terms of what they ate. Pariyar met not a single Gurkha household that had attempted to prepare English or any other Western dish for dinner; they always took Nepali food with beer at home. The second important rule for the Dasain party was about the genre of music: non-Nepali music and dance music was strictly banned, to the utter dismay of the younger boys and girls who prefer Hindi and English music. Nepali folk or country music was particularly emphasized. This tended to be the inclination of the organizers even in other events. For instance, there was an open dispute between the NCO leader and some young Gurkha boys at the Nepal New Year programme in 2010 because the former did not permit the latter to dance to Hindi and English tunes in the communal dance. Another important rule for Dasain was that people should wear, as far as possible, Nepali national dress—*daura* and *suruwal*[7] for men, and saree for women. Although almost every caste or tribal group has its own distinctive ethnic dress, this was not encouraged for the Dasain party. The overall aim was to maintain a distinctive Nepali flavour to the cultural programme, people's dress, and the cuisine. To a considerable degree, participants complied with the wishes of the organizers, though at least two young Gurkha daughters incurred their displeasure by appearing in miniskirts.

The event started in the BMW factory workers' club in the late afternoon. Light snacks were served with fried goat meat and beaten rice at the beginning; drinks were to be bought from the counter. This continued for a few hours with people drinking and socializing with each other while enjoying quite loud Nepali folk music. It was indeed an opportunity for many Nepalis to meet up. There was a cultural performance by some Gurkha children involving Nepali songs and dances on the stage. This was followed by a raffle draw. An announcer conducted the whole programme from the stage. Then people queued up for dinner at around 8 p.m. A Nepali catering company based in another town, Farnborough, was given the business of supplying and serving food as specified by the NCO. After this the official guest was

[7] A long-sleeved shirt, folded over and tied at the front, with trousers baggy at the top, and tight around the calves.

asked to address the gathering; this followed the NCO leader's speech in Nepali and English. The programme ended around 11 following communal dancing.

The greatest irony was that the event, organized for the celebration of a key religious festival of Nepal, did not include any associated ritual or religious observance. There were no Dasain rituals performed, no space or object consecrated, no worship of the goddess Durga, no red or white *tika* used. A small lamp was lit on the stage, but it was not sacralized, nor was it declared as an offering to the goddess. In fact, this could also be interpreted as purely secular, as ceremonial lamps are normally used as a way of opening any Nepali meeting. Most importantly, there was not even the mention of blood sacrifice. Of course, UK law does not permit the public slaughter of animals or birds, so blood sacrifice would not have been possible in any case. But fruits or vegetables can be used as surrogate victims when blood sacrifice is not possible. At the very least they could have put up posters or figurines of the goddess Durga and carried out worship with flowers, vermilion, and rice. There was in fact a total absence of discussion of the religious aspects of the event in the NCO meetings preceding the event. It was not just the activists who were not bothered with religious aspects of the function, there was no question raised by any of the over 300 participants. This could also be seen perhaps as a way of avoiding the problem of agreeing on what the appropriate practice would be. Given the widespread diversity of personal preferences and caste/ethnic traditions, it was better to conduct the event in terms of the most neutral and banal symbolism that could offend no one.

The communal, and even political, significance of the festival as celebrated, and the absence of direct religious importance, was evident also from the content of the formal proceedings. The official guests were seated on an allocated table close to the stage; there were formal speeches by the chief guest and officials of the NCO. The NCO leader spoke at length about Nepali culture and tradition, attempting to present the Nepalis in Oxford—Gurkhas and non-Gurkhas—as one community with a common culture, language, religion, and so forth. He did his level best to portray all Nepalis in Oxfordshire as one, united community. He refrained from mentioning internal divisions in terms of caste, tribe, class, education, language, religion, and so on. As a Magar he has his own ethnic language and speaks it well, but he did not utter a word of it. He deliberately attempted to hide the fact that Gurkhas and non-Gurkhas rarely met, that people socialized mostly with other Nepalis from their own caste or ethnic background. He made no reference to the many difficulties Gurkha families face in conducting their religious rituals in Oxford and in the UK generally.[8]

One example of such difficulties occurred during the second most important Nepali festival, Tihar, which follows Dasain a month later (it corresponds to the Indian Diwali). One of the popular ways of celebrating Tihar festival is through the public performance of Deusi and Bhailo—a special genre of music and dance—where groups of people go house to house chanting ritual songs and prayers. It is customary for host families to offer the performers cash, food, drinks, and so on. This is a popular practice in Nepal; several groups may visit and perform over several days. Some enthusiastic young people wanted to start the tradition and began visiting Nepali houses in Rose Hill. The normal way is to perform in front of the house in as loud a way as possible. They did not dare to do this, for fear that people nearby might complain and call the police. They felt constrained to come into the narrow hallway of the house itself and to sing just a few of the ritual songs in hushed tones. Everyone present knew that it was nothing like Deusi Bhailo in Nepal.

---

[8] One should also mention that there is a minority of Nepali migrants to the UK who choose not to participate in such communal events. A survey of 300 households for the VR project suggested that 12 per cent had not attended any religious event (festival) in the last two years and 9 per cent had not attended any non-religious event (e.g. barbecue, football tournament); only 4.3 per cent had attended no such event of either kind.

Belonging, the house, and animal sacrifice

A key site for the generation of one's sense of belonging is the home. One Oxford ex-Gurkha shared his personal experiences as follows:

> I have to not only keep visiting my place in Nepal but also do all I could to support it and my people. Even if I became very rich here and never went back to my society, my *atman* or spirit will go back where it came from when I die. It could not possibly hang around here because it will not get due respect and space in this country.

Chandra Limbu owned a house in Rose Hill that he had bought the previous year. When asked whether he liked it, his answer was—yes and no. He knew that it was a worthwhile investment. It was not small for his family of four; and he was quite happy with its physical outlook, shape, colour, size of the garden, and other facilities. The house was also close to other Nepali/Limbu houses. In fact, he had selected it after being shown many others in the area. Despite all this, he still did not feel that he truly owned this house or that he fully belonged to his house. He explained:

> I know the two could never be compared in terms of property values, but I always get the sense that my house in Rose Hill is never the same as my father's house in our ancestral village in Nepal. To my mind this house is not even equivalent to my father's buffalo shed. This is an important property in local terms and more so in Nepali terms, and yet I do not feel I fully belong here. I tend to think that my true home is in Nepal, and not this one; that it is nothing more than a temporary shelter.

One of the reasons for not feeling at home at his own house was that he believed only his family lived there, but his deities and ancestor spirits did not. He felt they did not have a space in his house because it had not been consecrated through 'house warming' rituals according to the Limbu tradition. As Hubert and Mauss (1964) famously claimed, at least occasional human intervention is essential for the very existence of the gods; there is a contractual and mutually beneficial relationship between the two worlds. The edited volume *Man and House in the Himalayas* (Toffin 1991), based on ethnographic study in a variety of locations in Nepal, amply demonstrates that for Nepalis the house is more than a mere physical space for dwelling: it is also the residence of ancestor spirits and deities. Generally the family starts living in a new house only after completing the ritual of installing their ancestor spirits and deities. These gods and deities protect the family, and in return the family has to regularly worship them, often involving blood sacrifice. For instance, Jest (1991: 158) shows, using the ethnography of a Majhi or fisherman house in eastern Nepal, that these deities cohabiting with the family can be malicious and can cause misfortunes, death, and destruction in the family if they are not treated well through mandatory rituals. In some cases, the house itself is believed to be a form of deity which should be appeased. Levy (1990: 331) describes how the Newars of Bhaktapur believe that people should not start living in a new house until blood sacrifice is performed (and the same is true much more widely within Nepal); people fear it could otherwise seek to draw human blood instead through fatal incidents like fire or earthquake or similar disasters. The same rule applies to new vehicles: blood sacrifice is required before using them so that they may not cause accidents and the resultant flow of human blood. Levy continues: "The close relation of animal sacrifice and threats to humans is experienced by some...individuals in their late childhood in a deeply felt way" (ibid.: 331–2).

As noted above, the biggest group within Oxford Nepalis is made up of Limbus, a group based in the far east of Nepal, with a largely shamanic religious tradition. According to Sagant (1976:

162–3), Limbu houses are no exception to the rules outlined above. Once a new house is built, or bought, a Limbu spiritual expert called Phedangma is summoned to perform the necessary rituals before the house is inhabited. He first ceremonially enters the house and performs elaborate rituals, including the sacrifice of a pig to the main pillar. Blood sacrifice and other domestic rituals are meant to make the key protector deity of the Limbus, Yuma, come and reside in the house; she is believed to live by the main pillar of the house and bear the burden of the house and the whole world. She is responsible for the overall welfare of the family in the house. "The Limbu calendar requires that every household make annual sacrifices, one in November and one in April, to the goddess Yuma; twice a year to Manguenna, to deceased ancestors, and to Nahangma" (Sagant 1996: 379).

Many Oxford Limbus used to perform some of these key rituals in their houses in Nepal towns, although the calendar would be followed more strictly in villages than in towns. They acknowledge the fact that the performance of these rituals, though mandatory according to their custom, is not possible in the UK. Firstly, there were no trained Phedangmas available in Oxford, or indeed in Britain. Even if they were available, UK laws forbid the slaughter of animals in domestic spaces or anywhere outside licensed venues run by professional butchers. The ban on animal slaughter makes many Limbu rituals—among those who wish to follow the tradition—incomplete. Unlike the Hindu sacrifice for the goddess Durga in Dasain, apparently fruits or vegetables cannot be used as surrogate victims in Limbu rituals. Even the simple act of burning a bundle of incense sticks could make the fire alarm go off, which inhibited many informants from performing this simple home ritual.

There was yet another aspect of their living arrangements that many Gurkhas found undermined their sense of belonging in Oxford and the UK. Many of their affinal and consanguineal relatives were in Nepal, and they were highly unlikely to visit their houses mainly because they would not normally be given visas to attend family rituals and functions in the UK. Of course, some of them did have a few close relatives living in the UK, but they did not always live close by. Many practical considerations prevented them from visiting friends and relatives even within the UK. Furthermore, the size of the UK houses that they could afford is too small for family gatherings. The design of UK houses is, in most cases, orientated towards accommodating a nuclear family and is not favourable to hosting an extended one. Most Gurkha houses in Nepal tend to be quite spacious. Besides, they can find places in neighbours' houses, or erect tents in the field, in order to host a large gathering. As the ex-soldiers recognized, such arrangements are normally not easy in the UK; one can certainly not keep guests in a tent in a nearby field.

It should be made explicit that the Limbu house is the epicentre of their rituals and other public functions. "The house is the sanctuary, almost the definition, of the cultural order. Beyond it there is almost nothing" (Sagant 1996: 9). In Nepal, when special guests arrive, the host family should ceremonially slaughter a pig or similar animal and offer the entire frontal half of the body to the guests to take home. The other half is cooked and eaten in an elaborate feast. This tradition, called *phudong*, is still popular among the Limbus in Nepal; there is an onus on families to observe it for important functions such as weddings and funerals. This cannot be practised in the UK, for the obvious reason that the killing of animals or birds in the house (or outside) is not permitted.

Oxford Gurkhas miss slaughtering animals so much that they have invented an interesting way of doing it whilst following the health and safety regulations. They have a special arrangement with pig farms in Didcot and Salisbury where they are offered a whole pig as soon as it has been slaughtered. Small groups of ex-Gurkhas took turns to drive to these places, cut and clean the pork themselves, and distribute the meat equally among the members of the pork-buying group. There were quite a few such groups of men in Oxford (women did not participate). It was certainly more than the mere provisioning of pork; everyone looked forward to it when he was on leave. They were prepared to travel long distances to chop a whole pig to pieces; this pork, they claimed, was much tastier than what they could buy in the local supermarkets.

Belonging and death rites in the UK

It is customary for the death of a Limbu due to unnatural causes like accidents and natural calamities to be treated by a ritual expert, specially trained for dealing with bad events, called Bijuwa; there is no elaborate funeral involved in such cases. Natural deaths are dealt with by Phedangmas who perform lengthy rituals.[9] According to Oxford Limbus, the very first thing he does is to go into a trance state in order to carry out direct verbal communication with the deceased. In an emotional invocation the spirit of the dead embodied in the Phedangma not only spells out the cause of his death, but also speaks about his personal experiences, interests, unfulfilled desires, and so forth. His family and friends, who find the words of the spirit medium entirely convincing, sometimes become hysterical. They ask the spirit about whether he or she has any last wishes and also sometimes about how they should perform the last rites.

Close members of the deceased's patriline act as chief mourners. As instructed by the Phedangma, the dead body is prepared in a special way and placed in the house with its head facing a certain direction. Then it is taken to the burial ground in a procession involving exclusively Limbus; people from other castes or tribes are not allowed to touch the body. After the burial chief mourners ceremonially shave their head, face, and body by the side of a river or stream. They then return and sit in a corner of the house on hay for three or four days, observing semi-

---

[9] The way in which death rituals are performed, and also the nomenclature used for the ritual specialist, varies from place to place within the Limbu region.

seclusion and food taboos, again under the supervision of the Phedangma.

Within a year of death the family should hold an elaborate final ritual called *khauma* that will help the spirit reach its final destination. All related households, consanguineal and affinal, support the family with a free supply of money, food, liquor, buffalo, pigs, chicken or meat. A pig or male buffalo is sacrificed and its raw head, together with liquor and other food items, is offered to the spirit. Whilst Phedangmas spend the nights chanting ritual texts, guests engage in merry-making, drinking, romantic love, and so on. Previously it was held over three nights but now it has been reduced to one for reasons of economy. This is a key ritual for any Limbu household. Although such elaborate rituals are not required in the case of unnatural deaths, the funeral involves the sacrifice of a piglet, which is often killed in a cruel manner.

Several Oxford Limbus told Pariyar: "It is easier in life but harder after death in the UK."[10] There was a sense among many Gurkhas and their spouses that they may live richer in the UK, compared to Nepal, but they would die poorer. It was not difficult to see that elaborate funerals following traditional custom were not going to be possible in the UK. It is not easy for people from countries like Nepal to fly to the UK for family visits; even when visa difficulties are overcome, many relatives simply cannot afford the cost of travel. The lack of space in the house for visitors and guests and the unavailability of ritual experts are other key problems. It is not Limbu custom to burn dead bodies, but not all can afford the traditional burial as it is comparatively more expensive in the UK. It is impossible to keep to the rule of not allowing a dead body to be touched by a non-Limbu, because the UK mortuary law requires that funeral officers do much of the work on the body, including its cleaning, before cremation.

---

[10] In August 2011 (issue 268), *Yuropko Nepalipatra*, a Nepali diaspora weekly, ran a front-page article about the difficulties Nepalis face in dealing with death in the UK, entitled 'It's not even easy to die'.

The Nepalis of Sikkim

We turn now to a very different diaspora population, equally originating from Nepal. This particular group also finds itself outside its homeland—indeed as the original inhabitants of the Kathmandu Valley they find themselves some hundreds of miles and at least a full day's journey away from their place of origin (in the 19th century it would have been two weeks' walk away). On the other hand, Sikkim shares a border with east Nepal. Sikkim had been a semi-independent kingdom, but was incorporated into the Indian Union, as its 22nd state, in 1975.

The people of Sikkim have mixed feelings about being part of the Indian Union: on May 16 1995, 20 years after the merger of Sikkim into India, Kaji Lhendup Dorji, who played a major role in engineering the merger of Sikkim into India and whose name has become a byword among Nepali-speakers for betrayal of one's nation, published a fierce statement urging the Indian Government to return Sikkim to its previous status. Yet on the whole most Sikkimese are reconciled to being part of India, if only because India has poured enormous resources into the fledgling state. There are roads to even the most remote hamlets and the poor receive subsidized rice and cooking gas. Some claim that this high level of government support has made the Sikkimese lazy and dependent.

Nepalis started migrating to Sikkim in the middle of the 19th century. A Newar from Bhaktapur, named Lakshmi Das, was able to lease land from the Chogyal, or King, of Sikkim in 1867. He was entrusted with mining copper in the 1870s and from 1882 with minting coins for the government. He encouraged many Nepalis to come to Sikkim to work in his enterprises. The Nepalis who settled in Sikkim faced no barriers to reconstructing their way of life and were able to carry on rituals as in Nepal. Despite its being a Buddhist country, they continued their own traditions, for example, sacrificing animals for Dasain, and it would appear that this practice died out only around the end of the 1980s. (Most temples in India forbid animal sacrifice.) Today some perform a sacrifice with a vegetable substitute. Locals in Sikkim ascribe the campaign against animal sacrifice to Sai Baba, who is very popular there. In general, Nepalis in Sikkim have assimilated to a larger Hindu-Nepali identity and have adopted the Nepali language as their mother tongue. There is a high degree of intermarriage between different caste and ethnic groups, as in nearby Darjeeling.

Today the population of Sikkim is over half a million, of whom nearly three quarters are of Nepali origin. The Lepchas and Bhutias, treated both in colonial times and after as indigenous to Sikkim, with various attempts to prevent their land being alienated to in-migrating Nepalis, form just one fifth of the total population.[11] In 1978 only the Lepchas and Bhutias were granted the status of Scheduled Tribes (ST), but Tamangs and Limbus were added to the list in 2002. 33 per cent of the post-matriculation educational places in the state are reserved for them. A further 5 per cent of the population are listed as Scheduled Castes (all members of the Nepali-speaking service castes) and 6 per cent of the educational seats are reserved for them. As the ST status is being diluted by additions to the category, the State Council of Sikkim gave Lepchas the status of 'Most Primitive Tribe' in January 2005. Shneiderman and Turin comment:

> [E]ven the most disadvantaged Lepcha settlements in Sikkim maintain a relatively high standard of living. Dzongu, an officially demarcated Lepcha reservation in north Sikkim, is remote by Indian standards, but still boasts electrified villages, well-run schools, and Community Information Centres with battery-powered computers and broadband satellite connections. Rather fittingly, the Indian reservation system has indeed created a 'reservation'—a discrete homeland territory

---

[11] For earlier studies of Sikkim and Darjeeling, particularly from the Nepali point of view, see Nakane (1966), Pradhan (1982, 2005), Chalmers (1983), Subba (1992), Hutt (2008), Steinmann (2003/04), Arora (2005, 2007), Shneiderman (2009), Vandenhelsken (2011).

> where only members of Sikkim's Most Primitive Tribe may settle and own land. (Shneiderman & Turin 2006: 58)

The OBC category was also diluted by adding Bahun, Chhetri, Newar, and Sanyasi in 2001, so the Sikkimese government simultaneously recognized a sub-category of Most Backward Classes (MBC). This included Bhujel, Gurung, Mangar (Magar), Kirat Rai, Sunuwar, Thamil, Jogi, and Dewan (Vandenhelsken 2011: 95–6).

Under the rule of Chief Minister Nar Bahadur Bhandari (1979-1994), differences within the Nepali-speaking population had not been encouraged, and civil servants who supported ethnic groups were discriminated against for promotion. However, when Pavan Chamling came in as Chief Minister in 1994 there was a change of policy in favour of multiculturalism. The various Nepali sub-groups were encouraged to re-learn their 'original' languages and for a year or so the Government of Sikkim published its proceedings in Newari, Tamang, etc.—which of course the vast majority of Sikkimese Newars, Tamangs, etc. were incapable of reading. Every group sought to have its own language and its own script in a process Arora (2007) dubs 'retribalization'. The obsession, strong in Nepal and even more so in Sikkim, with having one's own script is labelled 'scriptophilia' by Shneiderman and Turin. The *Sikkim Herald* weekly is still published in thirteen different languages, but, as Arora notes (2007: 206), all this is a question of "linguistic symbolism rather than linguistic proficiency". Some suspect that the encouragement of such retribalization is an elite Indian plot to divide the Nepalis of Sikkim and Darjeeling among themselves (Pradhan 2005: 22–4).

Very similar processes were occurring at the same time just over the state boundary in Darjeeling district, as has been described by Shneiderman and Turin (2006) and Shneiderman (2009) for the case of the Thangmis. The aim is to achieve the coveted protected status of Scheduled Tribe, though so far most

Nepali groups have only the lesser (but still desirable) status of OBC (Other Backward Class).

The Nepalis in Sikkim have been living there for well over a century now, and in some cases for over 150 years. Therefore they believe that they are no less indigenous people of Sikkim than the Bhutia and the Lepcha populations who have the coveted ST status. In so far as most of the Nepali communities, including the Bahuns, the Chhetris, the Rais, the Gurungs, the Magars and the Newars have not received ST status, they feel like outsiders. There is an unspecified line between Nepalese communities, on the one side, versus the Bhutias and the Lepchas on the other. All the Nepalese communities feel themselves somehow closer to each other than to the Bhutias and the Lepchas.

Nepalis in Sikkim show considerable respect and affection towards Nepal and visitors from Nepal. In the words of Suryabir Tuladhar, the priest of the Svayambhu Bhimakali temple in Gangtok, Nepalis in diaspora are fragments of Nepal, but abandoned and forgotten in foreign lands. Whether or not the mainland recognizes them, they believe that they are Nepali in their own right. One finds statues of the famous Nepali poet Bhanubhakta everywhere in Sikkim. Even more surprising, there seems to be a family portrait of the late King Birendra and his family in virtually every Nepali home in Sikkim. One informant said that during Dasain there was a tradition of offering a barley sprout (*jamara*) in the name of the King of Nepal before distributing them amongst themselves. The respect shown to the King of Nepal was surprising, because the people in Sikkim are physically and politically not bound to Nepal and their ancestors sought in India economic and educational opportunities and political and social freedoms not available in Nepal. It shows how, nevertheless, they are still attached culturally to Nepal.[12]

---

[12] Such respect was not extended to Gyanendra, who succeeded to the throne after the palace massacre of 2001.

Despite their love for Nepal and the Nepali people, Sikkimese Nepalis display not the slightest interest in returning to Nepal permanently. Among many reasons, their present prosperous economic and stable political position have given them confidence. For that matter, they are not attracted to other Indian states either. They are not very positive towards others migrating into Sikkim. People of Nepali origin who have migrated to Sikkim from other Indian states in recent times do not feel that the locals treat them well. For instance, Nepalis from West Bengal (Darjeeling, Kalimpong) and from across the border in Nepal come for work, but are not made welcome. Many people in Sikkim consider that people from other parts of India are attracted to Sikkim simply in order to get economic benefits from the state government.

Sikkimese Newars

Because there are some prominent Newars in Sikkim and there was a history of Newars working for the Chogyal as tax-collectors and contractors, it is believed that all Newars in Sikkim are well off; but in fact there are many who are poor and backward. A survey in 1989 showed a third of Sikkimese Newars to be illiterate. Even the numbers of those with prominent government jobs seems to be in decline as the reservations policy for STs begins to take effect. The Newars therefore are no less inclined to pursue ST status for themselves than anyone else, despite the fact that the Kathmandu Valley's sophisticated urban culture, from which they derive their culture, could be taken to be the very antithesis of tribal.[13]

Although individuals had been interested in the 1970s and 80s, the Newars of Sikkim did not become organized until 1993 when they established the Sikkim Newa Guthi, which was registered with the government the following year. By 1997 it had established branches in various places within Sikkim and had

---

[13] As argued, for instance, by Gellner (1986, 1991, 1997b: 30–4).

started to invite Newar activists from Kathmandu for help in reviving long abandoned or never-practised Newar customs. Of first importance was the observance of Mha Puja, which is the occasion for a motor-cycle rally and political speeches in Kathmandu. The Sikkim Newa Guthi also campaigned for OBC status for Newars. In 2003 the Guthi was renamed as the All-India Newar Organisation, Sikkim, in order to emphasize links with Darjeeling and elsewhere. In line with Chamling's language policy, there were attempts to teach Nepal Bhasa (Newari) to Newar children (whose parents spoke to them in Nepali or English); some young Sikkimese Newars were sent to Kathmandu to learn Newari as well.

Along with Bahuns, Chetris, Jogis, and Sanyasis, the Newars achieved OBC status in 2003. Khagendra Pradhan, Chair of the All-India Newar Organisation, Sikkim, wanted to go further. Generally, those seeking to achieve ST status need to demonstrate, in lines with the definitions of the 1965 Lokur Committee, "primitive traits, distinctive culture, geographical isolation, shyness of contact with the community at large, and economic backwardness" (Arora, 2007: 209).[14] With this in mind, Khagendra Pradhan wrote a paper in 2003 entitled 'Inclusion of Newars within the Provision of the Indian Constitution, Scheduled Tribes Status: provision Article 332 & 342'. He put forward the following eleven cultural arguments to demonstrate that the Newars should be considered a tribe:

> a) The great veneration shown by the Newars for serpent and the cult of Naga is similar to the tribes of South West India. b) Wa-vel-va and Sumaka sentences are perfectly the same in form and meaning in Newar and the dialect of the tribes of Nilgiri. c) It is to point out here that wooden pulveriser used as agricultural

[14] See also Middleton & Shneiderman (2008) on the ways in which these criteria of backwardness have affected Sikkim and Darjeeling, and are likely to affect Nepal.

> implement by the Newars is similar to that now being used in Malabar. In Newari it is called *Khatti Muga* and is called *Katta Kol* in Malayalam. d) Mulmi section among the Newars are drawn from the Murmi tribes. e) Newars are the descendants of the ancient Kiratas. f) Attention may be invited to the fact that Bhimsen, the epic hero, is regarded as an important deity both by the Newars and the Tamangs. g) Another cultural similarity with the Khasi is the settlement of dispute by water ordeal. h) The Newars' sub-clan Hayu or Vayu originally came from Lanka having left the country after the defeat of King Ravana. The sentimental attachment of the Newars is found to this mythological King. i) The exchange of betel-nuts in the marriage celebration is similar to the Khasi tribes. j) The ritual of disposing of the dead body of the Newar girl who dies during her first menstruation or Barha is similar to the dead body of Palaung woman of Shan States. k) Non-piercing of the nose and non-wearing of nose ornaments are similar to Lepcha, Bhutia and Tibet, women.[15]

Like the mouse-eating that the Thangmi of Darjeeling argued to be an original cultural trait of Thangmis in Nepal (Shneiderman 2009), many of these arguments might be looked at askance by Newars in Nepal. The point is that they are discursive arguments, aimed at achieving a particular bureaucratic classification within the Indian state's regime of preferential entitlements.

Conclusion

The two contrasting cases show particular diasporic populations adopting rather different strategies. In the Oxford case, cultural difference is ignored and played down in public forums in order to build a sense of identity that is useful in gaining resources from local government. Culture is objectified in public staging—

[15] Thanks to the author for providing Shrestha with the unpublished typed manuscript.

sometimes to the annoyance of the young people who do not want to be constrained by nationalist considerations. In more private spheres, however, members of the older generation have a clear sense that they do not belong, because they cannot carry out the rituals that they would at home—either at all (because animal sacrifice is not allowed) or properly (because they fear what the neighbours might say or do).

In the Sikkimese case, settlement goes back much longer. There has been a similar merging of different cultural identities to produce a pan-Nepali one, a process that has gone much further—but not so far as to obliterate internal cultural differences altogether. And that cultural difference is now at a premium, given the differential reservation policies that depend on being able to demonstrate a distinctive cultural identity combined with a history of exclusion. This means that, though in fact Sikkimese Newars (like other Nepalis in Sikkim) actually feel strongly that they do belong in Sikkim (to the extent that they do not welcome more recent Nepali arrivals), they are constrained (paradoxically) to try and demonstrate publicly that they do not fully belong and that the state should respond to their demand to allow them the most privileged category of citizenship (namely, that of ST) which they currently lack.

One context—the UK—may be characterized as weakly multicultural: there is a discourse that values cultural difference but there are no preferential rights. In the other strongly multicultural context—Sikkim—the state accords preferential treatment in matters of considerable import to anyone who values education or state employment, so that questions of group belonging and cultural classification are potentially crucial for almost every member of society.

7

From Kathmandu to Kent: Nepalis in the UK

David N. Gellner

Nepalis in Britain are one of the UK's most recent diaspora populations, younger and less visible than more established and better-known minorities from South Asia such as Pakistanis (approximately 1.2 million), Bangladeshis (around 450,000), Indians (1.4 million, whether from East Africa or India), or Sri Lankans (estimates up to 500,000).[1] The UK's 2001 census recorded a mere 5,943 people who had been born in Nepal. But beginning in 2004, Nepalis started to arrive in greater numbers and, for the next few years, they were one of the fastest-growing groups in the UK. Nepali restaurants began to appear in many British towns. Usually named after some variation on 'Gurkha' or 'Everest', they are decorated with posters of Swayambhu, Mount Machhapuchhre, or the living goddess Kumari, and tend to serve the long-established version of north Indian food adapted for British palates (usually served in 'Indian' restaurants run by

---

[1] This essay appeared originally in *Himal Southasian* (Gellner 2014a).

Bangladeshis). As a nod to Nepaliness, the menu usually lists among its starters *momos* and *choyala* (made from mutton or chicken, buffalo meat not being easily available—though it has started to be sold in areas with high Nepali population).

The 2011 census recorded 60,202 Nepalis in England and Wales. After a detailed sample survey, the Centre for Nepal Studies UK estimated in 2008 that there were 72,173 Nepalis in the UK as a whole, the vast majority living in southeast England. Community estimates, often repeated in the press, have ranged between 30,000 and 150,000.

Proliferation of associations

Whatever the true figure, for a newly arrived community, the Nepali diaspora is involved in an astonishing level of activity with a dizzying array of social groups formed on a variety of different bases. The groups inevitably have links with Nepal, but how close and intense these are depends very much on the personalities involved. Undoubtedly, these connections have been facilitated by social media in recent years. Some UK-based groups raise considerable amounts of money for charity or investment in Nepal. Other associations are primarily concerned with activity in the UK.

There are religious organizations (Hindu, Buddhist, Kirant, Bon, and Christian); ethnic organizations (Gurung/Tamu, Magar, Tamang, Sherpa, Newar, Chhetri, Thakali, Limbu, and Rai) with both central committees and branches in different parts of the UK; organizations based on a specific district, VDC (Village Development Committee), or cluster of villages back in Nepal; and organizations related to a particular locality in the UK (Burnt Oak Nepalese Community, Greater Rushmoor Nepali Community, etc.). A number of Gurkha organizations have also been formed: *numberi* or 'intake' associations, bringing together groups of Gurkha soldiers who were recruited and went through their basic training at the same time; and several competing ex-Gurkha associations, which campaign for Gurkha rights and support Gurkha welfare activities. Further, there are literary, musical, sports, and youth associations; professional organized (for doctors, nurses, caterers, engineers, business people, and media professionals); and political associations (both, issue-based and those linked to political parties in Nepal). There are also various pan-Nepali organizations and charities that attempt to unite all Nepalis, usually aiming to provide support for development work or education in Nepal. And the UK branch of the Non-Resident Nepali Association aspires to speak for all Nepalis and to incorporate them into a global movement that can negotiate with the government of Nepal, particularly on the issue of dual citizenship.[2]

In a surprisingly short time, Nepalis in the UK have created over 400 organizations that exist in a state of continual movement, mutual networking, and reciprocal support (and occasionally, conflict). Almost every Nepali in the UK belongs to or attends the public events of at least one of these organizations as research carried out as part of the VR project revealed. Some of these associations are large enough that there are elections every three years for a new team to run the organization. In others, it is a question of persuading respected and active figures to take on the task of running it. Leading figures of the community sit on the executive committee or act as advisors to a dozen associations or more; on Saturdays and Sundays they rush from one meeting to another.

Most of the organizations hold at least a summer barbecue and an annual festival or general meeting. Popular venues, such as Oak Farm Community School in Farnborough, Tamudhee Hall in Mytchett (a former church hall, bought for £500,000 and refurbished), or the Warehouse Community Centre in Reading are booked out every Saturday months in advance, especially in summer. During the annual Nepali Mela, organized by the Tamu Dhee UK, many groups come together and their numbers and

---

[2] On the NRN movement, see Adhikari & Gellner (2018).

activities—the sheer ebullience of the various parts of the Nepali community—are displayed for each other and for a wider UK audience at the Kempton Park Racecourse near London.

The Kirat Rai Yayokkha UK, to take one example, brings together all Rais from across the country to celebrate the Sakela-Ubhauli festival on a Saturday in May. Food and drinks stalls are set up in a large school playground. There is also that most English of institutions, an ice-cream van. Hundreds of people arrive by coach and by car. At the centre is a small shrine to Yalambar, cultural hero of the Rais as well as of Limbus and Sunuwars, with fruit and flower offerings in front of it. There is also a museum-style glass case displaying Rai cultural artifacts, such as cymbals, woven cloth, and sacred herbs. To one side is a set of seats for official guests, who give speeches, only half-listened to by most; the chief guests' main task is to judge the dance competition.

Groups from different towns in England such as Maidstone, Nuneaton, and Ashford compete for the prize of best dance group (see Plate 1.2, p. 21 above). The men are in spotless *daura suruwal* with matching coloured cummerbunds, bow and arrow slung on their backs; the women in identical *dhaka* blouses, gold jewellery in their hair, and matching skirts and silver anklets. Men and women alternate and dance in a circle. In the centre a man sits cross-legged, his white turban stuffed with feathers, a sacred flask in his lap; he mimes spirit possession. Once the formal competition is over, the entire group—old and young, Nepali-dressed and mini-skirted, male and female—all join in one enormous circle. Everyone who cares to join dances for hours to the hypnotic four-beat rhythm. Having displayed its segmented parts through the formal competition, the community now dances out its unity.

Ex-Gurkha communities

In Aldershot, well known as an army town, the Nepali population is believed to have gone from less than 2 per cent to more than 10 per cent (the census reports a figure of 6.5 per cent) within ten years. Many of them are ex-Gurkhas who came both in anticipation of and following the UK government's 2009 decision to allow all those with four years of service to settle in the country.

Rushmoor Borough (which includes Aldershot) is not a place one would immediately have associated with Buddhism, yet, at 3.3 per cent, it has the highest proportion of Buddhists in the UK—one of ten surprising facts revealed by the BBC following the 2011 census. It is appropriate, then, that the Buddhist Community Centre UK bought a disused building owned by British Telecom in Aldershot and remade it into a Tibetan Buddhist *gompa* (monastery) and community centre (see Plates 9.1 and 9.2). The campaign for a centre coincided with a visit by the Dalai Lama in 2012, when Aldershot Town Football Club was filled to capacity to welcome him.

One highlight of the calendar is the Gurkha Cup organized by Tamu Dhee UK in Aldershot in May every year. It is not just a knockout football competition between 48 nine-a-side teams (the 2013 poster specified a maximum of "three local native players" per team); there are also food stalls, charity displays, traditional Gurung dances, khukuri dances and a military wives' choir. The pattern of socializing around football is no doubt drawn from a tradition of football competitions within the Gurkha brigade itself. But the Nepali diaspora is not the first diaspora population in the UK to work out that creating ethnic football contests is a great way to involve the male youth of the second generation; Greek, Turkish, and Kurdish ethnic leagues, for example, have existed in London for many years. Other groups, such as the Yeti Nepali Association UK and the Magar Association UK, have launched similar football competitions.

What remains truly impressive is the sheer number of people devoting their time and energy for communal ends without any financial reward. It would be misleading, however, to suggest that everything is rosy and without friction. The desire for recognition sometimes leads to fierce competition in elections for the teams running the various organizations. Occasionally, such conflicts have been known to take on an ethnic tinge. They cannot always be managed through the politics of consensus; the losing side, alleging malpractice, may secede and set up a rival organization. Sometimes, organizations that are claimed as 'branches' behave with what the 'centre' believes is insufficient deference. Accusations of embezzlement are commonplace, probably far more common than actual embezzlement itself.

Local difficulties

There has also been friction with the local population. Again, Aldershot has been a flashpoint. Many of the ex-Gurkhas who settled there were elderly, spoke little or no English, and were coming directly from their villages to the UK. They had won the right to settle in the UK, but only had their pensions, which were set at a level that was supposedly generous for Nepal but was so little in the UK context that they immediately became eligible for welfare benefits.

Concerned about the growth of the Nepali population over the previous ten years, the local MP Gerald Howarth sent an open letter to the Prime Minister on 25 January 2011:

> This issue is of deep concern to the local authority and its Leader as their services are in danger of being overwhelmed by this influx, as are those provided by the National Health Service, Citizens Advice Bureaux and local schools.
>
> Some GP practices are struggling to cope. It is also causing immense tensions within the community which are exacerbated by the difficulties encountered by the Nepalese in integrating into the settled community, particularly given the low levels of literacy and often limited understanding of English.

Talk of an 'influx' was seen as provocative and labelled 'unhelpful' by local leaders of the Nepali community, but the MP was certainly articulating the feelings of his voters. They did not understand the Nepali custom of the 'morning walk' and somehow found it threatening that groups of diminutive old people, dressed quite differently, should hang around in parks and public spaces. Rumours about them spitting, urinating, and excreting in parks where local children played started to circulate. Around this time, Nepali troops serving in the UN in Haiti were accused of being responsible for a cholera outbreak there. Connections between Nepalis, TB, and cholera were flung about. At the same time, as the MP's letter claimed, doctors' practices in the area were finding it hard to cope with the sheer numbers of new patients, as well as with the fact that they did not have sufficient translators.

Perhaps encouraged by the MP's letter, there were a number of alarmist articles published in the popular British press describing the overcrowded conditions the elderly ex-Gurkhas were living in and blaming Joanna Lumley, a well-known actress who had spearheaded the 2009 campaign to win Gurkhas settlement rights, for luring them to the UK with false promises. Later in 2011, when a local woman could not get an appointment to see the doctor, her husband, Sam Phillips, set up a Facebook page called 'Lumley's Legacy' as a focus for concerns about the number of Nepalis in the area. It generated considerable debate and quickly put up a 'mission statement' emphasizing that:

> THIS IS IN NO WAY A RACIST GROUP WE HAVE GREAT APPRECIATION FOR THE SACRIFICES THAT THE GURKHAS HAVE MADE FOR OUR COUNTRY
>
> RACIST POSTS WILL BE DELETED AND THE MEMBER/MEMBERS FOUND RESPONSIBLE WILL BE REMOVED FROM THE GROUP WITHOUT PRIOR NOTICE

Indeed, those people who had been removed from 'Lumley's Legacy' "for having 'opinions'" set up another smaller and closed Facebook page some time later. And despite the non-racist intent, 'Lumley's Legacy' continues to provide an outlet for the kinds of concerns mentioned above, as well as for more mundane grumbles about noise, bad driving, political parties, rough sleepers, and so on. In response, a local Labour councillor, Alex Crawford, set up yet another Facebook page 'We Love the Gurkhas', to counter the negative publicity found elsewhere, which quickly acquired many more members.

When tensions between young people broke out into gang scuffles, fears of worse happening led to the involvement of the police and community workers. A big public event, named 'Best of Both', was organized at the King's Centre in Aldershot on 4 February 2012. Gerald Howarth attended, as did Tikendra Dewan, Chairman of the British Gurkha Welfare Society (BGWS) and President of the Greater Rushmoor Nepali Community. There were stalls displaying the work of ex-Gurkha charities, Rushmoor Borough Council, the local police, and charities operating in Nepal. Nepali and British dance groups performed. The formation of a new football team that would include both Nepali and local British youth was announced. And the compere of the whole event was none other than Sam Phillips, who had set up the 'Lumley's Legacy' Facebook forum.

Although peace seemed to have been established, and the worst of the threatened violence had been averted, current community relations are by no means perfect. The *Daily Mail*, one of the UK's most read newspapers, carried a long online article in November 2014 with the title "Joanna Lumley's legacy of misery: She fought to allow retired Gurkhas into Britain with her heart in the right place. Five years on, even they say it's backfired terribly" (Jones 2014).

Many elderly Nepalis still experience low-level harassment (verbal abuse or having food thrown at them) and many White people still resent their presence in Aldershot. But several community groups, such as Maddat Samuha, which helps newly arrived women, and Naya Yuva, a youth group, work with the council and other bodies to try and counteract polarization of the two communities.

Diversity

For its size and population, and thanks to its widely varying ecological zones and multiple histories of migration, Nepal is a leader in cultural diversity. Much of that diversity is reproduced in the UK, with the one big exception that Madheshis and Muslims from Nepal seem to be barely present. Dalits, who have fewer resources to migrate long distances, are also under-represented. As the work of Mitra Pariyar has shown (2011, 2018), the Dalits who do make it to the UK face many of the same problems as in urban areas of Nepal: refusal to rent rooms, share kitchens or offensive remarks. The idea, propagated by many, that there is no caste prejudice in the UK, is unfortunately wishful thinking, as UK Dalits from Indian backgrounds have also found.

This Gurkha connection makes the UK's Nepali population unusual when compared to other Nepali diaspora communities around the world. About two thirds of UK Nepalis are either ex-Gurkhas themselves or related to one. This means that those ethnic groups who were historically favoured for recruitment into the British Gurkha regiments—such as Magar, Gurung, Rai, Limbu—are present in the UK in much greater proportions than elsewhere or in Nepal (this historic recruitment policy no longer holds and the Ministry of Defence's official position today is that recruitment is ethnicity-blind). Gurungs, also known as Tamu, are only 1.9 per cent of Nepal's population, but are the biggest Nepali group in the UK with approximately 22 per cent. Limbus are 1.5 per cent in Nepal but 9.6 per cent of the Nepali population in the UK. Magars, Gurungs, Rais, and Limbus taken together are around 12 per cent in Nepal but over two thirds of the UK's Nepali population.

The Gurkha history is reflected in residence patterns. In the UK, just as in India, wherever there is a military base, you are likely to find ex-Gurkhas living nearby, whether in large or small numbers. The highest presence of Nepalis in relation to local population is in Rushmoor Borough, in northeast Hampshire, where there are several military bases. The county of Hampshire has the second-highest Nepali population after London. The third-largest is in Kent, mostly around Ashford, also near a base. Nepalis are found near military bases in Wales, Yorkshire, and Essex too. There are, of course, sizeable Nepali populations in some places without military connections: in west London (where there are many Indians) and in Plumstead in east London, as well as in towns such as Swindon, Carlisle, Oxford, and Reading.

Religious reconstruction

The different demography of the UK's Nepali population not only gives a new flavour to the community's politics; it also changes the religious complexion. The overwhelming dominance of Hinduism in Nepal does not hold in the diaspora. Even though Nepal is no longer the world's only Hindu kingdom and declares itself a secular federal republic, nonetheless, 81 per cent of the population is recorded as Hindu. This falls to 40 to 64 per cent in the UK, depending on whether or not multiple religious attachment is included (Table 2.2 above).

Just as many Nepalis are very happy to belong to multiple Nepali organizations, many are also quite comfortable with practising several religious traditions at once. In a video that was shown as part of an exhibition on the Nepali diaspora in Surrey Heath Museum in 2012, Dr Chandra Laksamba, a Limbu and ex-Gurkha, gave the following explanation:

> Nepalese people do not strongly stick with one religion, they are always with at least two or three. I do believe and practise in three religions: Hindu; I go the Pashupati temple in Kathmandu, a very famous Hindu temple, when I go to Nepal. I go to Swayambhu, and the birthplace of Lord Buddha, that is the Buddhist religion. And I do practise my Kirat religion. Even though I practise Hinduism and Buddhism in my day-to-day life, I have a small *puja* place [shrine] in my house. I have

> Hindu and Buddhist statues. On top of that, at the time of birth and death, death rituals mainly, when you do wedding ceremony or naming ceremony, we have to follow Kirat religion. Especially when we die, death ritual is based on Kirat religion. We don't use Hindu priests or Buddhist lamas. I practise, directly or indirectly, three religions. But we are not very hardcore fundamentalist type of thing. When I was in the army I used to go to church. We do celebrate Christmas as well, we Gorkhas [sic] celebrate all (laughs).

This religious tolerance or coexistence in everyday life rubs up against the notion that modern nation states usually require people to belong to one, and only one, ethnic group and one, and only one, religion. The UK census has evolved to the point where multiple responses are allowed and even encouraged to the nationality question (one is encouraged to be both English and British, for example). Though only one answer is allowed to the ethnicity question, at least there are the options of 'mixed race' and 'other' for those who feel they don't fit into the straitjacket of accepted responses. However, where religion is concerned, only one response is allowed and there are no hybrid options (although one is allowed to omit to answer it). Religion is the last refuge of modernist purity.

In Nepali censuses, multiple responses are not allowed either, nor are hybrid ethnic identities envisaged. In fact, in the early days of the Nepali census, people were not accustomed to being asked, 'What is your *dharma*?' The census enumerators had to be instructed to find out what people's one-and-only-one dharma was and fill out the form accordingly. Today, Nepalis are more used to the question and some ethnic organizations, such as the Nepal Magar Samaj, campaign for 'their' constituents to list their religion as 'Buddhist', regardless of their actual everyday practice—which in most cases is not Buddhist at all.

The VR project included a detailed survey of 300 Nepali households in the UK. The enumerator asked people what their religion was, and once they had responded, read out a series of options that included multiple identifications (Hindu + Buddhist, Kiranti + Hindu, Kiranti + Buddhist, and even Kiranti + Buddhist + Hindu). Given a singular choice, the respondents opted for Buddhism as their primary census identity. But once they were explicitly permitted to be both Hindu and Buddhist, they recognized that this was a better description of what they actually do. About a third of those who at first answered 'Buddhist' switched to 'Hindu + Buddhist' when given the option. A large proportion of these people were Gurungs and many others were Magars.

Generational shift

The older generation of Nepalis spend a lot of time worrying about their children: they may speak Nepali, but will they acquire the habit of reading it? Will they take advantage of the educational opportunities in the UK (the main justification many Nepalis give for migrating in the first place)? Will they ignore their parents' wishes, live separately, join gangs, or have dissolute lives, rather than working hard like their parents? Will they retain a connection to Nepal?

The younger generation are, of course, more at home in the UK than their parents. Campaigns for equal pensions for Gurkhas or for dual citizenship, which galvanize many of their parents' generation, are not pressing concerns for them. They are much more familiar with British popular culture, whether that concerns music or sport. One can do a lot of growing up even in five short years. But judging by their musical tastes, which include many top Nepali bands, they continue to think of themselves as Nepalis. Nepathya, a leading Nepali folk rock band, filled the Wembley Arena in 2013, the first Nepali band to do so. Their success was just the tip of a lively Nepali youth cultural scene that blends Nepali and global influences. For young people, the link to Nepal is likely to remain. Many traditional concerns about purity and caste are likely to fade away. At the same time, young Nepalis have taken the lead, both in social work in the UK, as with the Naya Yuva group mentioned earlier, and in raising money for charitable purposes in Nepal. That is a good sign for the future of the UK's Nepali diaspora.

8

The Performance of Ritual Identity among Gurungs in Europe

SONDRA L. HAUSNER

The performance of communal identity is a time-honoured way of representing a group to itself, as well as to others who may or may not belong to the same association.[1] Establishing the contours of any particular community—that is, demonstrating who

[1] This chapter was published originally in the *Journal of Ritual Studies* (Hausner 2016). My thanks to Linda Woodhead and the ESRC-AHRC Religion and Society award that funded the project on which this research is based, *Vernacular Religion: Varieties of Religiosity in the Nepali Diaspora*, and to my colleagues on that project: David Gellner, Bal Gopal Shrestha, Krishna Adhikari, Chandra Laksamba, and Raju Babu Shrestha. Thanks are also owed to Florence Gurung, who was awarded an AHRC doctoral award as part of the larger project, and who has been a steadfast and excellent researcher. Geoffrey Samuel encouraged this piece and was patient with its author, for which my gratitude on both counts. Mona Schrempf was a helpful interlocutor on the dynamics of ritual performance. Informants and hosts both in the UK, particularly Surya Gurung, Yarjung, and Bheg Tamu, and in Belgium, especially Rabindra Shrestha and his family and Ananta Gurung, were welcoming and helpful, always.

belongs and who does not—is accomplished in part through performance: participation in communal events is a way to see and be seen such that just being there is a mark of affiliation. Such a pattern is perhaps nowhere more apparent than in a diaspora setting, where newly arrived residents need and want to stick together.

In this article, we turn to the possibility of refracting further—or developing a taxonomy of—this open-ended field of performance: What kinds of performance effect a particular or desired political stance? Which kinds of identity emerge in which setting, and how does performance play a role in determining the preeminent or dominant category? And, perhaps most importantly for our ongoing attempts to establish generalizable theories of ritual, is there a difference between collective performance and individual practice?

Performance should not be taken only as the public presentation of identity category, or necessarily in opposition to personal ritual practice. But we know intuitively that performance and practice are not quite the same thing, overlap though they might in multiple and complex theoretical ways. Using the example of a relatively recently arrived immigrant population in Europe, Nepalis, and interrogating how changing internal demographics appear to have impacted the politics of belonging and representation, locally and globally, I argue here that practice must be understood at the level of the individual, while performance may be conducted by and for the sake of the individual self *or* by and for the purpose of consolidating the collective group. All ritual is in some sense performative (even if the audience is God, or a pantheon of deities, or the self), which implies collectivity, and multiplicity. Practice theory, by contrast, even as applied to ritual, takes the individual actor as the unit of analysis, even as he or she necessarily embodies a collective cultural stance. Ritual practice thus may be seen as conducted by the self, while ritual performance is understood as conducted for the other. The difference lies in the lens of the analyst, of course, not the practitioner.

This article is about Nepali Gurungs in particular, who comprise one ethnic group within the larger Nepali population, and the diaspora case study under discussion here thus represents the opportunity to assess ritual as it expresses the internal religious politics of Nepal, against the contemporary backdrop of national and global change. Gurung practices are highlighted here because, as one of a few ethnicities disproportionately recruited into Gurkha forces, they make up a much greater percentage of the Nepali population in the UK than they do in Nepal. This changing demographic landscape arises entirely out of a change in location, and offers a lens into both the specifics of the Nepali case and the wider principles at stake in ritual performance, whether or not it is explicitly understood (by the ritual actors or by the ritual theorists) as political.

Because Gurungs in the UK are represented in a larger proportion than they are in Nepal, they occupy a relatively majority status, instead of an exclusively minority one: Gurungs make up 17 per cent of Nepalis in the UK (the single largest group, along with Magars), compared to less than 3 per cent of Nepali population. Such a shift in position offers the possibility of new and formative identity politics that determine the particular set of combinative possibilities of ethnicity and religion for Nepalis globally (see Tables 1.1 and 4.1 above). A diaspora case thus affords, for the analyst, a forum where the changing *internal* politics of identity and alliance are on view. And we should not be surprised to learn that almost all of the debates around the appropriate links between religion and ethnicity will be precisely—and amply—expressed through ritual.

In short, among Gurungs in the UK, two largely opposing positions have emerged, basically divided between those that want to align themselves with Buddhism (generally drawn from historically 'higher'-ranked clans), and those who want to align themselves with a shamanic, nativist religion (generally drawn from historically 'lower'-ranked clans). Neither faction (if that is not too strong a word) positions itself in alliance with what was until recently state Hinduism, but each occupies a different oppositional stance. Part of the story is historical: in the first instance, once democracy came around in Nepal in 1990, it was critical to assert Buddhism as a collective identity that supported the stance of ethnic solidarity. An early political battle in Britain, a decade later, won the appointment of three Buddhist lamas to the Gurkha forces in addition to the three Hindu pandits that had been traditionally assigned to the chaplaincy roles of the Nepali regiments. But, since Buddhism does not account for the entirety of the religious activity of the Gurung population, a kind of nativist, shamanic ritual too has had to find its voice and make itself heard; today in Great Britain, many thousands of Nepali participants also participate in large, public shamanic rituals, which they classify as 'Bon', explicitly disavowing any links to popular or mainstream Buddhism.

Such an internal divide around issues of religious tension *within* one ethnic group of Nepalis is explicitly expressed through collective ritual, which demonstrates the terms of participation and publicly confirms the critical axis points of identity. And yet, moving into people's family homes and individual altars, one finds that individual ritual practice may—or may not—correlate with the public ritual identities collectively asserted as Buddhist or Bon. Indeed, images may be drawn from Hindu, Buddhist, or shamanic pantheons or representations in equal measure. Apparently public ritual performance does not easily correlate with individual or private ritual practice, at least at the level of symbolic display. That religious category as publicly identified is not necessarily congruent with people's personal practices should be of no surprise (Chaves 2010; Ch. 2 above), although we do well to recall it. The suggestion here is that such incongruence may help us understand the colloquial (and yet clearly meaningful) distinctions between ritual practice and ritual performance: our lens of analysis needs to account for the possibility of multiple or variegated identity at the level of individual ritual practice, even if collective ritual performance is often deliberately singular.

Gurungs in Europe

To move to our case, which is a complex one: Nepalis are an exceptionally diverse nationality, in Nepal and in the diaspora; they are also exceptionally mobile. A long history of migration characterizes the movement of Nepalis out of Nepal, almost always for livelihood or other activities that enable stability (such as, in the contemporary context, study and marriage). Definitions of diaspora vary widely (Cohen 2008), but the Nepali diaspora—however defined—is a large and widely dispersed population.[2] Different estimates exist regarding how many Nepalis are abroad; an open border with India, long the country with the most overseas Nepalis by far, means many thousands pass through uncounted every day. Some published figures suggest roughly 2-3 million of the total of 28 million Nepalis are overseas; other estimates calculate 6-7 million Nepalis are abroad, although half or more than half of that number are in India or the Gulf (see Seddon et. al. 2001 for an early analysis of these trends and Ch. 1 above). Overland migration to India is the old form of hard labour migration; this number is probably now rivalled by hard labour migration to the Gulf, while the UK, the US, continental

[2] One definition of diaspora is three generations in the so-called 'receiving' country (Khachig Toloyan, personal communication): in the UK, Nepalis generally have not yet been here for three generations—and yet consider themselves the heart of the Nepali diaspora. From such evidence, we may ask whether the notion of diaspora requires three generations of arrivals, or—perhaps theoretically more sound—three generations of departures? Is the question how long has a population been in a new place, or should it rather be how long they have been leaving the old one? Once again, the lens of the analyst (in this case locational) appears to determine the definition: if the receiving country is the point of interrogation, three generations of arrivals is logical; if, on the other hand, the sending country (often called the 'homeland') is the point of reference, three generations of departures would seem a more cogent descriptor of the term 'diaspora'.

Europe, and Australia remain the preferred destinations for professional labour migrants (see, for example, Hausner 2011)—that is, when visas can be procured.

One long-standing way for Nepali men to migrate abroad, with an assured source of income and professional status to match, was joining the British Gurkha forces (Caplan 1995). In the UK in recent years, a legal battle ensued to ensure citizenship rights for retired Gurkhas and members of their family: we now estimate 100,000 Nepalis in Great Britain (Adhikari 2012). 85 per cent of Gurungs in Britain were either Gurkhas themselves (20%) or related to Gurkhas (65%). Nepalis are scattered throughout other parts of continental Europe as well, although in much smaller numbers: in Belgium, our comparison case, where Nepalis could migrate relatively easily for a period between 2001 and 2006 on the grounds of political asylum, Nepalis number roughly a tenth of the number in the UK, or somewhere between five and ten thousand.

The picture of Nepali life in Europe is not always rosy; even in the UK, where migration under the Gurkha banner has been in some senses the most straightforward, some real 'assimilation issues' (as we might put it, using the sociological phrasing) have cropped up. Fears about service provision have emerged on both sides of the national divide (Cohen 2010): among Nepalis, concerns about whether they have reasonable access, linguistically and culturally, to health and social security benefits are palpable (Adhikari 2012); among so-called 'native' British, the predictable query about whether a migrant population densely concentrated around barracks areas are suddenly taking up too much social service space has sometimes painfully arisen (see Ch. 7 above). A number of attempts at community reconciliation appear to have been relatively effective: in February, 2012 in Aldershot, near a major barracks for Gurkha regiments, a grand event called 'Best of Both' was held by the local Council. 400 people attended, including both recent Nepali and long-term British residents; British MPs, Nepali Gurkha bands, and teenagers from both populations performed. Cross-cultural sporting events under the banner of a team called 'United Rushmoor' also appear to have allayed successfully community tensions (BBC 2012).

Religion

The ranks of Gurkha soldiers have, since the 19th century, been drawn from particular ethnic groups—seen as strong, resilient, and battle-worthy—that were historically *not* Hindu, although such a policy was never formally acknowledged. So, in Britain, the demographic balance of those ethnic groups whose religious practices have in some sense been subordinate to the religion of the state has shifted, and new possibilities for the assertion of religious identity have emerged. Nepal was formally a Hindu kingdom until 2007, when it became a Federal Democratic Republic and a secular state; regardless of location, then, the contemporary politics of historically underserved ethnic groups, many of whom never engaged in exclusively Hindu religious practices, are thus now increasingly articulated in terms of historically unacknowledged and state-limited religious discourse and practice. As it turns out, the Gurkhas won the right to settle, and claim settlement and attendant social service benefits, in the UK, in 2009, not long after Nepal became a secular republic rather than a Hindu state.

So diaspora terrain thus became doubly ripe for asserting religious identity: on one hand, Gurkhas, who were not historically Hindu, became the majority within the Nepali population in the UK and, on the other, Nepalis worldwide became newly convinced that religious minorities should have their ritual voices heard (and perhaps all the more so if, as in the UK, they were now majorities). Life in Europe (where ethnic and religious demographics would shift even in places where Gurkhas were not the majority) thus enabled a fresh set of religious identifications, implying newly displayed (although never acknowledged as new in innovation)—and vast—repertoires of collective ritual performances, including teachings, community events, and festival celebrations. These collective events invariably confirm a particular categorical identity, whether that of a world religion (Hindu; Buddhist), a particular group of disciples (to Sai Baba, for example), or a historically legitimate set of practices (shamanic blessings or exorcisms).

This complex of ritual and identity display is, of course, not limited to diaspora settings. Gurungs in Nepal have struggled with whether to subscribe to a unitary religious identity in opposition to the then-Hindu Kingdom since 1990, when democracy was ushered in. Roughly ten years ago, the Tamu Samaj (the Gurung Society) "decided" (as one informant told me) that Gurungs were Buddhists. But this unitary designation did not take into consideration clan differentials, and in the decade that followed, a breakaway Gurung group (largely but perhaps not exclusively constituted by lower-ranked clans) claimed shamanism as its true and native religion, in opposition to Gurung Buddhism, which was itself articulated in opposition to Nepali Hinduism. At the heart of ritual activity for both Buddhists and shamans is the centrality of two different kinds of ritual specialists, specifically at the time of death. These specialists are almost always lamas in the Buddhist context, and they are almost always shamanic practitioners known as *pachyu* and *klyepri* in the nativist context (sometimes called Bon, to signal the ostensibly earlier history of these practitioners) (Gurung 2018).

This internal split has travelled with Nepali Gurungs to Britain, where it has blossomed: the two different kinds of religious identification have bifurcated a previously otherwise solid ethnic identity. And here, where Gurungs are much more numerous or dominant as a percentage of the Nepali population in Britain, the stakes are arguably higher, and the numbers are too.[3] To be sure, most Gurungs actively participate in Vajrayana or Tibetan-style Buddhist ritual practice to affirm their religious identity as non-Hindu, but a solid and vocal minority continue to solicit actively the ritual teachings of Gurung Bon religion, which in turn rejects Buddhism out of hand. In the census conducted by our project on Nepali religion in the UK, almost 70 per cent claimed they were Buddhist, and this number increased when multiple identities were permitted; close to 80 per cent claimed they were in some part Buddhist (see Ch. 3 above), and 3 per cent claimed they were Bon. This figure seems small, but the percentage in Nepal is tiny (0.05%). In Britain, percentages are small, but Bon rituals are visibly popular, with a thousand or more attending collective events at a time.

Interestingly, among Nepali Gurungs in Belgium, however, where ethnic rather than religious affiliation remains the primary category of identity, this split among diaspora brethren in a nearby country is the cause of consternation. Being Gurung could accommodate any religious outlook or practice; one informant asked rhetorically but plaintively, "Why divide? That is the reason for *duhkha* [suffering]". While the demonstration of unified ethnic identity remains strong in Belgium, religious or ritual practice appears to have diminished as a communal or cultural priority (see Ch. 4 above). Not one informant in Belgium endorsed a split ethnic identity on the grounds of religion, arguing that ethnic

[3] The demographic shift in the diaspora context enables not only new kinds but also new and multiple modes of religious performance for non-Hindu groups of Nepalis in Britain—and new battles about what kinds truly belong to *that* ethnic identity. But of course they also refer to the representation of ethnic and religious identity, and the performances that both reflect and shape those identities, in Nepal, in a kind of feedback loop. These politics do not stay out of the 'homeland': they emerge from nascent debates there, and having taken full force in diasporic, slightly altered settings, are poised to travel right back in. In a sense, the argument here is that the debates start in Nepal, come to fruition in Europe where new dynamics have been exposed, and then travel back to Nepal, in a kind of circular migration pattern of ideas and identities.

unity would trump different inclinations toward religious practice. "Gurung is one," I was told emphatically, and any attempt to introduce religious factionalism would be stopped in its tracks. Division among Gurungs was not viable in Belgium: *chhaina pani; hundaina pani* ('there aren't any, nor would it be right'), I was told, meaning splinter organizations had not come to Belgium, and must not be permitted to infiltrate. Very few of the 50 organizations for Nepalis in Belgium were religious at all—and most Gurungs were happy to participate in the Sherpa Lhosar, affirming a collective, multi-ethnic Buddhist identity.

Ritual performance and ritual practice

As mechanisms of solidarity (and also for purposes of lobbying when needed), both in the UK and in Belgium, an enormous number of organizations or associations have sprung up, by ethnic identity, region, religion, and regiment, among others. In the UK, we have tabulated close to 500 organizations (or one organization per 200 people); in Belgium in 2011, we calculated around 50 (or one organization per 100 people) (see Tables 4.2 and 4.3 above). These organizations serve as strong forums for collective mobilization and representation, but they also are the fulcrum of social activity, in both celebratory and ritual life-cycle modes, for most Nepalis (Gurungs and others) in Europe.

Collective performance I: New Year's celebrations

Seasonal collective celebrations naturally become a way for diaspora Nepalis to gather, and major Nepali festivals are always an occasion to do so. Since the advent of democracy and the rise of ethno-religious representational politics in Nepal, the New Year festival known as Lhosar or Lhochhar has become the largest festival for groups that identify as other than Hindu (see Holmberg 2016). Lhosar used to be a Tibetan Buddhist (Vajrayana) New Year festival, but now is celebrated by Sherpas, Tamangs, and Gurungs—in both Buddhist and Bon renditions—as well as other groups, each on a separate day, with large and sometimes ebullient displays of national (read ethnic) dress, dancing, stalls, and eateries sporting national (read ethnic) cuisine, not to mention ritual activity. As just one example, in 2011, I asked a young friend who had just returned from a large (many thousands) public celebration of Gurung Lhosar in the centre of Kathmandu, "What do you do at Gurung Lhosar?" "We wear Gurung dress; we eat Gurung food," she replied. "What's Gurung food?" I pressed. "Well, it's Nepali food but we call it Gurung because it's Gurung Lhosar." To participate in the performance of Gurung identity in Nepal at that time was not, for her, to subscribe to the idea that there was a difference, necessarily, between Gurungs and other Nepalis. But it was to attend the call of ethnic identification as a salient differential that must be tended to—performed, and thereby acknowledged—in a contemporary, multi-religious, multi-ethnic Nepal.

These celebrations in London and in Leuven (as well as in Kathmandu) have, over the past ten years, become a very prominent mode of public performance and collective belonging: they delineate a collective as occupying a temporal universe markedly distinct from the one that starts with the Nepali New Year (now read as oppressively Hindu), normally in April. Lhosar, or Lhochhar, is rather celebrated in mid-winter (sometimes coincident with the Chinese New Year) and has become the dominant mode of articulating a particular ethnic group affiliation; Tamangs celebrate Tamang Lhochhar (Holmberg 2016); Gurungs celebrate Gurung Lhochhar—or two Gurung Lhochhars, as the case may be, as in the UK the Buddhists and the shamans have fallen into complicated and sometimes acrimonious debates about whether Lhosar should be marked by one unified or two separate celebrations (Ch. 9 below).

Even separately, Gurung Lhosar celebrations are the largest of the year by far, numbering many thousands. Over the past few years, the two kinds of Gurung religious collectives could not resolve their differences, and Buddhist Gurungs celebrated their New Year on one day, while Bon Gurungs celebrated theirs on another. (One year the two organizations refused to compromise and chose to have their respective celebrations on the same day, thus disabling the possibility that someone could attend both.) Lhosar has in itself become a marker of (ethno-)religious identity, such that the ritual performance of either a lama or at least one shamanic specialist (but more often a group of them, represented by the main shaman and a set of his disciples) becomes the central theme of the day, marking the collective as legitimate and enduring, followed by cultural performances, games, dances, and copious amounts of food and drink. These events are good opportunities for the display or performance of heritage—as far as the objects of shamanic trance and action, for example, which are laid out in elaborate offering form every year among the Gurung Bon community, carefully constructed by UK-based Gurung shamans. By performing Bon ritual activities on this calendrical cycle, Gurung shamanic leaders offer an opportunity for Gurungs who identify as shamanist to attend and participate in a collective event of affirmation and demarcation.

Collective performance II: Funerals

Arguably the most important kind of ritual event the world over is a funeral, which reconsolidates a social world in the absence of one of its own. And there is no doubt that a funeral is only a ritual performance: no degree of correctness or acuity will bring the deceased person back into the world of the living, although a funeral may assuage the universal experience of mourning. The importance of ritual at the time of death means that the choice of specialist takes on particular importance, and it is precisely around the question of whether Buddhist lamas or Bon *pachyu* and *klyepri* are more appropriate as ritual facilitators at funerals that the heart of the religious debate within Gurung worlds lies, in both the UK and Nepal (Gurung 2018; Ch. 9 below). (In Belgium, where there is still fierce resistance at the idea of a divided Gurung community, a lama who could officiate in both contexts was called a *lama-kegi*.)

As the numbers of elderly Nepalis in Europe increase, funeral arrangements have become an even more obvious priority of diaspora ethnic and religious associations. Providing assistance to immigrant groups who need to attend to these rituals (so particularly Nepalis in areas where they are concentrated) has also become a priority—or at least a facility—of local British councils, who have set up parallel offices to help facilitate. At one New Year's festival, a local council representative in attendance stood to tell the assembled crowd that funeral assistance was a service that the UK Government was able to provide, information that was regarded with hesitation among the participants: funeral arrangements are an intensely personal (and cultural) affair, and strict rules govern who may see or tend to a body. At a different New Year's celebration, I was asked by a local hospice worker *what*, precisely, Nepali funerals entailed, as appropriate linguistic and cultural provisions increasingly needed to be found for Nepali residents who died in the area.

A Gurung funeral rite is centred around an event known as an *argaun*, and, once again, in the British context, most (but not all) Gurungs will seek a Vajrayana or Tibetan-style Buddhist lama to conduct purificatory rituals, although the choice of who to call for the various ritual events required is a complex and often contested one (Gurung 2018). At a funeral rite I witnessed in Hampshire, presided over by a Buddhist lama (one of the Buddhist chaplains for the Gurkha forces), the end of the ritual was marked by a Gurung re-purification of the next of kin, who could now be properly reintegrated into social worlds, in an idiom quite distinct from a classically Tibetan-style Buddhist ritual. Undoing ritual impurity at the very conclusion of a funeral rite clearly acts in defiance of or opposition to the purity polarities of Hinduism, but, in this case, the Vajrayana-trained lama suggested that the last phase of the ritual was not Buddhist practice, either. Although he had recited the entire Tibetan liturgy appropriate for the funeral at the request of the family, he was frustrated that the ethos of the hall was noisier than he expected, and in the end had to characterize the event not as Buddhism but as 'Gurungism'.

Members of the Bon Gurung community would not have agreed that these acts constituted classical 'Gurungism' insofar as the ritual officiant was not a traditional Gurung practitioner. At the headquarters of the Bon movement (known as the Tamu Pye Lhu Sangh, or TPLS) just outside Pokhara in Nepal, many rooms and much effort is devoted to training qualified ritual practitioners to officiate at ritual events, and most importantly at funerals. While some families in both the UK and Belgium have made the choice to repatriate the body of the deceased to Nepal, the importance of having trained ritual specialists to facilitate Gurung funerals in Europe has been clear to community members, and the question of how best to officiate a Bon funeral in the UK when most trained practitioners are in Nepal has been an active one. There are now a core number of qualified (or qualifying) Bon *pachyu* and *klyepri* practitioners in the UK, and they have attended, in what they call a traditional way—despite time limits at crematoriums and constraints on the number of days that can be given over to death ceremonies—multiple funerals (Gurung 2018).

The kind of specialist employed for either celebratory seasonal events or significant life- or death-cycle rituals is thus at the heart of the intra-ethnic tension about ritual performance (Gurung 2018). In this regard, the symbolic valences around the performance of correct ritual procedures in England do not appear to be different from those in South Asia: lamas reflect an elite, cosmopolitan tradition, while shamans reflect a village, home-base—nativist—model of indigeneity and thus original or primary (even ontological) claim to place and method (Balikci 2008; see also Mumford 1989 and Samuel 1993), even if, in this case, shamans are performing ritual blessings in a land far from their own. (Still, ritual implements such as drums and costumes and crowns are specifically made in and flown from Nepal, and training for ritual specialists is thought best done there, although the exigencies of overseas life mean that it is possible to apprentice in the UK.) Conceptually, we might push the polarity between the ritual performance of Buddhism and shamanic Bon further still: lamas, in their emphasis on right action, appear to align with the value of purity in the Indic model; shamans, in their capacity to take on or in bodily from the poisons or forces latent in social dynamics, use the physical or material world as the vehicle for social healing, and thus represent an arm of medical religion that largely focuses on nature, and is now giving rise to environmentalist movements among eastern Nepalis as well.[4]

Individual practice: Altars and shrines

Funerals are almost always collective events, necessarily, and New Year's celebrations are usually large, public social occasions. Interestingly, a minority—only about a third—of Gurung respondents to our survey reported being actively involved in social organizations, and a small fraction (8%) had ever held an office in such an organization. Participating in a collective event is not the same as managing it. By contrast, a very high percentage (88%) reported having a shrine or a holy place at home. Such a figure indicates that religion features strongly in the private lives—and practices—of Gurungs in the UK.

What is more, the religious categorization that tends to be quite starkly performed in the context of public occasions appears to dissipate in the context of private display. Personal practice, as articulated by Gurung respondents and as evidenced by the posters, statues, and religious objects in their shrines, is easily and comfortably—and often—multivocal, defying category. To be sure, there are many individuals whose public persona correlates perfectly with private display (and whose participation in collective performance, I am suggesting, tallies easily and with no

[4] In some sense, this same polarity (purity versus control over nature) is also reflected in the Hindu disparity between Brahmans and ascetics (on which see, for example, Das 1977).

contradiction with their private practices): for example, the secretary of the Tamu Dhee, the main Gurung cultural organization to which most of those identifying as Vajrayana Buddhists belong, has in his home an entire wall dedicated to the statues of different manifestations of the Buddha, behind glass, with a set of devotional water bowls in front, kept full and clean, along with bowls of fruit and, on ritual occasions, freshly made *tormas*. And a number of shamanic adherents deliberately kept their altars spare, with only the brass pot (iconic of natural forces?) displayed.

But the vast majority of personal shrines—and locations of personal practice—were multiply adorned, in that they displayed images or icons from both Hindu and Buddhist registers. Religious identity—and religious practice, too—at the level of the individual respondent was much more muddied, or multivalent, or multiple (Ch. 3 above). Indeed, when explicitly given the opportunity to choose a multiple religious identity, four times as many of our Gurung respondents did so, almost half of them opting, interestingly, for the religious category of 'Hindu AND Buddhist'. In parallel, the number of people who chose a single category, once aware that they did not have to select only one, dropped by nearly half. If Gurungs in the UK are particularly religious, they are also happy to identify multiply—as individual practitioners, if not as members of a collective performance. As conscious as people might be of their ethnic identity, and as important as it might thus be to perform particular attendant religious identity in public, in private, as far as religious practices go, the more the merrier.

In Belgium, where the public performance of religious categories was generally given short shrift, this panoply of religious iconography at the personal or individual level was all the more apparent. For example, at a restaurant owned by a Gurung woman, public images downstairs were consistently Buddhist (as befit a public Gurung identity in that context—and as generally thought proper in Nepali restaurants), but Sai Baba featured in an image in a private upstairs room, adorned with red tika powder. When asked if she wasn't Buddhist, my hostess was entirely nonplussed, and claimed not only could she worship many kinds of deities, but she could also conduct her religious practice anywhere, including a church. Others, too, claimed they could go to any location to do religious practice—a church, a mosque—and that people's religious identities didn't matter to them at all.

Individual ritual precisely need not be so taken with categories of religious identity, of course, because a practitioner does not have to be a specialist. Here we see Weber's classification between lay and virtuosi religion. Virtuosi are required in the performance of ritual identity, while an individual practitioner may conduct his or her ritual as he or she sees fit, to a large degree, as long as s/he is also a participant in the collective ritual events that are facilitated by a specialist who is clear about his or her mandate and identity. Again, the exception—the outside to this perfect matrix of 'individual : lay : practice :: collective : virtuosi : performance'—is the ritual specialist who is a healer, or instrumentalist, who, in his or her practice, may mix and match his or her identity categories in the practical performances of healing—and whose seemingly muddled categories do not put off his or her patients or disciples: what is at stake is of a different order. But for the majority of ritual participants, individual practice is free from the constraints of identity performance, in that it is personal, for the self, or for the upkeep of a private or internal relationship with God or the divine.

Practice and performance

Ritual practice and ritual performance are subjects of exhaustive critical literatures, although almost all scholars of the subject acknowledge at some point that we are talking semantics.[5] Still,

---

[5] See, most famously, Clifford Geertz (1973), whose articulation still rings true when he speaks of the Balinese performance of ritual as "a story

the construction of ritual identity is a complex and close to universal business, and the question of internality and externality—of experience and performance—intersect with core anthropological questions about practice or praxis, and the ways consciousness and self-consciousness relate to how we exist as cultural human beings who are both formed by our environments and surroundings and aware of our actions, such that we need to confirm our senses of who we are with ritual action. But ritual is also about seeking outcomes, and this kind of performance has a different kind of audience. Also writing about Nepalis in a diaspora context (India in this instance), Sara Shneiderman (2011) distinguishes between practice and performance (cultural or ritual or otherwise) on these grounds: if it is for yourself, it is practice; if it is for someone else, it is performance.

Shneiderman suggests that the analytical divide between practice and performance might be constructed such that the former (practice) speaks most usefully to an indigenous cosmological action—where the audience is a pantheon of deities and force—and the latter refers to external political and economic structural constraints—where the audience is presumably a recognizable social world (2011). Both spheres, she argues, "are necessary for groups and individuals to maintain the pragmatic and emotional well-being that derives from a sense of belonging to a shared … identity … recognized by others" (2011: 208). She draws upon Guneratne's distinction, too, of action within a particular context, untheorized as such by the actor, and the kind of political identification that may then be layered upon those actions (1998), within the broader transnational frames of ethnicity and nation, or, here, religion. Moving into the particular sphere of religion, we may understand the distinction she draws between performance and practice as largely adhering to the distinction of religious category and religious practice (Ch. 2

they tell themselves about themselves" (1973: 448); Catherine Bell (1992); and the ever-eminent Durkheim (1995).

above), where performance is about demonstrating the identity category to which one belongs in public. In a sense, in all these renderings, the question is one of self-consciousness, where the actor is understood to be swept up in the action in the context of practice, but aware of the ways in which it might be read externally (by other humans) in the context of performance. Other parallel binaries that might be invoked here are emic/etic, or private/public, although each takes on a slightly different frame and speaks to a different scale.

Into this dialectical analytical frame, I want to insert a new binary—or at least a dyad—that is left somewhat alone in both Guneratne's and Shneiderman's analyses, that between the collective and the individual. It would be too simple to suggest that ritual practice is an individual's act and ritual performance is a collective's, but I am tempted to suggest that while an individual may engage in either ritual practice or in ritual performance (and that there may not be much to distinguish the two at that level), a collective or association may really only engage in ritual performance. When ritual is conducted for the sake of other human beings, there is a performative or self-conscious element that is, in a classic Durkheimian rendering, about confirming group identity, whatever it may look like, in whatever manifestation it might have at that particular place and time.

This is not to say that ritual experience in a group setting is not genuine. On the contrary: the very presence of other human beings may precisely enable what Durkheim called collective effervescence (1995), which is at the heart of religious life. Performance does not refer only to external or public display; it may invoke or infuse private or internal aspects of the self. Rather, the point is that the individual—interested not only in the group/s to which he or she belongs and the cementing of that bond but also the instrumental logic of personal well-being—has been left out of the equation (Hausner 2013b). I suggest therefore that group identity (although it undeniably constitutes not only our senses of self but also the cultural frames through which we articulate our desires) is not the be all and end all of individual ritual practice, which may also seek personal help and enablement, and that it is at this level of religious action that we may more accurately use the term ritual practice. Individuals may practice; groups will perform.[6]

Practice may really only be understood at the level of the individual (*pace* Bourdieu 1977), while performance probably encompasses all forms of ritual, private and public, individual and collective, for the individual is almost certainly performing it to him or herself, or reminding him or herself who he is—possibly in terms of multiple identification, but certainly in terms of wholeness and integrity. By understanding ritual practice in this way—in contradistinction to but also a subset of performance—we "concentrate on embodied cognition rather than on symbolic expression", as Sax (2010: 8) puts it—although in this piece I have focused equally on symbolic expression as the mode of ritual performance and affirmation of collective identity. Very simply, I am suggesting that ritual action at the level of individual interiority may productively be called ritual practice, while ritual action in order to confirm identity to anyone (from any realm, human or divine, natural or super-natural), where there is a shared or at least partially overlapping or aspirational notion of who one is meant to be, is necessarily ritual collective performance.

---

[6] Shneiderman is right to suggest that a distinction should be made between actions intended for supernatural forces or deities and actions intended for humans; evidence that humans are 'hard-wired' to look for supernaturality implies that they know a human when they see one (e.g. Barrett 2004). But there are plenty of *gurus* or teachers (or witches or shamans) who occupy some kind of middle ground between human and divine, as far as capacity to manipulate the material world goes, and as far as the respect that is owed them among members of their constituent communities. These larger-than-life figures—human beings, in life and in lore, and yet perceived as able to press natural limits—appear to confound the analytical binary of human/supernatural; the extra-ordinary power they are said to accrue would seem to emerge from their capacity to do so, and transcend categorization.

Returning to Claude Lévi-Strauss' famous analogy of music to culture in *Overture* (1969), consider the colloquial distinction: one practises one's art in the privacy of one's own emotional realms, until such time as one's cumulatively built-up internalized capacity may be brought to bear, and come to full fruition, in public performance.

Conclusion: Individual and collective

Researching collective identity in a newly established diasporic setting lays out in unusually clear terms the emergence of social worlds at the moment of their formation. First, new lobbying possibilities arise—and are needed—in new terrain, and in these sometimes uncharted political contexts, shifts in identity and affiliation may be particularly marked: the field is open, and religious—or ethnic or national or regional—associations can crop up in many forms. Which ones do crop up—and in relation to which battle—can point us to new configurations of the perennial power plays inherent in identity politics.

Second, recent immigrants may be particularly concerned to transmit ostensibly long-held cultural values to the next generation. These values may indeed be 'traditional,' or they may be more recent constructs that, in order to confirm status, longevity, and legitimacy, present themselves as if they are indigenous, archetypal, or have historical primacy. Either way, performance of a particular kind of religious identity in a public setting may take a ritual form as a way of confirming it.

With increased awareness in Nepal about the salience of religion as an identity category in the modern world, especially since democracy in 1990 and the fall of the Hindu Kingdom in 2007, ritual performance has taken on new meaning and new importance for Nepalis globally. The debates about Gurung identity have precisely taken ritual and performative form in Britain, but ritual practice among this same population does not appear to have been limited to particular idioms, easily encompassing multiple frames. Such a complex set of ritual actions—that both articulate and evade identity categories—gives us new material with which to think through old theoretical problems about the possible distinctions to be drawn between ritual performance and ritual practice. We may give ourselves more tools of analysis in the study of ritual if we delineate practice from performance by looking to that old question of social science, and distinguishing action at the personal level of the individual, which should be viewed primarily as practice, from that at the public level of the collective, which will usually fall under the head of performance.

9

State-Level Representation versus Community Cohesion: Competing Influences on Nepali Religious Associations in the UK

FLORENCE GURUNG

Introduction

Patterns of religious identification in Nepal have long been influenced by ethnic politics.[1] Nepal was, for many years, a Hindu state, and until recently the vast majority of the population identified as Hindu, at least in official contexts. Since the 1990s, however, there have been increasing demands for equality of representation and opportunity amongst the numerous minority ethnic groups, many of which now claim a non-Hindu origin.[2]

---

[1] This chapter was first published in *Religion in Diaspora*, eds Hausner & Garnett (Gurung 2015).

[2] There is a vast literature on Nepali ethnic politics since 1990. See, for example, Des Chene (1996), Gellner et al. (2008), Fisher (2001), Minami (2007), Lecomte-Tilouine (2009), Hangen (2010).

This movement directly challenges the state-promoted vision of national identity which apparently privileges the culture of the Hindu high castes and marginalizes those groups which, historically, may have followed Buddhism and/or their own tribal religion. In this context, asserting a Buddhist identity can be a statement of belonging to a particular ethnic group, or of solidarity with other minority ethnic groups in defiance of alleged Hindu domination and oppression, as much as a purely 'religious' statement. It may, or may not, reflect the nature of actual religious practice and belief (Ch. 2 above).

In addition, while most of these groups are agreed on being not Hindu, there are debates within some as to what religious identity they should assert instead. There is, nonetheless, widespread agreement that each group should have a 'religion of identity', that they should be able to claim one particular religious tradition as a distinct part of their ethnic culture. While a large proportion now claim a Buddhist heritage, many have also preserved some shamanic or animistic practices and there are sections within some groups who argue that these should be revived and reclaimed as their indigenous religion or religion of identity in place of either of the two world religions on offer. While many individuals have retained elements of these traditions, and continue to follow them alongside Hindu or Buddhist practices, the idea of claiming such local customs as a primary religious identity is a comparatively new one and, to many, a somewhat alien concept. Those who do so, therefore, tend to be relatively politically aware. In other words, the explicit assumption of a Bon (Gurung) or Kirati (Rai/Limbu) identity, as opposed to the less explicit or self-conscious following of elements of that tradition in person's daily life, has only become a possibility because of a particular political context. In practice, as has been much commented on before, Nepalis, like many South Asians, can be religiously quite mixed (Carrithers 2000). Many individuals follow elements of Hinduism, Buddhism, and some kind of shamanic tradition in different contexts. However, the idea that, at least at an official level, one should claim a singular religious identity, and that that identity is at least partly defined by *jat* (caste/ethnic group), is now widely accepted.[3]

In the UK, formal associations have been established both on the basis of *jat*[4] and of religious affiliation. While clearly influenced by political agendas in various ways, most claim to be non-political. Their stated aims, more often, are to do with the needs of the diaspora community. They are formed to bring the community together, and to provide welfare and support, financial or emotional, to those struggling in the UK. They also aim to preserve religious or cultural traditions, so that they might retain their ethnic identity and so that the younger generation, brought up in the UK, may not lose the connection with their ancestral land and cultural heritage.

This chapter looks at the ways in which the form and priorities of Nepali religious associations in the UK have been influenced by these two spheres: Nepali ethnic politics on the one hand, and the needs of community-building in the UK on the other. I explore the ways in which these two rival influences both support one another but also conflict. At one level they seem be much in congruence for they promote similar interests: both encourage the recreation and preservation of threatened cultural traditions and the uniting of a community which shares them. However, there are areas in which they appear to clash, where political issues create divisions within religious or social groups,

---

[3] Gellner and Hausner (Ch. 3 above) have demonstrated that while most Nepalis (in the UK) are ready to claim a singular religious identity when asked, assuming this to be expected or required in official contexts, when given the option of a multiple religious identity ('Hindu-Buddhist' or 'Hindu-Kiranti' for example) a significant number will take it.

[4] The term '*jat*' can be used to signify 'caste' in the Hindu sense (with the understanding of hierarchy) but in many contexts can also be translated as 'tribe' or 'ethnic group' or even 'clan'. Literally it means 'species' or 'type'. Because of the ambiguity of the term, and the sensitivity around the appropriate English term to use (many do not consider their own *jat* do be part of the caste system), I will use the Nepali term throughout.

or where social divisions obstruct political unity. Where conflict is identified it sometimes reveals a degree of tension between openly declared and tacitly pursued goals. Contrary to what might be expected, this is by no means always a case of stated religious or social priorities masking deeper political motivations. While there is a sense in which the political context has influenced conceptions of religion and religious identity in such a way that it is very difficult for purportedly religious or social organizations to divorce themselves from politics absolutely, there are also cases where essentially political goals are subverted by the realities of local community needs.

I begin by providing some background on the range of Nepali associations operating in the UK. I discuss the continuing salience of *jat* or ethnicity as a basis on which such associations are formed, and the way that religion is understood and utilized in defining and expressing ethnic identity. I then introduce the Gurungs, as the representative ethnic group on which this discussion is based, and the principal associations in which they are involved. I continue with a discussion of the debates between the major Gurung organizations Tamu Dhee UK and TPLS UK over the proposed joint Lhosar celebrations, considering the ways in which political concerns and the needs of the diaspora community both supported and obstructed the cause. I then turn to an examination of the Buddhist Community Centre UK, considering how far its rejection of ethnic concerns in favour of what it regards as the religious needs of the diaspora population really represents a distancing from politics and the concerns of the Nepali state. The research is based on participant observation and in-depth interviews with leaders of the various associations and members of the Gurung community carried out over two years of fieldwork in Farnborough, Hampshire.

Nepali associations in the UK and the continuing salience of *jat*

The Nepali diaspora in the UK is a relatively new one. Although there have been a few Nepalis settled in the UK since the 1960s and 70s, significant numbers only started to arrive after the government granted ex-Gurkhas the right to settle in the UK in 2004, with a further boost after that right was extended from only those who had retired after 1997 to all ex-Gurkhas with at least four years' service, in 2009. As the population has expanded, numerous associations have sprung up with the aims of strengthening social networks, providing mutual support and welfare and preserving cultural traditions. Some of these associations bring together people from a particular region or district in Nepal (Lamjung Samaj, Ilam Samaj, etc.), or a smaller geographical area, be it a single village or group of villages (Kolma Bahakot Samaj, Mardi Khola Samaj, etc.). Others represent all the Nepalis living in a particular area in the UK, most common or at least most active in areas where there are relatively few Nepalis (Nepalese Community Winchester, Tonbridge Nepalese Community, etc.). There are also professional organizations (Nepalese Doctors' Association UK, Society of Nepalese Engineers in the UK) and many ex-Gurkha associations, both campaigning organizations such as the Gurkha Army Ex-Servicemen's Association (GAESO) and the British Gurkha Welfare Society (BGWS), and less formally structured groupings of '*numberi*', those who joined up in the same year, which do little more than hold annual get-togethers. A few are defined specifically by religion, such as the Lumbini Nepalese Buddha Dharma Society, the Buddhist Community Centre UK, and Shiva Culture, but many of the largest and most influential associations in the UK are those defined by *jat*. Tamu Dhee UK, for example, is one of the only Nepali associations in the UK to own property, a hall in Mytchett used for a variety of Nepali community gatherings, and is also responsible for organizing two of the most widely-attended events in the Nepali social calendar: the Gurkha Cup and the Nepali Mela. All of those *jats* most highly represented in the UK (so all those traditionally favoured for Gurkha recruitment)[5] have their own *jat* association (Tamu Dhee UK, Magar Sangh, Kirat Yakthung Chumlung (Limbu), Kirat Rai Yayokkha, etc.), and there are now smaller associations of sub-*jats* (the Ghale Samaj, or Lila-Phung UK) and even of clan (Pachyu Bhai Khalak).

The salience of *jat* organizations in the UK is related to (although not fully explained by) the growth of ethnic politics in Nepal.[6] As stated above, ethnic rights and equal opportunities for all Nepal's ethnic groups have been big political priorities since the first People's Movement of 1990, which introduced multi-party democracy in Nepal. For much of the country's history, Nepal was officially a Hindu state and citizens were encouraged to adopt and assert a Hindu national identity. In addition, government and the professions had been dominated by Hindu elites (*bahun* and *chhetri*, or Brahmin and Ksatriya, castes), and the *janajati* (a term which emerged during this period to describe hill ethnic groups most of whom claim a non-Hindu origin but have been gradually 'Hinduized' over the years) claimed to have been marginalized and oppressed. Following the 1990 movement they pressed for Nepal to lose its status as a Hindu kingdom and

---

[5] The British army has been recruiting Nepalese soldiers into a special wing, the Brigade of Gurkhas, since 1815. In the past, the British would only recruit from certain ethnic groups, those they regarded as 'martial races' (Caplan 1995). This criterion excluded Bahun/Chhetri castes and favoured, particularly, Gurungs, Magars, Rais and Limbus. Although there is now apparently no caste discrimination in the recruitment process it is still predominantly those *jats* with a history of Gurkha service who seek to join up. The majority of Nepalese migrants in the UK are ex-Gurkhas and their dependents (around 60%) and consequently these *jats* are, proportionately, more highly represented in the UK than they are in Nepal.

[6] It is noteworthy that *jat* distinctions are not of equal importance in all parts of the Nepali diaspora. In Belgium, for instance, while *jat* associations do exist, associations with links to Nepali political parties are more salient (Ch. 4 above).

to recognize the many religions practised in Nepal (finally achieved in 2008), for *janajatis* to get equal representation in the government and equal opportunities in education and employment, and for their languages and cultures to be recognized and preserved alongside mainstream Nepali culture.[7] In order to lobby for such rights, ethnic associations were formed to press the government for recognition but also to enable and encourage these groups to rediscover and preserve lost or disappearing traditions. Part of their demand for greater representation was based on the claim that these groups are indigenous to Nepal, that Hindu populations entered Nepal later, and that their own cultural traditions are thus more authentically Nepali than that which had been promoted as the national culture in recent years.

In this way, notions of Nepali citizenship have come to be tied up with notions of ethnic identity: a distinctive ethnic culture viewed as evidence of indigeneity, of belonging to the land, and representation at the level of government increasingly being through *jat*, with *jat* associations apparently best able to stand up for collective interests. The culmination of this trend is seen in the current demands for ethnic federalism. Under this system each ethnic group would be responsible for governing its own ethnically-based state where it is argued that the interests of that *jat*, including the preservation of its unique language and culture, could be best served (Hangen 2007b).

Notions of religious identity have also been moulded by this discourse. As noted above, while, in reality, many Nepalis are quite mixed in their religious practice, following aspects of Hinduism, Buddhism, and sometimes their own tribal religion,

---

[7] The development of a mainstream Nepali culture, in which Nepal's status as the world's only Hindu kingdom was a central feature, and an attempt by the state to inculcate a sense of Nepali national identity through such a shared culture, only really began during the Panchayat period. See Burghart (1984) on the historical development of the concept of the nation-state in Nepal. See, for example, Onta (1996b) and Pigg (1992) on the Panchayat style of nation-building.

the discourse around ethnic rights assumes that each ethnic group has a distinctive and singular religious identity. This is in part related to the rejection of Hindu domination, as *janajati* groups insist that their indigenous religion is something other than Hinduism. However, more than simply rejecting Hinduism, there is an expectation that each *jat* should be tied to an alternative religious tradition which forms an integral part of its ethnic culture. While some have found it difficult to agree on what religion that should be, there is nonetheless a general consensus that agreement should be sought, that each ethnic group must have a single religious identity which defines them and distinguishes them from other ethnic groups. The umbrella organization NEFIN (Nepal Federation of Indigenous Nationalities) has made this an explicit criterion of membership. It states that in order to be recognized as an indigenous nationality, each ethnic group must have their "own language, culture and religion different from the rulers".[8]

While the *jat* associations in the UK are, by and large, not directly affiliated with their Nepal-based counterparts, the inclination to organize along *jat* lines, and the principal objectives of the preservation of ethnic culture and identity, are clearly influenced by the centrality of ethnic issues within Nepali political life. Some are also influenced by debates going on within Nepal-based ethnic associations regarding the nature of their indigenous culture, as the process of reasserting and rediscovering lost history, customs, and religious practices has, in many cases, caused considerable controversy. Either way, *jat* associations feel impelled to identify a singular religion as one source of their shared identity.

---

[8] www.nefin.org.np.

The Gurungs

In this chapter I focus on one ethnic group, the Gurungs, as one of the most highly represented groups in the UK and one with a very mixed religious heritage, and on three quite different associations in which they are involved. First, Tamu Pye Lhu Sangh (TPLS) UK is primarily a *jat* association: its membership is (almost) entirely Gurung and its principal aim is the preservation of Gurung culture. However, it may also be described as a religious organization as Gurung culture is defined according to the oral texts of the Gurungs' traditional shamanic priests, the *pachyu* and *klyepri*. It is the only one of the three organizations discussed here which is a branch of a Nepal-based (although now transnational) organization and so, in some ways, is most closely tied to the Nepali ethnic political agenda. Although the Nepal-based organization also claims to be non-political, its formation in 1990 was very much a product of the political climate of that time and it has been instrumental in the rediscovery of Gurung history and consequently in determining how Gurung ethnic identity should be represented at the national level (Pettigrew 1995). However, while strongly connected to TPLS headquarters in Nepal, the UK organization is also a community organization, formed to meet the needs of Gurungs in the diaspora. The initial impetus for its establishment was the conviction of a few individuals that Lhosar, the Gurung's major annual festival, was not being celebrated according to Gurung tradition, but they also identified a need to support *pachyu* and *klyepri* (Gurung shamanic priests) in the UK, making it possible for them to officiate at life-cycle rites and other Gurung ritual occasions.

Secondly, Tamu Dhee UK, is the other major Gurung *jat* association. Although avowedly non-religious, and non-political, the majority of its membership identify as Buddhist. Its relationship with the other major *jat* organization, TPLS, is also determined by religious questions. The two associations disagree as to how Gurungs should represent their religious identity, whether Tibetan Buddhism or Bon (as TPLS now term the religion of the *pachyu* and *klyepri* priests) is their indigenous religion, and even whether their indigenous religion and religion of identity need be the same. These debates were recently brought to the fore as the two associations attempted to come to an agreement over how to celebrate Lhosar together, united as one *jat*. Attempts to unite the community in this way made reference both to the need for unity in order to secure rights and representation in Nepal as well as in order to provide mutual support in the UK. However, both competing views about the place of religion within ethnic identity and the mechanics of how communities actually form in the diaspora created barriers to unity and ensured that the two associations continued to act independently and to celebrate Lhosar in their own separate ways.

Finally, the Buddhist Community Centre UK at first sight appears to be at a much greater remove from the concerns of Nepali ethnic activists. It is quite firmly a religious and not a *jat* association, and explicitly tries to be pan-Nepali, appealing to and welcoming all *jats*, although a large proportion of the membership is Gurung. However, there are ways in which it too is shaped and influenced by political concerns. Its responses to those concerns however, differ considerably.

Tamu Pye Lhu Sangh UK, Tamu Dhee UK, and the campaign for Tamu unity

Tamu Pye Lhu Sangh UK and Tamu Dhee UK both represent the Gurung (or Tamu)[9] *jat* in the UK. While Tamu Dhee is primarily a social organization, Tamu Pye Lhu Sangh is more concerned with the preservation of traditional Gurung religion, the traditions of the *pachyu* and *klyepri* priests, and research into, and the dissemination of knowledge about, Gurung history and culture. Although adamant that the existence of two major *jat* organizations is justified as they fulfil different roles, there has

[9] 'Tamu' is the Gurung word for 'Gurung'.

been some uneasiness that it may appear to some (to British-born or raised Gurung children as well as members of other *jats*) that there is a split within Gurung society, that they are divided.[10] The fact that each organization hosts their own separate, and apparently competing, community event to celebrate their most important festival, Gurung Lhosar, has added to this impression.

Consequently, in 2011, a number of influential Gurung community leaders got together and began a campaign for Tamu unity. The chief proposal was that the two organizations should come together for the celebration of Lhosar, and organize a joint event for all Gurungs. Lhosar has become, both in Nepal and the UK, the main occasion at which to publically display and celebrate Gurung culture. It is slightly ironic that it is considered a uniquely Gurung festival, given that Lhosar, in some form, is also celebrated by a large number of other Janajati communities, who have also adopted it as the appropriate opportunity to display and celebrate their own unique culture.[11] A large, public Lhosar celebration, to which political leaders can be invited, has become almost a requirement of any significant Janajati group in Nepal as well as the UK, and such events have quite overtly political aims. The

[10] There are two largely endogamous clan groups within Gurung society and it has been alleged in the past that these groups were caste-like, in that there was hierarchy between them, and that this hierarchy has been the cause of considerable tension in some regions (see, especially, Messerschmidt 1976, whose claims about caste tension within Gurung society were publicly refuted by Gurung leaders). These claims are now extremely controversial and it is widely agreed that any sense of hierarchy which did exist was not indigenous to Gurung culture but introduced by Hindu rulers in a strategy of divide and rule. Most are adamant that today all Gurungs are equal.

[11] Holmberg (2016) has described the revival of Lhochhar among the Tamang community, where it has also been raised to the status of the Tamangs' major annual festival, replacing other local ritual occasions. He observes that in most Tamang accounts "the revival of Lhochhar is directly tied to the push for a multi-cultural Nepal and the de-Hinduization of the state" (2016: 308) and that it is also linked to the movement to boycott Dasain, the major Hindu festival celebrated in Nepal.

Everest Times, a Nepali-language newspaper in the UK, ran an article which stated quite explicitly the political relevance of Lhosar celebrations. The headline ran "For obtaining our rights: Lhochhar festival" with the subheading, "Lhochhar is also a festival for putting pressure on the state".[12]

Lhosar marks the changing of the *lho*, the animal year according to the Gurung, or Tibetan, calendar and so is often described as New Year. It is celebrated with various rituals to cast out the bad planetary influences of the year before, and to bring health and prosperity in the coming year, but as important as the ritual elements in the new Lhosar celebrations are the official and cultural programmes which follow them. In the former, members of the community are felicitated on their own personal achievements such as exam successes, or their contributions to the association or the wider Gurung community, while in the latter, guests are entertained with cultural performances, celebrations of Gurung (and Nepali) song and dance.

The campaign for Tamu unity proceeded with articles in the Nepalese press, discussion at community events, and private meetings among the leaders of the respective organizations and culminated in an open meeting in Reading to negotiate whether and how to proceed with the plans for a joint Lhosar. In emphasizing the importance of achieving unity within the community, campaigners referred both to the political situation in Nepal and to the needs of the Gurung community in the diaspora. With regard to the former, the campaign made explicit reference to the proposed formation of a Tamuwan state, an ethnically defined self-governing federal state in Nepal, if and when proposals for ethnic federalism are agreed. It was argued that unity was vital in order to win sufficient seats in the federal government, and even to govern their own state effectively. A Gurung community leader summed up the urgency of realizing Gurung unity in an article for the *Everest Times*:

---

[12] *Everest Times*, Thursday 8th December 2013, pp. 10–11.

> If Tamuwan is established, as long as we are not united it seems that it will not be possible for us to get, on the cultural level, the identity that we have been searching for, on the political level the necessary representation, and on the economic and policy level, a state formed on the basis which we need for progress and growth.[13]

These same issues were being discussed in Nepal, and a similar campaign for united Lhosar took place there. In Pokhara and Kathmandu various Gurung *jat* organizations did manage to celebrate Lhosar together, although most would hesitate to declare that Tamu unity had been achieved.

In the UK, the campaign also emphasized the benefits of unity for the diaspora community. For many campaigners, it was the support that could be offered to fellow migrants if the whole Gurung community were brought together, that was at the heart of the campaign. One campaigner explained to me that if the Gurungs were united they could support each other in the UK instead of pulling each other's legs (*khutta tannu*),[14] and resenting each other's successes. The Gurung community could provide a support network, as many of the smaller organizations and kinship groups were already doing, helping fellow Gurungs find work or housing and coming together to provide financial or other support in times of crisis such as death or ill health. In this way, the political situation in Nepal and the needs of the diaspora appear to be in support of one another. Both point to the benefits of Tamu unity, of forming a broad and cohesive community of mutual support and shared interests along *jat* lines. They accept notions of citizenship based on ethnic identity, and encourage that sense of identity to be maintained in the diaspora. However, ultimately unity was not achieved. The reasons for this can be

---

[13] *Everest Times*, 25th October 2011, p. 6.

[14] A common Nepali expression, meaning to attempt to hold your peers back from getting ahead; to begrudge and obstruct the achievements of others.

related to both spheres—the political landscape and the social exigencies of being in the diaspora—which have held up the achievement of this goal in different ways.

Barriers to unity

From an analysis of the public discourse, it would appear that the campaign for unity failed because the two associations were unable to agree on how Lhosar should be celebrated, which itself was the result of a failure to agree on a common vision of Gurung culture, and how that ought to be displayed on this symbolic public occasion. The lack of consensus was purportedly over religion. As noted above, there has been an ongoing debate amongst the Gurungs as to whether their indigenous religion and/or their religion of identity should be Tibetan Buddhism or Bon (the religion of the *pachyu* and *klyepri* priests). Tamu Pye Lhu Sangh argued that, as a uniquely Gurung festival, the Lhosar ritual should be performed by *pachyu* and *klyepri* priests only and that Buddhist lamas should not be invited to participate. They reasoned that as Gurung Lhosar was not a Tibetan festival it would be inappropriate to invite a Tibetan lama, equivalent, they suggested, to inviting a Hindu pandit or imam to officiate at a Christmas service. Tamu Dhee, on the other hand, argued that the majority of their members are now Buddhist, and so to deny any role to the lamas, would be to alienate large parts of the Gurung community.

Some individuals suggested that religion might be left out of the whole affair, and that Lhosar could be marked together as a celebration of culture without any ritual performance. However, for representatives of Tamu Pye Lhu Sangh, religion could not be so easily separated from culture. For them, the religion of the *pachyu* and *klyepri* priests is the very foundation of Gurung culture. The knowledge contained in their oral texts is the key to Gurung ethnic identity and thus to celebrate their major festival in a purely secular fashion would be to devalue their own traditions and deny their unique identity. In this way, they agree on the way in which ethnic identity defines a citizen's relationship with the state, that ethnic associations can represent the collective interests of an ethnic group, and that the group have common interests because they share a history, a cultural identity, and a similar experience of marginalization, but they disagree on the place of religion within that shared identity. Tamu Dhee sympathisers say it can be separated: we are Gurungs and share a culture, but our faith is our own personal/individual concern; TPLS argue that religious traditions define that shared culture and without them identity is lost.

While the terms of this public discourse represent a significant aspect of the barrier to unity, there were other undercurrents which arguably had an equal part to play. One of these has to do with the way that community building actually occurs in the diaspora, the way in which people gravitate towards and associate with particular organizations. The immediate goal of the unity campaign was joint Lhosar, but the deeper goal was greater cooperation, cohesion, and support between all Gurungs in the UK. The apparent division within Gurung society was represented by the existence of two Lhosar events, but many suspected this was the outward manifestation of a deeper division related to *jat*. There are a large number of Gurung sub-*jats*, or *thar* (176 identified by TPLS), and these form two endogamous clan groups. There has been a great deal of controversy in the past as to the terms used to describe these clan groups and whether there is any hierarchy between them. The general consensus now is that there is no hierarchy and that any hierarchy that existed in the past was not indigenous but was a corruption of Gurung culture, introduced by the Hindu rulers as a strategy of divide and rule.

Although there has been a concerted effort to erase this aspect of the Gurung past, and to combat any lingering prejudice or discrimination, the mechanics of community building in the diaspora appear to be undermining these efforts. In the UK, networks form primarily through clan and kin connections. The majority assert that their primary allegiance is to their village society or *bhai khalak* (clan or patrilineage), and that involvement in either of the larger Gurung associations is relatively superficial. When asked why they attend one or the other of the Lhosar events, almost all referred to family commitments. Some claimed that one of their *aphno manche* (own people) had a leadership position in one association and invited them, others merely that they knew that this particular Lhosar was where they would meet others from their extended family or clan. Very few related that it was the presence of a Tibetan Lama or *pachyu* and *klyepri* which decided their attendance. As a result it is very difficult for either association to claim to represent all Gurungs, or to satisfy all parts of the community that they are not intentionally exclusive or discriminatory in their membership. Both organizations claim to represent all Gurungs and to reject and oppose any hint of hierarchy or inequality. Many individuals amongst the unity campaigners would even promote greater intermarriage between the two groups, insisting that all Gurungs are one and there should therefore be no division, hierarchical or not. However, this goal is obstructed by the tacit goals of many community members. For many, kin and clan ties, and the sense of belonging which such connections help to create, have an immediacy and relevance to their lives, with which the pan-Gurung leadership, in their attempts to strengthen a much broader Gurung community, cannot compete.

The Buddhist Community Centre UK

The Buddhist Community Centre (BCC) UK appears to represent an attempt to steer away from this *jat*-based view of community membership and to distance itself from Nepal's ethnic politics. The organization is dominated by Gurungs: of the 18 Executive Committee members for 2009–2011, 10 were Gurung (16/20 area representatives), 23 out of 27 members of the *ama samuha* (women's group) were Gurung (and all 8 of their area representatives), and Gurungs made up around two thirds of

Trustee Members (those who had donated £1000 or more).[15] The *ama samuha* was comprised mainly of women from the *ama samuha* of the Gurungs' main gompa in Pokhara (Ram Ghat/ Bouddha Arghaun Sadan), and a number of leaders of Tamu Dhee, which is overtly non-religious, are also involved with BCC UK. However, BCC UK is decidedly not a *jat* association, and has made every effort to welcome all *jats* and represent all Nepalis. The chairman, who was also one of the founders of the organization and the main mover behind many its activities, is a Sherpa, and they approached many of the UK *jat* associations to ask them to send a representative to sit on their committee so they might be truly representative of all *jats*. The high number of Gurungs is at least partially explained by the disproportionate number of Gurungs within the Nepali community in the UK.[16]

If BCC UK saw itself as involved in the maintenance and preservation of culture, it was pan-Nepali culture, rather than that of any particular ethnic group. There were some indications that it did see Buddhism as a unifying feature of Nepali culture, and viewed itself as a Nepali cultural association. Buddhism was associated with Nepali national identity in a number of ways. First, much was made of the status of Lumbini as the birthplace of Buddha and this was regarded as a source of national pride. When it was discovered that a London museum had stated that the Buddha was born in India there was much concern and discussions about what action should be taken. Individual members had also suggested to me that their own attachment to Buddhism, and to the association, was influenced by the fact that Lumbini belonged to Nepal. They felt that Nepal had a special connection with Buddhism and with the Buddha Sakyamuni in particular.

Secondly, one of the first actions taken by BCC UK when it was established was to campaign (and this campaign was

[15] www.bccuk.co.uk.

[16] Gurungs comprise 22.2 per cent of the Nepali population in the UK but only 2.4 per cent of the population of Nepal.

9.1 The Buddhist Community Centre gompa (temple-monastery), Aldershot, which was officially inaugurated by the Dalai Lama in June 2015. (D.N. Gellner)

ultimately successful) for the appointment of a Buddhist lama to the Brigade of Gurkhas. Up until that time, the religious needs of the brigade were served only by a Hindu pandit and in the past Gurkha soldiers had been required to register as Hindu and to follow Hindu customs, such as the celebration of Hindu festivals, whilst in the army (Uesugi 2007). The BCC sent numerous letters to the MoD to convince them that the majority of Gurkhas are Buddhist, not Hindu. They collected statements from many of the *jat* associations in the UK (including Tamu Dhee, alongside groups representing the Tamang, Sherpa, Magar, and others), asserting that their respective *jat* historically followed Buddhism and not Hinduism. The point they were attempting to make was that Nepal may have been, until recently, a Hindu state, but that a large proportion of its citizens, especially those traditionally recruited to the Gurkhas, are Buddhist.

9.2 Dashami ('tenth-day') ritual to Guru Rinpoche in the BCC gompa, Aldershot, 16 March 2019. (D.N. Gellner)

In presenting itself to the world beyond the Nepali community, the BCC was also often happy to be represented as a Nepali cultural association. On one occasion, when asked to have a stand at the Surrey fair, a local community event, the BCC first proposed organizing a performance of Nepali cultural dance. This idea was only dropped when someone pointed out that the Greater Rushmoor Nepalese Society were already doing this and that it might therefore be better to create a display purely about Buddhism instead. The assumption was that their organization was viewed from without as representative of Nepali culture and they were initially prepared to accept this characterization. When the Dalai Lama came to speak in Aldershot in June 2012, the BCC's largest and most high-profile event to date by far, they arranged for each Nepali *jat* group in the UK to perform their own cultural dance while the audience awaited the Dalai Lama's arrival. These performances were seen as an opportunity to showcase for the wider community Nepali cultural diversity, while also showing that these diverse groups were united by a common attachment to Buddhism.

The BCC UK also recognized the wider relevance of Buddhism, readily acknowledging its status as a World Religion, with adherents in many different cultures. It had forged links with Japanese and Thai Buddhists, and invited speakers representing a range of Buddhist traditions to their annual celebration of Buddha Jayanti. There were also intimations that many members, while proud of Nepal's connection with the historical Buddha, had particular respect for Buddhism because of its international following. It was compared favourably with Gurung Bonism, which some considered only 'culture', because it appeared that the truth within Buddhism had been recognized across the globe, and crucially, because it was a textual religion with ancient, and apparently authoritative, scripture.[17]

To return to the central dichotomy between the demands of Nepali ethnic politics and those of community-building, however, it must be noted that the main stated aims of the organization concerned the needs of the Nepali Buddhist community, rather than the representation of Buddhism or Nepali culture to the world beyond. These aims were to promote Buddhism and to provide the resources to enable Nepali Buddhists in the UK to continue to practise according to their traditions. The most important and urgent goal was to purchase a property to establish a gompa and bring a lama from Nepal to reside there. This gompa would be a place where Buddhist Nepalis could carry out life-cycle ceremonies, especially death rites, according to their traditions and would also be an important meeting place and teaching centre.

---

[17] The denigration of local traditions regarded as 'merely culture' and elevation of those apparently global traditions which are thought to legitimately fall into the category of 'religion' by some Gurungs, parallels the findings of Jacobsen (1997) regarding the attitudes of Muslim Pakistani youths in Britain.

Many emphasized how important it could be for the elderly especially, a place where they could congregate for *puja* (worship), meditation, and religious instruction. There are a large number of elderly migrants within the Nepali community and much concern that with little knowledge of the English language and, in many cases, no family in the UK they could easily become isolated. At present, many meet at English classes provided by the council, churches, and others, and gather in the parks on summer evenings because, as one lady sadly pointed out, they have nowhere else to go. The gompa would provide that community base, and purposeful activity appropriate to their stage of life, which so many of them need. Many described how their lives in Nepal, particularly those living in Pokhara, were filled with visits to local gompas for various religious programmes. For those who had leisure time, religious activity was their main occupation and the way they connected with others in their community. It was this kind of social activity which many reported they missed on coming to the UK.

It is tempting, therefore, to see the BCC UK as a purely religious organization, as it asserts itself to be, which works to bring together the Nepali diaspora community, or the Buddhist-leaning sections of that community, to preserve shared customs and encourage a strengthening of knowledge in and attachment to shared religious teachings. But it is also clear that, however non-political it claims to be, it is yet influenced and shaped by the Nepali state's—and civil society's—understanding of the relationship between ethnic and religious identity. It is significant that the BCC endeavours to be not just pan-Nepali but specifically multi-*jat*. In seeking to be inclusive and open to all it has insisted on finding representatives from each *jat*. Both in its calls to the various *jat* associations for representative trustee members and in its request for letters to present to the Ministry of Defence, the BCC is tacitly accepting both the proposition that religious affiliation is tied to ethnicity and the idea that *jat* groups are best able to protect or represent the interests of their members.

At the same time, it is of note that, while BCC claims to include all Nepali *jats,* only certain *jats*, all of which are amongst the Janajatis, are associated with Buddhism. In linking Buddhism with Nepali national culture, they are making a claim that the Janajatis are the true representatives of Nepali national culture and that Hindu culture should not be seen as dominant. This implication, while not explicitly stated, is inherently political. The letters to the Ministry of Defence are more markedly so, for here they are dealing with a policy of the British government which was formed in conjunction with the Nepali state. It was the Nepali government that first demanded that Gurkhas continue to follow Hinduism while in British service and this demand formed part of the Tripartite Agreement of 1947, which set out principles of Gurkha terms and conditions of service (Uesugi 2007). The campaign which set out to prove that the majority of Gurkhas were in fact Buddhist was thus a direct challenge to this and a contradiction of the Nepali state's previous characterization of national identity.

Conclusion

Each of the associations discussed in this chapter claims to be non-political. Each further claims to exist, primarily, to encourage the creation of new and preservation of existing social bonds within the Gurung or Nepali community in the UK, to help community members support one another, and to enable them to preserve valued traditions and some sense of ethnic or religious identity. The expressed goals are thus focused inwards, on the diaspora community and its social and religious needs.

While none is political in an overt sense—none is affiliated with any political party, nor has actively lobbied the government on any particular issue—each is influenced by the political context in Nepal and the way that that context has shaped conceptions of Nepali citizenship and the connection between citizenship and ethnic and religious identity. The very form of Tamu Dhee and TPLS, as *jat* associations, is an outcome of the predominance of ethnic politics in Nepal and even the BCC, which attempts to be pan-Nepali, accepts the assumption that religious affiliation is, to some extent, determined by *jat*.

Occasionally the concerns of the state impact more directly on the priorities of these diaspora associations, as in the negotiations regarding the organization of a joint Lhosar celebration and the campaign for Tamu unity. In this case, direct reference was made to the process of state formation in Nepal and the importance of showing a united front if the Gurungs, seen as a unit with the same political interests, are to get the representation and economic advantages they are seeking. Here Lhosar was publicly acknowledged to be not only an opportunity to share and celebrate traditional Gurung culture for the sake of creating a sense of belonging in the diaspora, but also a chance to demonstrate to the wider world, and particularly to those in positions of power in the Nepali state, the strength, unity, and unique indigenous culture of the Gurung *jat*. The debates over the religious aspect of ethnic identity, both over what religion the Gurungs should claim as their own, and whether religion is central or peripheral to ethnic identity, are shaped by past and current debates over the form of the future Nepali state.

Very often the respective influence of political concerns and the needs of the diaspora community can be hard to disentangle as they support and reinforce one another. Preserving or recreating endangered cultural traditions and instilling a sense of belonging to a broadly based Gurung community with an awareness of a shared culture are aims of diaspora community leaders hoping to unite a disparate community in the UK, but are likewise the aims of Gurung ethnic activists in Nepal. The achievement of Tamu unity was seen to have tangible benefits both for the community trying to establish themselves in the UK, and for the Gurung leadership in Nepal, hoping to gain leverage in political negotiations at the centre. While most of the campaign leaders would argue that community concerns were higher on their agenda than political ones, many were doubtless influenced by both to some degree.

Occasionally, however, these two influences clashed. The Tamu unity campaign, seeking to do away with outdated notions of division and hierarchy between different Gurung clans, required people to abandon clan loyalties in deference to a loyalty to a broader conception of the Gurung community, united by a common culture and identity. However, in the diaspora, it seems that kin and clan connections matter to people a great deal, and it is on the basis of these kinds of association that communities naturally form in the UK.

For those associations that see themselves as purely religious, involvement in politics is viewed as inappropriate, and yet they cannot divorce themselves entirely from the political context which has encouraged the development of particular religious identities. TPLS is adamant that the issues which have prevented their union with Tamu Dhee are purely religious, representing only a difference of opinion on the authentic way to celebrate their primary religious festival and yet that fixation with authenticity, indigeneity, and antiquity is itself a product of the discourse on ethnic rights. The BCC, meanwhile, scorns any kind of association with Nepali ethnic politics, emphasizing instead the broad appeal of Buddhism which cuts across *jat* distinctions and unites adherents even of different nations. But its championing of a national identity based on a common commitment to Buddhism has strong overtones of political activism. An examination of religious practice at the individual level may reveal a different picture, a picture of immense diversity within and across the various ethnic and religious categories. However, the religious associations operating in the UK, although overtly aimed at meeting the needs of the diaspora community, can only imagine those needs within a frame dictated by a political context where ethnic rights, religious affiliation, and national identity are inextricably tied together.

10

नेपाली बहुआयामिक धार्मिक अभ्यासः छोटो मन्थन

कृष्ण प्र. अधिकारी

नेपाल र अझै भनौं दक्षिण एसियामा पाइने बहुधार्मिक अभ्यास पश्चिमा र अन्य अब्राहमिक (यहुदी, इसाई, मुस्लिम) धर्ममा जस्तो एकल 'फ्रेममा' बाँधिएको हुँदैन ।[1] नवआयातित इसाई र इस्लामलाई छाडेर, ऐतिहासिकरूपमा यो क्षेत्रमा भएका अरू सबै धार्मिक अभ्यास तथा परम्पराहरू परस्परमा द्वन्द्वात्मक नभएर एउटै बृहत्तहर परिधिभित्रका अन्तरसम्बन्धित विविधता हुन भन्ने मान्यता थियो । यसकारण नेपालमा केही राज्यप्रदत्त कठिनाइका बाबजुद पनि धार्मिक विविधता दिगो हुन गई सहिष्णुता र सहअस्तित्व कायम हुन सम्भव भएको हो ।

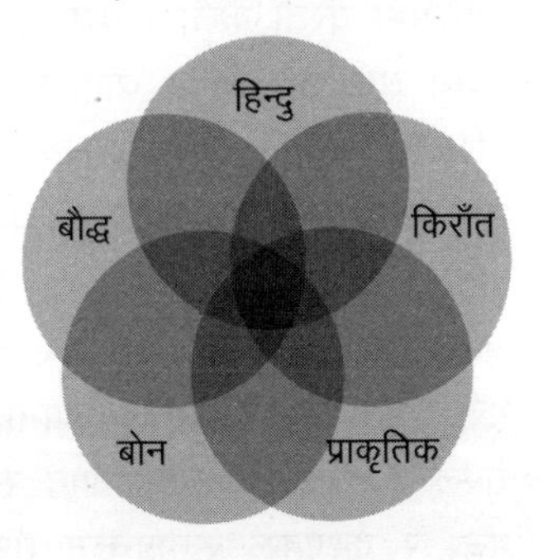

[1] यो लेखमा व्यक्त विचार लेखकमा निजी हुन् । यिनले लेखक आवद्ध कुनै पनि संस्थाको विचारलाई प्रतिबिम्बित गर्छन् भन्ने जरुरी छैन । यो लेख नेपाल पत्रकार महासङ्घ, बेलायत शाखाबाट सन् २०१३ मा प्रकाशित प्रवासी पत्रकारितामा छापिएको 'नेपाली बहुआयामिक धार्मिक अभ्यासः छोटो मन्थन' को परिमार्जित रूप हो (Adhikari 2013)।

जनगणनाहरूले यस्तो यथार्थलाई उतार्न सक्नु पर्दछ र धार्मिक पहिचान र पुनरुत्थानका प्रयासहरू पनि यसबाट सुसूचित हुनु उपयुक्त देखिन्छ ।

धर्मको प्रश्नमा आफ्नै कमजोरी

सन् २००० तिरको कुरा हो । स्विडेनको गोथेन्बर्गमा एक बङ्गाली साथीको घरमा दालभातको तिर्सना मेट्न गएको थिएँ । जाँदासाथ अत्यन्त चलाख १२ वर्षे उनको छोरासँग भेट भयो । परिचयसँगै उनले एकदम जिज्ञासा राख्दै थुप्रै प्रश्नको गोला वर्षाए । तीमध्ये केही धर्मसम्बन्धी घतलाग्दा प्रश्नहरू थिए । 'तिम्रो धर्म कुन हो?' 'तिम्रो प्रोफेट को हो?' आदि । मैले उनलाई हामी धेरै किसिमका धर्म मान्छौं, र हाम्रा तेत्तिस कोटी अर्थात तेत्तिस करोड देवी देवता पनि छन् भनेपछि उनले जिब्रो काडे । मैले राम्ररी उत्तर दिन नजानेका र प्रायजसो टार्न खोज्ने यस्ता प्रश्नहरूको टालटुले उत्तर दिएर उम्कैँ ।

यस्तो असमञ्जस्य अवस्थामा परेको म एकल नेपाली पात्र भने होइन होला । मैले विदेशी भूमिमा आफ्ना छोराछोरीले सोधेका धर्मसम्बन्धी प्रश्नहरूको उपयुक्त जवाफ दिन नसकेर अल्मलिएका कयौं नेपाली बाबु आमा भेटेको छु । अनादिकालदेखि आध्यात्मिक साधनाको केन्द्र बनेको कैलाश पर्वत र ज्ञानका ज्योति गौतम बुद्धको पावन भूमिमा जन्मेर पनि मजस्ता कयौं नेपालीहरूमा आध्यात्मिक ज्ञानको न रुचि छ न त राम्रो जानकारी नै । फेरि अरूलाई आफ्नो धर्मबारेमा प्रचार गर्ने न हाम्रो सिद्धान्त छ, न त आम मानिसमा यस्तो कला । यसो हुनुमा तीन कारण छन् जस्तो लाग्छ : पहिलो, पूर्वीय धर्म संस्कृति र व्यवहार पश्चिमा र अन्य अब्राहमिक (यहुदी, इसाई, मुस्लिम) धर्महरूजस्तो एकल 'फ्रेममा' बाधिएको छैन र यस्ता पाश्चात्य अभ्यासमा परिचितहरूलाई आध्यात्मिक बहुल अभ्यास हुन्छ भन्ने कुरा बुझ्न र बुझाउन गाह्रो पर्छ । दोस्रो, पुरानो गुरूकुल र कथावाचन प्रक्रिया हाम्रो आध्यात्मिक जीवनको अङ्ग भएपनि दैनिक धार्मिक संस्कारलाई पुरोहितीकरण गरी जीवनयापनको स्रोतकोरूपमा मात्र लिइएको छ र आध्यात्मिक सिद्धान्तलाई सरल र व्यवस्थितरूपमा आम सञ्चार गर्ने संरचना विकास गरिएको छैन । मन्त्र र कथाहरू सुनाइन्छन् तर तिनको अर्थ वा गुह्य खुलाईदैन । तेश्रो चाहीँ व्यक्तिगत कारण हो : मेरो पुस्ताका कयौं मानिसहरूमा धर्मप्रतिको अरुचि ।

धर्मको प्रसङ्ग आउँदा यी माथिका कुरालाई यहाँ सामान्यरूपमा जोड्दै यो लेखमा मैले नेपालीहरूको धार्मिक बहुलता, यसको स्रोत र व्यवहारिक

पक्षका साथै जनगणनाका विषयमा छोटकरीमा छलफल गर्ने जमर्को गरेको छु । यो लेखमा विशेषतः चारओटा स्रोतहरूबाट केही तथ्याङ्क प्रस्तुत गरिनुको साथै चर्चा पनि गरिएको छ । पहिलो सन् २००८ मा मेरो संलग्नतामा भएको नेपाल अध्ययन केन्द्र (सिएनएसयुके) को नेपाली जनगणना (सर्वे) । उक्त सर्वेमा बेलायतमा नेपालीले मान्ने मुख्य धर्महरूको मोटामोटी आँकडा समेटिएको थियो र त्यसको लागि केही नौलो विधि पनि प्रयोग गरिएको थियो । त्यही नौलो विधिलाई दोस्रो स्रोत, अर्थात् अक्सफोर्ड विश्वविद्यालय र सिएनएसयुकेको तत्त्वाधानमा बेलायत र बेल्जियममा बस्ने नेपाली डायस्पोराका चलनचल्तीका धार्मिक व्यवहारहरूको अध्ययनमा पनि प्रयोग गरिएको थियो । उक्त अध्ययन सन् २००९ देखि २०१२ को बिचमा चलेको थियो । तेस्रो स्रोत, सन् २०११ को बेलायती जनगणना हो । इङ्लैन्ड र वेल्सबाट जनगणनामा ६०,२०२ जना नेपालीले भाग लिएका थिए र ५२,७८५ ले आफ्नो धार्मिक आस्था उल्लेख गरेका थिए । हाम्रो विशेष अनुरोधमा जनगणना गराउने संस्था अफिस फर नेसनल स्टाटिस्टिक्स (ओएनएस) बाट नेपालीसम्बन्धी तथ्याङ्कलाई तालिकीकरण गरी हामीलाई उपलब्ध गराइएको थियो । यो जनगणनाका केही सीमाहरू छन्, तर बेलायतमा नेपालीहरूको धर्मअनुसार जनसङ्ख्याको पछिल्लो चित्र थाहा पाउन यो नै ठूलो र भरपर्दो स्रोत हो । चौथो, यहाँ तुलनाका लागि सन् २०११ को नेपालको जनगणनाका केही तथ्याङ्कहरू पनि प्रस्तुत गरिएको छ (तलको तालिका १०.१ हेर्नुहोस्) । यीनै संलग्नता, तथ्य तथ्याङ्क र व्यक्तिगत अवलोकन तथा अनुभवहरूको आधारमा यहाँ केही निजी विचारहरू प्रस्तुत र छलफल गरिएको छ ।

धार्मिक बहुलता र मापनको नयाँ प्रयोग

बेलायतको सन् २०११ को जनगणनामा नेपालीहरूको सहभागिता बढाउने उद्देश्यले सिएनएसयुकेले जनजागरण अभियान चलाएको थियो । जनगणनाको प्रायः सबै प्रश्नहरूमा कतिवटा विकल्प छान्ने भन्ने खुलाइएको थियो तर धर्मको प्रश्नमा यस्तो केही उल्लेख थिएन । अन्य प्रश्नहरू अनिवार्य भएता पनि धर्मको प्रश्नमा उत्तर दिन वा नदिन स्वतन्त्रता दिइएको थियो । हामीले विगतमा गरेका दुवै अध्ययनहरू (सन् २००८ को सिएनएसयुकेको गणना, र २००९-१२ को सिएनएसयुके - अक्सफोर्ड विश्वविद्यालयको अध्ययन) मा धेरै नेपालीहरूले एकभन्दा बढी धार्मिक अभ्यास गर्ने गरेको पाइएको कारण बेलायती जनगणनाको फाराम कसरी भर्ने भन्ने अन्यौलता देखिएको थियो ।

यससम्बन्धी स्पष्टीकरणको लागि ओएनएसको ग्राहक सेवा केन्द्रमा एकजना सल्लाहकारसँग सम्पर्क भयो । 'एकभन्दा बढी धर्ममा टिक लगाउन पाउने कि नपाउने?' भन्ने प्रश्नमा सर्वप्रथम त 'यस्तो पनि हुन्छ र ?' भनेर उनले आश्चर्यपूर्वक प्रतिप्रश्न गरेकी थिइन् । त्यसपछि, 'यदि हुन्छ भने चाहे जति सबैमा टिक लगाउन मिल्छ' भन्ने सूचना दिइन् । हामीले पनि सोहीअनुसार प्रचार गर्न थाल्यौं । तर पछि अस्पष्ट भएका थप विषयहरूसमेत समावेश गरेर लिखितरूपमा ओएनएससँग जानकारी मागियो । जवाफ आउँदा माफी मागेर पूर्व सूचनालाई सच्याउँदै धर्मको प्रश्नमा एकभन्दा बढी विकल्प छानेमा एउटा र पहिलो मात्र मान्य हुने जानकारी मिल्यो । पश्चिमा र अरू अब्राहमिक धार्मिक परम्परा (यहुदी, इसाई, मुस्लिम) हरूमा धर्मलाई प्रायजसो एकलरूपमा लिइएको हुन्छ । यस्तो एकलवादी धर्ममा मान्यता के हुन्छ भने कि त तपाईं आस्तिक (धर्म मान्ने) हुनुहुन्छ, कि त नास्तिक (धर्म नमान्ने)

तालिका १०.१: धर्मअनुसार बेलायतमा र नेपालमा नेपाली जनसङ्ख्या

धर्म	प्रतिशत बेलायतमा (सिएनएसयुके सर्वे २००८, नमूना जनसङ्ख्या ७,८८१)	प्रतिशत बेलायतमा (२०११ इङ्लैन्ड र वेल्सको जनगणना, जनसङ्ख्या = ६०,२०२; उत्तरदाता = ५२,७८५)	प्रतिशत नेपालमा (२०११ को जनगणना, जनसङ्ख्या = २ करोड ६५ लाख)
हिन्दु	४१.४	५३.५०	८१.३४
हिन्दु र बौद्ध	९.२	यो विकल्प छैन	यो विकल्प छैन
बौद्ध	२९.३	२७.७२	९.०४
किराँत	१०.१	यो विकल्प छैन	३.०४
हिन्दु तथा किराँत	४.९	यो विकल्प छैन	यो विकल्प छैन
बौद्ध तथा किराँत	२.३	यो विकल्प छैन	यो विकल्प छैन
मुसलमान	०.०१	०.५६	४.४३
इसाई	२.२	३.६४	१.४१
यहुदी		०.०४	यो विकल्प छैन
अन्य		०.१९	०.२३
सिख		०.११	०.०१
उल्लेख नगरेको		१२.५	
धर्म नमान्ने		१.३४	यो विकल्प छैन

स्रोतः सिएनएसयुके सर्वे २००८, बेलायत (इङ्लैन्ड र वेल्स) जनगणना सन् २०११ (ओएनएस) र नेपाली जनगणना २०११ (राष्ट्रिय तथ्याङ्क विभाग) ।

हुनुहुन्छ; तपाईं धर्म मान्नु हुन्छ भने एउटा मात्र मान्नु हुन्छ र आफ्नो धर्म के हो भन्ने बारेमा तपाईं स्पष्ट हुनुहुन्छ । त्यसै मान्यतामा रहेर जनगणनामा प्रश्न बनाइएको हुन्छ ।

धर्मको सन्दर्भमा नेपालको जनगणनामा पनि एउटा मात्र विकल्प छान्न पाइने नियम छ । यस अर्थमा जनगणनाका नतिजाहरू विवादित मात्र छैनन् तिनले मानिसको वास्तविक धार्मिक व्यवहारलाई पनि समेट्न सकेका छैनन् । धार्मिक र सामाजिक सहिष्णुतालाई नेपालमा व्यापक महत्त्व दिँदै आइरहेको भएता पनि त्यसलाई सोहीअनुसार समेट्ने र चित्रित गर्ने परिपाटी नभएको सन्दर्भमा बेलायतमा पहिलो पटक सिएनएसयुकेले गरेको जनगणनामा यस्तो विशेष विधि प्रयोग गरिएको थियो । एकभन्दा बढी विकल्प छान्न पाउने मौका दिँदा मानिसहरू त्यसो गर्न चाहन्छन् कि चाहदैनन् भनेर जाँच गर्ने हाम्रो ध्येय थियो ।

तालिका १०.१ मा उल्लेख गरेअनुसार सिएनएसयुकेको सर्वेमा बेलायतमा हरेक छ जनामा एक जना नेपालीले एकभन्दा बढी धार्मिक आस्था रहेको वा अभ्यास गर्ने गरेको जनाएका थिए । यिनीहरूमा सबैभन्दा बढी (लगभग हरेक १० मा एक) ले आफू हिन्दु र बौद्ध दुवै धर्म मान्ने जनाएका थिए । कुलको पाँच प्रतिशतले किराँत र हिन्दु दुवै, अनि दुई प्रतिशतले किराँत र बौद्ध दुवै मान्ने जनाएका थिए ।

माथिको तालिका हेर्दा नेपालको जनगणनाले देखाउने धर्मको वितरणको अनुपात र बेलायतमा नेपालीहरूको जनसङ्ख्याको धर्मको अनुपात मेल खाएको देखिँदैन । यसको प्रमुख कारण बेलायतको नेपाली जनसङ्ख्याको जातिगत संरचनाको अनुपात नेपालको भन्दा फरक हुनु हो । सिएनएसयुकेको सन् २००८ को गणनाले देखाएअनुसार नेपालमा १४ प्रतिशतभन्दा कम जनसङ्ख्या भएका पहाडी र हिमाली क्षेत्रका जनजातिहरू (मूलतः गुरूङ, मगर, राई र लिम्बू) को बेलायतमा दुई-तिहाई भन्दा बढी जनसङ्ख्या छ । यसो हुनुको मूल जड गोर्खा भर्ती नै हो । बेलायती गोर्खामा माथि उल्लिखित जनजातिहरूलाई 'सैन्य कौशलता भएका लडाकु नश्ल' मानेर विगत दुई शताब्दीभर प्राथमिकताका साथ भर्ती गरिने गरिएको थियो । बेलायती सरकारको सन् २००४ र २००९ को निर्णयबाट गोर्खाहरूलाई बेलायतमा नै बस्न पाउने अधिकार प्राप्त भएपछि निश्चित जनजातिहरूको बेलायतको नेपाली जनसङ्ख्यामा बाहुल्यता बढेको हो । यही कारण त्यहाँ अरू जातजातिको उपस्थिति तुलनात्मकरूपमा न्यून देखिएको हो ।

यो बहुधार्मिक आस्था वा बहुआयामिक धार्मिक अभ्यासलाई समेटने गरी तथ्याङ्क सङ्कलन गर्ने प्रक्रिया आफैमा नीतिगत सरोकार भएको एउटा रोचक प्रयोग थियो । त्यसैकारण सिएनएसयुकेको अध्ययनमा आधारित भएर बहुधार्मिक अभ्यासलाई पुनः व्यवस्थित तरिकाले अध्ययन गर्न अक्सफोर्ड विश्वविद्यालय र सिएनएसयुकेले सन् २००९ र २०१२ को बिचमा बेलायत र बेल्जियममा बस्ने नेपाली डायस्पोराहरूको चलनचल्तीका धार्मिक व्यवहारहरूको अध्ययन गरेका थिए (तालिका १०.२) । बेलायतमा ३०० घर परिवारका १,१९७ जनासँग गरिएको सर्वेमा हामीले अझै व्यवस्थितरूपमा माथिको विधिलाई प्रयोग गरेका थियौं । यसक्रममा उत्तरदाताहरूलाई दुइओटा प्रश्न सोधिएको थियो । पहिलो प्रश्नमा विकल्पहरू नदिइकन, 'यदि धर्म मान्नु हुन्छ भने कुन कुन धर्म मान्नु हुन्छ?' भनेर सोधेका थियौं । लगभग १० जनामा एकजना उत्तरदाताले स्वभाविकरूपले एकभन्दा बढी धार्मिक आस्था र अभ्यास गर्ने बताएका थिए । त्यसपछि पूर्वअध्ययनहरूबाट प्राप्त विभिन्न (मिश्रितसमेत) विकल्पहरू पढेर सुनाएपछि उनीहरूलाई पुनः आफ्नो धार्मिक

तालिका १०.२ः बेलायतमा नेपालीहरूको धार्मिक अभ्यास (विकल्प सुनाउनुअघि र पछि)

अभ्यास गरिएका धर्महरू	विकल्प सुनाउनुअघि		विकल्प सुनाएपछि		फरक दर (प्रतिशत)
	उत्तर सङ्ख्या	प्रतिशत	उत्तर सङ्ख्या	प्रतिशत	
हिन्दु	५७८	४८	४६६	३९	-१९.३८
बौद्ध	२९५	२५	२००	१७	-३२.२०
किराँत	१०४	९	१०३	९	-०.९६
इसाई	७२	६	७२	६	०
बोन			६	१	-१००
हिन्दु तथा बौद्ध	६०	५	१८५	१५	२०८.३३
हिन्दु तथा किराँत	४९	४	१०९	९	१२२.४५
बौद्ध तथा किराँत	४	०	२४	२	५००.००
हिन्दु, बौद्ध तथा किराँत	५	०	५	०	०
बौद्ध तथा बोन	४	०	४	०	०
धर्म नमान्ने	१३	१	१५	१	१५.३८
अन्य	१३	१	८	१	-३८.४६
जम्मा	१,१९७	१००	१,१९७	१००	

स्रोतः चलनचल्तीका धर्महरूको सर्वे, अक्सफोर्ड विश्वविद्यालय र सिएनएसयुके (२००९-१२)

अभ्यासको बारेमा प्रश्न सोधिएको थियो र दुई वा सोभन्दा बढी धर्म सँगसँगै रोज्नसक्ने विकल्पबारे प्रष्ट्याइएको थियो । यस पटक आफ्नो धार्मिक परिचयसम्बन्धी जवाफ बदलेर हरेक चार जनामा एक जना (अर्थात एक चौथाई) ले दुई वा सोभन्दा बढी धार्मिक आस्था रहेको वा सोहीअनुसार अभ्यास गर्दै आएको बताएका थिए । यसपछि बौद्ध धर्म मात्र मान्ने र हिन्दु-बौद्ध दुवै मान्नेको सङ्ख्या लगभग समानजस्तो हुन गयो; अनि जतिले किराँत धर्म मान्ने जनाएका थिए, अर्को त्यति नै सङ्ख्याले हिन्दु-किराँत दुवै मान्ने बताएका थिए । आफूलाई एकल धार्मिक पहिचान दिनेहरूमा अधिकांशको दैनिक धार्मिक गतिविधिहरू र पूजा कक्षका विभिन्न सामग्रीहरूको अवलोकन गर्दा बहुधार्मिक प्रकृति स्पष्ट देखिएको थियो ।

धार्मिक बहुआयामिकताको स्रोत

माथिका अध्ययनका नातिजाहरूले के देखाउँछन् भने समग्रमा नेपालीहरू धेरै हदसम्म बहुआयामिक वा बहुल धार्मिक आस्था राख्दछन् र सोअनुसार व्यवहार गर्दछन् । उनीहरू धार्मिकरूपमा बढी सहिष्णु र कम कट्टर मानिनुको कारण पनि यही हो । तर यसको पनि सीमा हुन्छ । उनीहरू एकै साथ प्राकृतिक, किराँत, बौद्ध वा हिन्दु धर्म त अभ्यास गर्न सक्छन् तर सँगसँगै यहुदी, इसाई वा इस्लाम मान्न भने सक्दैनन् । यद्यपि एकाध अपवाद नभेटिएका भने होइनन् । बेलायतमा नेपालीले क्रिस्मस मनाउनु र नेपालमा गैरहिन्दुले दशैं मनाउनु एउटा सामान्य सामाजिक ऐकवद्धताको कुरा हुन सक्छ तर धर्मको अवलम्बन गर्नु नितान्त अर्को । भर्खरै परिवारका एक वा केही सदस्य इसाई धर्म लिएर बाँकी पुरानो धर्म छाड्न नचाहेको परिवारमा देखिने बाध्यकारी धार्मिक बहुलतालाई अपवाद मान्नु पर्छ । यहाँ उल्लेख गर्न खोजिएको सीमा के हो भने नेपालीहरूको बहुआयामिक धार्मिकता पुराना मानिएका र अस्तित्वमा रहेका 'रैथाने' धर्म संस्कृतिहरू, जस्तै प्राकृतिक धर्म, किराँत धर्म, कुल धर्म, बौद्ध धर्म, हिन्दु धर्म, आदि (जसलाई कतिपयले ओमकार परिवार पनि भन्दछन्) का बिचमा मात्र सम्भव देखिन्छ । नेपालको सन्दर्भमा तुलनात्मक हिसाबले यिनीहरूलाई पुराना धार्मिक आस्था वा व्यवहारबिचको सामञ्जस्यताको रूपमा पनि लिन सकिन्छ ।

इतिहासकालदेखि घोषित वा अघोषितरूपमा हिन्दु धर्मलाई राज्यबाट संरक्षण र संवर्द्धन गरिँदै आएको पाइन्छ । खास गरी बि.सं. १८५४ को मुलुकी ऐनद्वारा सबै जातजातिलाई केही हदसम्म हिन्दु धर्म संस्कृति थोपरिएको थियो । तर यहाँ हेक्का राख्नु पर्ने कुरा के छ भने केही हदसम्म

विभिन्न जातजातिका चल्दै आएका रीतिथितिहरूलाई मान्यता दिँइदै आएको पनि देखिन्छ । अर्को विचारणीय कुरा के छ भने नेपालमा पुरानो अस्तित्वमा रहेका विभिन्न धर्म वा सांस्कृतिक अभ्यासहरूको बिचमा तात्विक द्वन्द्व थिएन र छैन । यसको कारण खोज्न हामीले हिन्दु शब्दलाई ऐतिहासिक र बृहत्तर परिवेशमा हेर्नु आवश्यक हुन्छ । दक्षिण एसियामा धर्मलाई बुझाउने अरू नै नाम थिए । हिन्दु शब्दले पहिलो पटक अङ्ग्रेजको शब्दकोशमा सन् १८१५ तिर मात्र प्रवेश पायो । शुरूमा हिन्दु शब्द कुनै धर्म विशेषलाई बुझाउने अर्थमा प्रयोग गरिएको थिएन । यसले भारतीय उपमहाद्वीपका सबै मूल बासिन्दा भन्ने अर्थ राख्दथ्यो । पछि यसैको आधारमा तिनले मानेका र अभ्यास गरेका प्रायः सबै धर्महरू हिन्दु मानिए ।

नेपालमा सुरुका दिनमा मकवानपुरे राजा राघव नगेन्द्र सेनले आफूलाई हिन्दुपति घोषित गरेका थिए । आफूलाई मगरको राजा हुँ भनी बताउने गोरखाली राजा पृथ्वीनारायण शाहले त नेपाललाई असली हिन्दुस्तान नै बनाउने ध्येय राखेका थिए । पछिल्ला दिनहरूमा यी ऐतिहासिक तथ्यहरूलाई राजनीतिक मनसायले आफ्नो अनुकूल व्याख्या गर्ने चलन बढेको भएता पनि तत्कालीन अवस्थामा हिन्दु शब्दको अर्थ अलि फरक थियो । तात्कालिक सबै स्थानीय धर्महरूलाई परस्पर अन्तरविरोधी नभएर एक अर्काका परिपुरकको रूपमा हेरिन्थ्यो । यसैकारण पनि एउटा निश्चित भौगोलिक क्षेत्रभित्रका सबै धर्महरू चाहे ती बौद्ध हुन् वा जैन, प्रकृति पूजा हुन वा कुल पूजा सबैलाई एउटा हिन्दु भन्ने बृहत्तर परिभाषाभित्र समेटिएको थियो । यसबाट हिन्दु भन्नु एउटा बहुधार्मिक अभ्यासको नामजस्तो हुन गयो । भलै कुनै निहित स्वार्थले अभिप्रेरित भएर यसो गरिएको किन नहोस् वैदिक धर्मावलम्बीहरूले भगवान गौतम बुद्धलाई भगवान विष्णुको दशौँ अवतारकोरूपमा व्याख्या गरे । यसबाट विभिन्न धर्म तथा परम्पराको स्वतन्त्र विकासमा नेतृत्वदायी भूमिकामा केही बाधा त भयो होला तर बृहत्तर हिन्दुको परिभाषामा समेटिएर तमाम धार्मिक सम्प्रदाय र व्यवहारहरू आपसी सामञ्जस्यताका कारण अस्तित्व जोगाउन सफल भए । व्यापारको नाममा दक्षिण छिमेकी भारतमा तुलनात्मकरूपमा पछि प्रवेश गरेका मुसलमान र इसाई धर्महरूबाट तत्कालीन नेपालमाथि खतरा हुनसक्ने महसुस गरिएको थियो । भारतमा शासन सत्ता पहिले मुगलले कब्जा गरेका थिए भने, पछि इस्ट इन्डिया कम्पनीले । नेपाललाई 'असली हिन्दुस्तान' बनाउने कुरा हिन्दु धर्म लाद्नेभन्दा पनि स्वाधीनतासँग सम्बन्धित विषय थियो । बृहत्तर हिन्दुको परिभाषाभित्र जसरी जुन हदसम्म परम्परागत धार्मिक सांस्कृतिक व्यवहार बाँच्न सकेका छन्, सम्भवतः यदि मुसलमान वा इसाई

धर्मको आक्रमण भएको भए त्यो सम्भव हुने थिएन । निसन्देह आजको विविधता पाउन सकिँदैनथ्यो भन्ने कुरा अनुमान लगाउन कठिन छैन ।

नेपाली धर्म संस्कृतिहरू यसरी मिसिएका छन् कि यिनलाई फुकाएर कुन स्रोतबाट कुन कुरा मिसियो भनेर छुट्ट्याउन लगभग असम्भव छ । रैथाने आदिवासी धर्म संस्कृतिहरू हिन्दुमा मिसिएका छन्, र हिन्दु आदिवासीमा । किराँत हिन्दुमा अनि हिन्दु किराँतमा । हिन्दुहरू लुम्बिनी पसेर शान्तिको महसुस गर्छन्, बौद्धहरू पशुपति पसेर । माथि उल्लिखित विभिन्न धर्महरूको वर्गीकरणमा आफूलाई एकभन्दा बढी धार्मिक समूहमा नराख्ने व्यक्तिहरूसमेत व्यवहारमा एकभन्दा बढी धार्मिक अभ्यास गरिरहेका भेटिन्छन् । के जात, के सम्प्रदाय वर्षभरी प्रकृति पूजा, बालीनालीसम्बन्धी चाडवाड, थानिमानी, डाँडाकाँडा, देवी देउरालीको पूजा गर्ने, बलि दिने गरेको पाइन्छ । एकार्काका चाडपर्व मनाउने, मन्दिर दर्शन गर्ने मात्र हैन हिन्दु भन्नेहरूको पूजा कक्षमा बुद्धको पोस्टर पाइन्छ, बौद्धहरूकोमा शिव, लक्ष्मी, गणेश आदिको । त्यस्तै दैनिक जीवनका समस्याको निदानमा पनि यस्तै सीमारहित आदानप्रदानका अभ्यासहरू गरिन्छन् । कसैले तिनै देवतालाई रक्सी चढाउँछन्, त कसैले दुध, कसैले सुँगुर चढाउँछन् त कसैले कुखुरा, राँगा, बोका, अनि कसैले नरिवल मात्र । धार्मिक बहुलताभित्र आआफ्ना परम्पराअनुसार व्यवहार गर्न त्यहाँ छुट छ ।

विनिर्माणको अनपेक्षित तर सम्भावित नियति

बि.सं. २०१७ सालमा आएर संवैधानिक रूपमा नेपाललाई हिन्दु अधिराज्य घोषणा गरिएको भएता पनि ऐतिहासिक कालदेखि नै हिन्दु धर्मलाई राज्यको संरक्षण प्राप्त हुँदै आएको कुरा निर्विवाद छ । यहाँ स्मरणीय के छ भने जनगणनाअनुसार केही दशक अगाडिसम्म लगभग हरेक १० मा नौ जना र अहिले पनि हरेक पाँचमा चार जना मानिसहरू हिन्दु भएर पनि नेपाल आश्चर्यजनकरूपमा बिना कुनै अवरोध धर्मनिरपेक्ष राष्ट्र भइसकेको छ । यद्यपि धर्मको मामिलामा राज्यको भूमिका पहिले जति विवादित थियो (र केही हदसम्म अझै पनि छ) त्यति नै सरकारी जनगणनाका आँकडाहरू पनि विवादित छन् । प्रजातान्त्रिक वातावरण बनेपछि सन् १९९१ को जनगणनामा हिन्दुबाहेकका अरू रैथाने स्थानीय धर्म संस्कृतिहरूले आफ्नो स्थान र भूमिका विस्तार गर्ने मौका पाए । तर अर्कोतर्फ अध्ययनहरूबाट के देखिन्छ छ भने कतिपय संस्थाहरूले आफ्ना सदस्यहरूलाई हिन्दु धर्मबाट आफ्नो जातीय स्वधर्महरूमा फर्कन उर्दी त दिए तर उनीहरूको पहिचानको राजनीतिबाट

प्रेरित यो सैद्धान्तिक आव्हानले जनव्यवहार र अभ्यासलाई आत्मसात् गर्न सकेको देखिँदैन । सदियौंदेखि गर्दै आएका, चल्दै आएका र परस्परको सांस्कृतिक आदानप्रदानबाट निमार्ण गरिएका मिश्रित धार्मिक सांस्कृतिक आस्था तथा अभ्यासहरूप्रति बेवास्ता गर्दै 'फर्कन' त भनियो तर गन्तव्य कुन हो, किन हो ? र कसरी फर्कने हो? भन्ने चित्त बुझ्दो तार्किक मार्गदर्शन गरिएन । यसबाट फलस्वरूप यहाँ खासगरी दुईओटा अवस्था सिर्जित भएको देखिन्छः पहिलो, व्यवहार एउटा तर राजनीतिक 'करेक्टनेस'को लागि पहिचान अर्कै देखाउनु पर्ने बाध्यता । पछिल्लो समयमा कयौं मानिसहरूलाई आफूले व्यवहारमा एक किसिमको अभ्यास गर्दै आईरहेको भएता पनि दबाबको कारण 'पोलिटिकल करेक्टनेस' को लागि अर्कै किसिमको पहिचान उल्लेख गर्न बाध्य हुनुपरेको अवस्था देखिएको छ ।

दोस्रो, यस्तो जनव्यवहार र राजनीतिक दबाबको बिचमा देखिने असामञ्जस्यताले गर्दा कतिपय मानिसहरूमा आफ्नो धार्मिक स्वाभिमानप्रति हीनभावना विकास हुनु स्वभाविकै हो । यसबाट उनीहरू धर्म परिवर्तनको लागि सक्रीय विदेशी तथा स्वदेशी समूहहरूको चक्करमा परेका र पर्नसक्ने बढी सम्भावना देखिन्छ । नेपाली परम्परागत धार्मिक व्यवहारहरू बहुलताको जगमा अडिएका छन् र यिनीहरूको पश्चिमा धर्महरूजस्तो एकलवादी र विस्तार (प्रचार)वादी परम्परा छैन । यसर्थ रैथाने धर्मको उत्थान हुँदा निसन्देह धार्मिक विविधताको विस्तार हुन्छ र सहिष्णुता पनि मजबुत हुन्छ । तर राज्यले काखी च्यापेको धर्मप्रति विकर्षण र विनिर्माणमा जति शक्ति खर्चिएको देखिन्छ त्यति आफ्नो परम्परागत (प्राकृतिक, कुल आदि) धर्म व्यवहारलाई पुनरुत्थान गर्न ध्यान पुर्याउन सकेको देखिँदैन । एउटा विनिर्माण हुने तर विकल्पको निर्माण गर्न नसक्ने कारण पनि मानिसहरू बिचमा अलपत्र पर्ने सम्भावना हुनसक्छ । यसकारण पनि नेपालमा इसाई धर्मको द्रुतगतिमा विस्तार हुन पुगेको छ । नेपालको पछिल्लो जनगणनाले देखाएअनुसार किराँत र प्राकृतिक लगायत प्रायजसो स्थानीय परम्परागत धर्म मान्नेको संख्या घटेको छ, जसलाई जनगणनाको त्रुटीकोरूपमा मात्र लिनु आफैंमा एक महङ्गो त्रुटी हुनसक्छ । पछिल्लो प्रवृत्तिको आधारमा समग्रमा भन्नु पर्दा नेपालीहरूको धार्मिक बहुआयामिक अवस्थाबाट यस्तो क्षेत्रमा शिघ्र अवतरण भइरहेको छ जहाँ एकलबाहेक अन्य आस्था र अभ्यास अटाउन सक्दैनन् । एकलवादी धार्मिक व्यवहार र अभ्यासमा केवल एक मात्र आस्था मौलाउन सक्छ र अन्य व्यवहारहरू त्यहाँ स्वाभाविकरूपमा विस्थापित हुँदै जानुपर्ने हुनसक्छ ।

अन्तिम कुरा

लेखलाई छोटो सारांशसहित टुङ्ग्याउनु पर्दा निम्न चार कुराहरू दर्शाउन सकिन्छः (क) नेपालीहरू सामान्यतया बहुआयामिक धार्मिक आस्था राख्छन् र सोहीअनुसार व्यवहार अपनाउछन् । (ख) सामान्यतया नेपालका विभिन्न पुराना परम्पराहरू एकापसमा द्वन्द्वात्मक नभएर सामञ्स्यात्मक वा समन्वयकारी छन् र सोहीरूपमा स्वीकार गरिएका छन्, तर्सथ कतिपय प्रतिकूल परिस्थितिमा पनि विभिन्न रैथाने धार्मिक, सांस्कृतिक अभ्यासहरू अस्तित्वमा रहिरहेका छन् । साथै विगतमा राज्यद्वारा प्रायोजित धर्मको विरोधमा आफ्नो मौलिक संस्कृतिको रक्षार्थ चलाइएका अभियानहरूले यी यथार्थलाई आत्मसात् गर्दा मात्र बढी सार्थकता पाउनसक्ने देखिन्छ । (ग) पश्चिमा र अन्य गैरबहुलवादी साँघुरो धार्मिक दार्शनिक 'लेन्स'बाट नेपालीहरूको बहुआयामिक धार्मिक अभ्यासलाई पूर्ण विश्लेषण गर्न सकिँदैन, र त्यस्ता असामञ्स्यात्मक परिवेश रैथाने परम्पराहरूको विकासको लागि प्रतिकूल हुने देखिन्छ । (घ) नेपालीहरूको जनगणना गर्दा बहुआयामिक धार्मिक अभ्यास र पद्धतिलाई चित्रण गर्ने विधिको प्रयोग गर्नु उचित देखिन्छ ।

References

Adhikari, A. 2014. *The Bullet and the Ballot Box: The Story of Nepal's Maoist Revolution*. London: Verso.

Adhikari, J. 2001. 'Mobility and Agrarian Change in Central Nepal' *Contributions to Nepalese Studies* 28(2): 247–67.

Adhikari, K.P. (ed.) 2012. *Nepalis in the United Kingdom: An Overview*. Reading: Centre for Nepal Studies UK.

Adhikari K.P. 2013. 'The Multi-dimensional Religious Practices of Nepalis: A Brief Analysis' *Diaspora Journalism* 1(1): 20–2. (In Nepali) (= Ch. 10 above).

Adhikari, K.P. 2018. 'The First Nepali in England: Motilal Singh and PM Jang Bahadur Rana' *European Bulletin of Himalayan Research* 50–51: 58–76.

Adhikari, K.P. & D.N. Gellner 2016a. 'New Identity Politics and the 2012 Collapse of Nepal's Constituent Assembly: When the Dominant becomes "Other"' *Modern Asian Studies* 50(6): 2009–40.

Adhikari, K.P. & D.N. Gellner 2016b. 'Ancestor Worship and Sacrifice: Debates over Bahun–Chhetri Clan Rituals (*kul puja*) in Nepal' in D.N. Gellner et al. (eds), pp. 226–61.

Adhikari, K.P. & D.N. Gellner 2018. 'The Non-Resident Nepali Movement' in Gellner & Hausner (eds), p. 437–66.

Adhikari, K.P. & C.K. Laksamba 2018. 'Counting Ourselves: CNSUK's 2008 Survey of Nepalis in the UK' in Gellner & Hausner (eds), pp. 303–31.

Adhikari, K.P., C.K. Laksamba, & L.P. Dhakal 2016. 'Social Mobility of Nepalis in the UK: A Case Study of Nepali Migration in Fairfax Road, Farnborough' *Britain–Nepal Society Journal* 40: 26–31.

Allen, M.R. 1987 (1975). *The Cult of Kumari: Virgin Worship in Kathmandu* (2nd ed.). Kathmandu: Mandala Book Point.

Allen, N.J. 2008 (1997). 'Hinduization: The Experience of the Thulung Rai' in Gellner, Pfaff-Czarnecka, & Whelpton (eds), pp. 303–24.

Ammerman, N.T. 2007. *Everyday Religion: Observing Modern Religious Lives*. New York: OUP.

Appadurai, A. 1996. *Modernity at Large: Cultural Dimensions of Globalization*. Minneapolis, MN: University of Minnesota Press.

Arora, V. 2005. 'Being Nepali in Sikkim' *Contemporary India* 24(1): 54–64.

Arora, V. 2007. 'Assertive Identities, Indigeneity, and the Politics of Recognition as a Tribe: The Bhutias, the Lepchas and the Limbus of Sikkim' *Sociological Bulletin* 56(2): 195–220.

Asad, T. 1993. *Genealogies of Religion: Discipline and Reasons of Power in Christianity and Islam*. Baltimore: Johns Hopkins University Press.

Balikci, A. 2008. *Lamas, Shamans and Ancestors: Village Religion in Sikkim*. Leiden: Brill.

Ballard, R. 1996. 'Panth, Kismet, Dharm te Qaum: Continuity and Change in Four Dimensions of Punjabi Religion' in P. Singh & T. Shinder (eds) *Globalisation and the Region: Explorations of Punjabi Identity*. Coventry: Coventry University Press.

Barrett, J.L. 2004. *Why Would Anyone Believe in God?* Walnut Creek CA: Alta Mira Press.

Basch, L.G., N. Glick Schiller, & C. Szanton Blanc 1994. *Nations Unbound: Transnational Projects, Postcolonial Predicaments, and Deterritorialized Nation-States*. Amsterdam: Gordon and Breach.

Baumann, G. 1996. *Contesting Culture: Discourses of Identity in Multi-Ethnic London*. Cambridge: CUP.

BBC 2012. 'Aldershot Football Team Helps Nepalese Integration' www.bbc.co.uk/news/uk-england-hampshire-16796228 (accessed 24 March 2014).

Bell, C. 1992. *Ritual Theory, Ritual Practice*. Oxford: OUP.

Bennett, L. 1983. *Dangerous Wives and Sacred Sisters: Social and Symbolic Roles of High-Caste Women in Nepal.* New York: Columbia University Press.

Bourdieu, P. 1977. *Outline of a Theory of Practice*, tr. R. Nice. Stanford: Stanford University Press.

Brekke, T. 2002. *Makers of Modern Indian Religion in the late Nineteenth Century.* Oxford: OUP.

Briggs, G.W. 1973 (1938). *Gorakhnath and the Kanphata Yogis.* Delhi: Motilal Banarsidass.

Brubaker, R. 2004. *Ethnicity without Groups.* Cambridge, Mass.: Harvard University Press.

Brubaker, R. 2005. 'The "Diaspora" Diaspora' *Ethnic and Racial Studies*, 28(1): 1–19.

Bruslé, T. 2010a. 'Who's in a *labour camp*? A Socio-economic Analysis of Labour Migrants in Qatar' *European Bulletin of Himalayan Research* 35–36: 154–70.

Bruslé, T. 2010b. 'Living In and Out of the Host Society: Aspects of Nepalese Migrants' Experience of Division in Qatar' *Forum Qualitative Social Research* 11(2) (www.qualitative-research.net).

Bruslé, T. 2012a. 'What's New in the Gulf? New Technologies, Consumption and Display of Modernity among Nepali Workers in Qatar' *e-migrinter* 8: 59–73.

Bruslé, T. 2012b 'Nepalese Diasporic Websites: Signs and Conditions of a Diaspora in the Making?' *Social Science Information* 51(4): 593–610.

Bruslé, T. 2014. 'Geographical, Cultural, and Professional Belonging of Nepalese Migrants in India and Qatar' in Toffin & Pfaff-Czarnecka (eds), pp. 159–82.

Burghart, R. 1984. 'The Formation of the Concept of Nation-State in Nepal' *Journal of Asian Studies*, 44: 101–25; reprinted in C.J. Fuller & J. Spencer (eds) (1996) R. Burghart *The Conditions of Listening: Essays on Religion, History and Politics in South Asia.* Delhi: OUP.

Campbell, B. 1995. 'Dismembering the Body Politic: Contestations of Legitimacy in Tamang Celebrations of *Dasai*' *Kailash* 17(3–4): 133–46.

Caplan, L. 1995. *Warrior Gentlemen: 'Gurkhas' in the Western Imagination*. Oxford: Berghahn.

Caplan, L. 2000 [1970]. *Land and Social Change in East Nepal: A Study of Hindu-Tribal Relations* (2nd ed.). Lalitpur: Himal Books.

Carrithers, M. 2000. 'On Polytropy: Or the Natural Condition of Spiritual Cosmopolitanism in India: The Digambar Jain Case' *Modern Asian Studies* 34(4): 831–61.

Chalmers, R. 2002. 'Pandits and Pulp Fiction: Popular Publishing and the Birth of Nepali Print-Capitalism in Banaras' *Studies in Nepali History and Society* 7(1): 31–97.

Chalmers, R. 2003. '"We Nepalis": Language, Literature and the Formation of a Nepali Public Sphere in India, 1914–1940'. Unpublished PhD thesis, SOAS, University of London.

Chandra, B. 1984. *Communalism in Modern India*. Delhi: Vikas.

Chau, A.Y. 2011. 'Modalities of Doing Religion and Ritual Polytropy: Evaluating the Religious Market Model from the Perspective of Chinese Religious History' *Religion* 41(4): 547–68.

Chaves, M. 2010. 'Rain Dances in the Dry Season: Overcoming the Religious Congruence Fallacy' *Journal for the Scientific Study of Religion* 49(1): 1–14.

Chemjong, I.S. 2003 (1948). *History and Culture of Kirat People*. Lalitpur: Kirat Yakthung Chumlung.

Clarke, P.B. & P. Byrne 1993. *Religion Defined and Explained*. Houndmills: Macmillan.

CNSUK 2011. *Directory 2011 of Nepali (Individuals, Businesses and Organisations) in the UK*. Reading: Centre for Nepal Studies UK.

Cohen, N. 2010. 'A Happy Ending for the Gurkhas? Think Again' *The Observer*, 7 March www.theguardian.com/commentisfree/2010/mar/07/nick-cohen-gurkhas-resettlement (accessed 24 March 2014).

Cohen, R. 2008 (1997). *Global Diasporas: An Introduction* (2nd ed.). Abingdon & New York: Routledge.

Dahal, D.R. 2003. 'Social Composition of the Population: Caste/Ethnicity and Religion in Nepal' *2003 Population Monograph Volume I*, Nepal Central Bureau of Statistics website (www.cbs.gov.np).

Das, V. 1977. *Structure and Cognition: Aspects of Caste and Ritual*. Delhi: OUP.

Day, A. 2011. *Believing in Belonging: Belief and Social Identity in the Modern World*. Oxford: OUP.

Des Chene, M.K. 1991. 'Relics of Empire: A Cultural History of the Gurkhas 1815–1987'. Unpublished PhD thesis, Stanford University.

Des Chene, M.K. 1996. 'Ethnography in the Janajati Yug: Lessons from Reading Rodhi and Other Tamu Writings' *Studies in Nepali History and Society* 1(1): 97–161.

Dolfuss, P., M. Lecomte-Tilouine, & O. Aubriot 2001. 'Un araire dans la tête: Réflexions sur la répartition géographique de l'outil en Himalaya' *Techniques & Cultures* 37: 3–50.

Droogers, A. 1989. 'Syncretism: The Problem of Definition, the Definition of the Problem' in J.D. Gort, H.M. Vroom, R. Fernhout, & A. Wessels (eds) *Dialogue and Syncretism: An Interdisciplinary Approach*, pp. 7–25. Grand Rapids, MI: Eerdmans.

Droogers, A. 2009. 'Defining Religion: A Social Science Approach' in P.B. Clarke (ed.) *The Oxford Handbook of the Sociology of Religion*, pp. 263–79. Oxford: OUP.

Durkheim, Emile. 1995 (1912). *The Elementary Forms of Religious Life*, tr. K. Fields. Glencoe IL: Free Press.

Fisher, W.F. 1993. 'Nationalism and the Janajati: Diversity in Ethnic Identity Strengthens Nepali Nationalism' *Himal* 6(2): 11–14.

Fisher, W.F. 2001. *Fluid Boundaries: Forming and Transforming Identity in Nepal*. New York: Columbia University Press.

Fitzgerald, T. 2000. *The Ideology of Religious Studies*. New York: OUP.

Fürer-Haimendorf, C. von 1966. 'Unity and Diversity in the Chetri Caste of Nepal' in C. von Fürer-Haimendorf (ed.) *Caste and Kin in Nepal, India and Ceylon: Anthropological Studies in Hindu-Buddhist Contact Zones*, pp. 11–67. Bombay: Asia Publishing House.

Gaborieau, M. 1972. 'Muslims in the Hindu Kingdom of Nepal' *Contributions to Indian Sociology* 6: 84–105.

Gaborieau, M. 1993. *Ni Brâhmanes, ni ancêtres: colporteurs musulmans du Népal*. Nanterre: Société d'Ethnologie.

Gaenszle, M. 2000. *Origins and Migrations: Kinship, Mythology, and Ethnic Identity among the Mewahang Rai*. Kathmandu: Mandala Book Point & The Mountain Institute.

Gaenszle, M. 2002a. *Ancestral Voices: Oral Ritual Texts and Their Social Contexts among the Mewahang Rai in East Nepal*. Münster, Hamburg, London: LIT Verlag.

Gaenszle, M. 2002b. 'Nepali Kings and Kasi: On the Changing Significance of a Sacred Centre' *Studies in Nepali History and Society* 7(1): 1–33.

Gaenszle, M. 2011. 'Scripturalisation of Ritual in Eastern Nepal' in C. Brosius & K.M. Polit (eds) *Ritual, Heritage and Identity: The Politics of Culture and Performance in a Globalised World*, pp. 281–97. London: Routledge.

Gaenszle, M. 2016. 'Redefining Kiranti Religion in Contemporary Nepal' in Gellner et al. (eds), pp. 326–52.

Gaige, F.H. 2009 (1975). *Regionalism and National Unity in Nepal*. Kathmandu: Himal.

Garnett, J. & G. Rosser 2013. *Spectacular Miracles: Transforming Images in Italy from the Renaissance to the Present*. London: Reaktion.

Geertz, C. 1973. *The Interpretation of Cultures*. New York: Basic Books.

Gellner, D.N. 1986. 'Language, Caste, Religion and Territory: Newar Identity Ancient and Modern' *European Journal of Sociology* 27(1): 102–48.

Gellner, D.N. 1991. 'Hinduism, Tribalism, and the Position of Women: The Problem of Newar Identity', *Man* (N.S.) 26(1): 105–25. Republished as Ch. 13 in Gellner (2001a).

Gellner, D.N. 1992. *Monk, Householder, and Tantric Priest: Newar Buddhism and its Hierarchy of Ritual*. Cambridge: CUP.

Gellner, D.N. 1997a. 'For Syncretism: The Position of Buddhism in Nepal and Japan Compared' *Social Anthropology* 5(3): 275–89. Republished as Ch. 14 in Gellner (2001a).

Gellner, D.N. 1997b. 'Introduction' in D.N. Gellner and D. Quigley (eds) *Contested Hierarchies: A Collaborative Ethnography of Caste among the Newars of the Kathmandu Valley, Nepal*, pp. 1–37. Oxford: Clarendon.

Gellner, D.N. 1999. 'Religion, Politics, and Ritual: Remarks on Geertz and Bloch' *Social Anthropology* 7(2): 135–53. Republished as Ch. 4 in Gellner (2001a).

Gellner, D.N. 2001a. *The Anthropology of Buddhism and Hinduism: Weberian Themes*. Delhi: OUP.

Gellner, D.N. 2001b. 'From Group Rights to Individual Rights and Back: Nepalese Struggles with Culture and Equality' in J. Cowan, M. Dembour, & R. Wilson (eds) *Culture and the Anthropology of Rights*, pp. 177–200. Cambridge: CUP.

Gellner, D.N. 2005. 'The Emergence of Conversion in a Hindu-Buddhist Polytropy: The Kathmandu Valley, Nepal, c. 1600–1995' *Comparative Studies in Society and History* 47(4): 755–80.

Gellner, D.N. 2007. 'Ethnicity and Inequality in Nepal' *Economic and Political Weekly* 42(20): 1823–8.

Gellner, D.N. (ed.) 2009. *Ethnic Activism and Civil Society in South Asia*. New Delhi: Sage.

Gellner, D.N. 2011. 'Belonging, Indigeneity, Rights, and Rites: The Newar Case' in Pfaff-Czarnecka & Toffin (eds), pp. 45–76.

Gellner, D.N. 2013. 'Warriors, Workers, Traders, and Peasants: The Nepali/Gorkhali Diaspora since the Nineteenth Century' in D. Washbrook & J. Chatterji (eds) *Routledge Handbook of South Asian Diasporas*, pp. 136–50. Abingdon & New York: Routledge. (= Ch. 1 above.)

Gellner, D.N. 2014a. 'From Kathmandu to Kent: Nepalis in the UK' *Himal Southasian* 27(4): 38–51. (= Ch. 7 above.)

Gellner, D.N. 2014b. 'The 2013 Elections in Nepal' Asian Affairs, 45(2): 243–61. (bit.ly/1pe2hal)

Gellner, D.N. & S.L. Hausner 2013. 'Multiple versus Unitary Belonging: How Nepalis in Britain Deal with Religion' in A. Day, G. Vincett, & C.R. Cotter (eds) *Social Identities between the Sacred and the Secular*, pp. 75–88. Farnham & Burlington VT: Ashgate. (= Ch. 3 above.)

Gellner, D.N., S.L. Hausner, & C. Letizia (eds) 2016. *Religion, Secularism, and Ethnicity in Contemporary Nepal*. Delhi: OUP.

Gellner, D.N. & S.L. Hausner (eds) 2018. *Global Nepalis: Religion, Culture, and Community in a New and Old Diaspora*. Delhi: OUP.

Gellner, D.N., S.L. Hausner, C. Laksamba, & K.P. Adhikari 2016. 'Shrines and Identities in Britain's Nepali Diaspora' *Diaspora* 19(1) (2010): 116–47. (= Ch. 5 above.)

Gellner, D.N., S.L. Hausner, & B.G. Shrestha 2014. 'Buddhist, Hindu, Kirati, or Something Else? Nepali Strategies of Religious Belonging in the UK and Belgium' in E. Gallo (ed.) *Migration and Religion in Europe: Comparative Perspectives on South Asian Experiences*, pp. 131–53. Farnham: Ashgate. (= Ch. 4 above.)

Gellner, D.N., J. Pfaff-Czarnecka, & J. Whelpton 2008. *Nationalism and Ethnicity in Nepal.* Kathmandu: Vajra Books; previously published as *Nationalism and Ethnicity in a Hindu Kingdom*, 1997, Amsterdam: Harwood.

Graner, E. & G. Gurung 2003. 'Arab ko Lahure: Looking at Nepali Labour Migrants to Arabian Countries' *Contributions to Nepalese Studies* 30(2): 295–325.

Guneratne, A. 1998. 'Modernization, the State, and the Construction of a Tharu Identity in Nepal' *Journal of Asian Studies* 57(3): 749–73.

Gurung, F. 2015. 'State-level Representation versus Community Cohesion: Competing Influences on Nepali Religious Associations in the United Kingdom' in S.L. Hausner & J. Garnett (eds) *Religion in Diaspora: Cultures of Citizenship*, pp. 158–77. Houndmills: Palgrave Macmillan. (= Ch. 9 above.)

Gurung, F. 2018. 'Death and Society: The Performance of Gurung Death Rites in the UK' in Gellner & Hausner (eds), pp. 360–86.

Gurung, H. 1998. *Nepal: Social Demography and Expressions.* Kathmandu: New Era.

Gurung, H. 2003. *Social Demography of Nepal: Census 2001.* Lalitpur: Himal Books.

Haaland, G. 2008. 'Explaining Causes in Evolving Contexts: From Nepali Hill Farmers to Business Managers in Thailand' in B.B. Walters, B.J. McCruy, P. West, & S. Lees (eds) *Against the Grain: The Vayda Tradition in Human Ecology and Ecological Anthropology*, pp. 43–66. Lanham MD: Altamira.

Haaland, G. & P. Gurung 2007. 'Globalization of Interaction Systems and the Culture in Ethnicity: Popular Songs and the Production of Nepali Ethnoscapes in South-East Asia' *The International Journal of Diversity in Organizations, Communities and Nations* 7(3): 77–84.

Hachhethu, K. & D.N. Gellner 2010. 'Nepal: Trajectories of Democracy and Restructuring of the State' in P. Brass (ed.) *Routledge Handbook of South Asian Politics*, pp. 131–46. Abingdon & New York: Routledge.

Hangen, S.I. 2005. 'Boycotting Dasain: History, Memory, and Ethnic Politics in Nepal' *Studies in Nepali History and Society* 10(1): 105–33.

Hangen, S.I. 2007a. 'Between Political Party and Social Movement: The Mongol National Organization and Democratization in Rural East Nepal' in M. Lawoti (ed.) *Contentious Politics and Democratization in Nepal*, pp. 175–98. London: Sage.

Hangen, S. 2007b. *Creating a 'New Nepal': the Ethnic Dimension* (Policy Studies 34). Washington: East-West Center.

Hangen, S.I. 2010. *The Rise of Ethnic Politics in Nepal: Democracy in the Margins*. London: Routledge.

Hausner, S.L. 2005. *The Movement of Women: Migration, Trafficking, and Prostitution in the Context of Nepal's Armed Conflict*, Kathmandu: Save the Children USA.

Hausner, S.L. 2007a. *Wandering with Sadhus: Ascetics in the Hindu Himalayas*. Bloomington: Indiana University Press.

Hausner, S.L. 2007b. 'Pasupatinath at the End of the Hindu State' *Studies in Nepali History and Society* 12(1): 119–40.

Hausner, S.L. 2011. 'Nepali Nurses in Great Britain: The Paradox of Professional Belonging' (COMPAS Working Paper WP-11-90) (www.compas.ox.ac.uk/publications). Republished in Toffin & Pfaff-Czarnecka (eds) 2014, pp. 185–208.

Hausner, S.L. 2013a. 'The Category of the *Yogini* as a Gendered Practitioner' in I. Keul (ed.) *'Yogini' in South Asia: Interdisciplinary Approaches*, pp. 32–44. Milton Park: Routledge.

Hausner, S.L. 2013b. 'Is Individual to Collective as Freud is to Durkheim?' in S.L Hausner (ed.) *Durkheim in Dialogue: A Centenary Celebration of* The Elementary Forms of Religious Life, pp. 167–79. New York & Oxford: Berghahn.

Hausner, S.L. 2016. 'The Performance of Ritual Identity among Gurungs in Europe' *Journal of Ritual Studies* 30(1): 99–108. (= Ch. 8 above.)

Hausner, S.L. & D.N. Gellner 2012. 'Category and Practice as Two Aspects of Religion: The Case of Nepalis in Britain' *Journal of the American Academy of Religion* 80(4): 971–97. (= Ch. 2 above.)

Hitchcock, J.T. & R.L. Jones (eds) 1976. *Spirit Possession in the Nepal Himalayas*. Warminster: Aris & Phillips.

Höfer, A. 1979. *The Caste Hierarchy and the State in Nepal: A Study of the Muluki Ain of 1854.* Innsbruck: Universitätsverlag Wagner. (Reissue 2004, Kathmandu: Himal Books.)

Hoftun, M., W. Raeper, & J. Whelpton 1999. *People, Politics, and Ideology: Democracy and Social Change in Nepal.* Kathmandu: Mandala Book Point.

Holmberg, D. 1989. *Order in Paradox: Myth, Ritual, and Exchange among Nepal's Tamang*. Ithaca, NY: Cornell University Press.

Holmberg, D. 2016. 'Tamang Lhochhar and the New Nepal' in D.N. Gellner, S.L. Hausner, & C. Letizia (eds) *Religion, Secularism, and Ethnicity in Contemporary Nepal*, pp. 302–25. Delhi: OUP.

Hubert, H. & M. Mauss 1964 (1898). *Sacrifice: Its Nature and Function*, tr. W.D. Halls. Chicago: University of Chicago Press.

Huntington, S.P. 1993. 'The Clash of Civilizations?' *Foreign Affairs* 72(3): 22–49.

Huntington, S.P. 2002. *The Clash of Civilizations and the Remaking of World Order*. London: Simon and Schuster.

Hutt, M.J. 1988. *Nepali: A National Language and its Literature.* London/Delhi: SOAS/Sterling.

Hutt, M.J. 1989. 'A Hero or a Traitor? The Gurkha Soldier in Nepali Literature' *South Asia Research* 9(1): 21–32.

Hutt, M.J. 1998. 'Going to Mugalan: Nepali Literary Representations of Migration to India and Bhutan' *South Asia Research* 18: 195–214.

Hutt, M.J. 2003. *Unbecoming Citizens: Culture, Nationhood, and the Flight of Refugees from Bhutan*. Delhi: OUP.

Hutt, M.J. (ed.) 2004. *Himalayan 'People's War': Nepal's Maoist Rebellion.* London: Hurst & Co.

Hutt, M.J. 2008 (1997). 'Being Nepali without Nepal: Reflections on a South Asian Diaspora' in Gellner et al. (eds), pp. 101–44.

Jacobsen, J. 1997. 'Religion and Ethnicity: Dual and Alternative Sources of Identity among Young British Pakistanis' *Ethnic and Racial Studies* 20(2): 238–56.

Jaffrelot, C. 1996. *The Hindu Nationalist Movement and Indian Politics, 1925 to the 1990s: Strategies of Identity-Building, Implantation and Mobilisation*. London: Hurst.

Jest, C. 1991. 'How I Built my House' in G. Toffin (ed.) *Man and his House in the Himalayas: Ecology of Nepal*, pp. 155–60. New Delhi & Bangalore: Sterling Publishers.

Jha, P. 2014. *Battles of the New Republic: A Contemporary History of Nepal*. London: Hurst; Delhi: Aleph.

Jones, D. 2014. 'Joanna Lumley's Legacy of Misery' *Daily Mail* 15 Nov. (www.dailymail.co.uk/news)

Joshi, B.L. & L. Rose 1966. *Democratic Innovations in Nepal: A Case Study of Political Acculturation*. Berkeley: University of California Press.

Kirkpatrick, Col. 1969 (1811). *An Account of the Kingdom of Nepaul*. New Delhi: Manjusri.

Knott, K. 1991. 'Bound to Change? South Asian Religions in Britain' in S. Vertovec (ed.) *Aspects of the South Asian Diaspora*, pp. 86–111. Delhi: OUP.

Krauskopff, G. & M. Lecomte-Tilouine (eds) 1996. *Célébrer le pouvoir: Dasain, une fête royale au Népal*. Paris: CNRS/Maison des Sciences de l'Homme.

Laksamba, C.K. 2012. 'Battlefields to Civvy Street: Gurkha Struggles in Britain' in K.P. Adhikari (ed.), pp. 102–22.

Lawoti, M. 2005. *Towards a Democratic Nepal: Inclusive Political Institutions for a Multicultural Society*. Delhi: Sage.

Lawoti, M. & A. Pahari (eds) 2010. *Maoist Insurgency in Nepal*. New York: Routledge.

Lecomte-Tilouine, M. 2003. 'Sur le de-Sanskritisation des Magars: ethno-histoire d'une groupe sans histoire' *Purusartha* 23: 297–327.

Lecomte-Tilouine, M. 2004. 'Ethnic Demands within Maoism: Questions of Magar Territorial Autonomy, Nationality and Class' in Hutt (ed.), pp. 112–35.

Lecomte-Tilouine, M. 2009. 'Ruling Social Groups—From Species to Nations: Reflections on Changing Conceptualizations of Caste and Ethnicity in Nepal' in Gellner (ed.), pp. 291–336.

Lecomte-Tilouine, M. 2010. 'To Be More Natural Than Others: Indigenous Self-Determination and Hinduism in the Himalayas' in M. Lecomte-Tilouine (ed.) *Nature, Culture, and Religion at the Crossroads of Asia*, pp. 118–57. Delhi: Social Science Press.

Letizia, C. 2005. 'Retourner au Bouddhisme moderne des origines: Remarques sur la diffusion du Bouddhisme Theravada chez les Tharu et les Magars du Népal' *Annales de la Fondation Fyssen* 20: 69–77.

Letizia, C. 2011. 'Shaping Secularism in Nepal' *European Bulletin of Himalayan Research* 39: 66–104.

Letizia, C. 2014. 'Buddhist Activism, New Sanghas and the Politics of Belonging among Some Tharu and Magar Communities of Southern Nepal' in Toffin & Pfaff-Czarnecka (eds), pp. 289–325.

Levine, S. & D.N. Gellner 2005. *Rebuilding Buddhism: The Theravada Movement in Twentieth-Century Nepal.* Cambridge: Harvard University Press.

Lévi-Strauss, C. 1969. *The Raw and the Cooked*, tr. J. & D. Weightman. New York: Harper & Row.

Levitt, P. 2001. 'Between God, Ethnicity, and Country: An Approach to the Transnational Study of Religion' Transcomm Working Paper WPTC-01-13. (www.transcomm.ox.ac.uk)

Levy, R. (with K. Rajopadhyaya) 1990. *Mesocosm: Hinduism and the Organization of a Traditional Newar City in Nepal.* Berkeley: University of California Press.

Lorenzen, D.N. 1972. *The Kapalikas and Kalamukhas: Two Lost Saivite Sects*. Los Angeles: University of California Press.

Lorenzen, D.N. 1999. 'Who Invented Hinduism?' *Comparative Studies in Society and History* 41: 629–59.

Macfarlane, A. 2008 (1997). 'Identity and Change among the Gurungs (Tamu-mai) of Central Nepal' in Gellner et al. (eds), pp. 185–204.

Masuzawa, T. 2005. *The Invention of World Religions, or How European Universalism was Preserved in the Language of Pluralism.* Chicago: University of Chicago Press.

Messerschmidt, D.A. 1976. *The Gurungs of Nepal: Conflict and Change in a Village Society*. Warminster: Aris & Phillips.

Michaels, A. 2016. 'Blood Sacrifice in Nepal: Transformations and Criticism' in D.N. Gellner et al. (eds), pp. 192–225.

Middleton, T. & S. Shneiderman 2008. 'Reservations, Federalism and the Politics of Recognition in Nepal' *Economic and Political Weekly* 43(19): 39–45.

Minami, M. 2007. 'From *tika* to *kata*? Ethnic Movements among the Magars in an Age of Globalization' in H. Ishii, D.N. Gellner, & K. Nawa (eds) *Nepalis Inside and Outside Nepal: Social Dynamics in Northern South Asia*, pp. 443–66. Delhi: Manohar.

Monier-Williams, M. 1877. *Hinduism*. London: Society for Promoting Christian Knowledge.

Moya, J.C. 2005. 'Immigrants and Associations: A Global and Historical Perspective' *Journal of Ethnic and Migration Studies* 31(5): 833–64.

Mumford, S.R. 1989. *Himalayan Dialogue: Tibetan Lamas and Gurung Shamans in Nepal*. Madison: University of Wisconsin Press.

Nakane, C. 1966. 'A Plural Society in Sikkim: A Study of the Interrelations of Lepchas, Bhotias and Nepalis' in C. von Fürer-Haimendorf (ed.) *Caste and Kin in Nepal, India and Ceylon: Anthropological Studies in Hindu-Buddhist Contact Zones*, pp. 213–63. New Delhi: Sterling.

Neupane, G. 2000. *Nepalko Jatiya Prasna: Samajik Banot ra Sajhedariko Sambhavana* (Nepal's Nationality Question: Social Structure and the Possibilities of Compromise). Kathmandu: Centre for Development Studies.

Neupane, G. 2005. *Nepalese Migrants in Delhi*. Kathmandu: Centre for Nepalese Studies.

Onta, P.R. 1996a. 'Creating a Brave Nation in British India: The Rhetoric of Jati Movement, Rediscovery of Bhanubhakta and the Writing of Bir History' *Studies in Nepali History and Society* 1(1): 37–76.

Onta, P.R. 1996b. 'Ambivalence Denied: The Making of Rastriya Itihas in Panchayat Era Textbooks' *Contributions to Nepalese Studies* 23(1): 213–54.

Onta, P.R. 2006. 'The Growth of the *Adivasi Janajati* Movement in Nepal after 1990: The Non-Political Institutional Agents' *Studies in Nepali History and Society* 11(2): 303–54.

Orsini, F. 2002. *The Hindi Public Sphere 1920–1940: Language and Literature in the Age of Nationalism*. Delhi: OUP.

Ortner, S.B. 1990. *High Religion: A Cultural and Political History of Sherpa Buddhism*. Princeton: Princeton University Press.

Ortner, S. 1998. 'The Case of the Disappearing Shamans, Or: No Individualism, No Relationalism' in D. Skinner, A. Pach III, & D. Holland (eds) *Selves in Time and Place: Identities, Experience, and History in Nepal*, pp. 239–67. Lanham: Rowman & Littlefield; also in *Ethos* 23(3), 1995.

Ortner, S. 1999. *Life and Death on Mt Everest: Sherpas and Himalayan Mountaineering*. Princeton: Princeton University Press.

Pandey, G. 1990. *The Construction of Communalism in Colonial North India*. Delhi: OUP.

Pariyar, M. 2011. 'Cast(e) in Bone: The Perpetuation of Social Hierarchy among Nepalis in Britain' (COMPAS Working Paper WP-11-85) (www.compas.ox.ac.uk/publications/).

Pariyar, M. 2018. 'Caste Discrimination Overseas: Nepali Dalits in England' in Gellner & Hausner (eds), pp. 404–34.

Pariyar, M., B.G. Shrestha, & D.N. Gellner 2014. 'Rights and a Sense of Belonging: Two Contrasting Nepali Diaspora Communities' in Toffin & Pfaff-Czarnecka (eds), pp. 134–58. (= Ch. 6 above.)

Pettigrew, J. 1995. 'Shamanic Dialogue: History, Representation and Landscape in Nepal'. Unpublished PhD, University of Cambridge.

Pettigrew, J. 2013. *Maoists at the Hearth: Everyday Life in Nepal's Civil War*. Philadelphia: Pennsylvania University Press.

Pfaff-Czarnecka, J. 1995. 'Migration Under Marginality Conditions: The Case of Bajhang' in Interdisciplinary Consulting Group (eds) *Rural–Urban Interlinkages: A Challenge for Swiss Development Cooperation*, pp. 97–108. Zurich/Kathmandu: INFRAS.

Pfaff-Czarnecka, J. 1996. 'A Battle of Meanings: Commemorating the Goddess Durga's Victory over the Demon Mahisha as a Political Act' *Kailash* 18 (3–4): 57–92.

Pfaff-Czarnecka, J. & G. Toffin (eds) 2011. *The Politics of Belonging in the Himalayas: Local Attachments and Boundary Dynamics*. Delhi: Sage.

Pigg, S.L. 1992. 'Inventing Social Categories Through Place: Social Representations and Development in Nepal' *Comparative Studies in Society and History* 34(3): 491–513.

Pinney, C. 2004. *'Photos of the Gods': The Printed Image and Political Struggle in India*. London: Reaktion.

Pradhan, K. 1982. *Pahilo Pahar* (First Watch). Darjeeling: Shyam Prakashan.

Pradhan, K. 1991. *The Gorkha Conquests: The Process and Consequences of the Unification of Nepal with particular reference to Eastern Nepal*. Calcutta: OUP.

Pradhan, K. 2005. *Darjeelingmā Nepālijāti ra Janajātiya Cinārikā Nayā Adānharu* (M.C. Regmi Lecture 2004). Lalitpur: Social Science Baha.

Pradhan, R. 1994. 'A Native by any other Name' *Himal* 7(1): 41–5.

Ragsdale, T. 1990. 'Gurungs, Goorkhalis, Gurkhas: Speculations on a Nepalese Ethno-history' *Contributions to Nepalese Studies* 17(1): 1–24.

Ramirez, P. 1993. 'Drama, Devotion and Politics: The Dasain Festival in Argha Kingdom' in G. Toffin (ed.) *Nepal, Past and Present*, pp. 47–59. Paris: Editions du CNRS.

Ratanapruck, P. 2007. 'Kinship and Religious Practices as Institutionalization of Trade Networks: Manangi Trade Communities in South and Southeast Asia' *Journal of the Social and Economic History of the Orient* 50(2–3): 325–46.

Reader, I. 1991. *Religion in Contemporary Japan*. Basingstoke: Macmillan.

Regmi, M.C. 1984. *The State and Economic Surplus: Production, Trade, and Resource-Mobilization in Early 19th-Century Nepal*. Varanasi: Nath.

Regmi, M.C. 1999. *Imperial Gorkha: An Account of Gorkhali Rule in Kumaon (1791–1815)*. Delhi: Adroit.

Roos, H. 2014. 'The Mobility of Religion: Settling Jainism and Hinduism in the Belgian Public Sphere' in E. Gallo (ed.) *Migration and Religion in Europe: Comparative Perspectives on South Asian Experiences*, pp. 77–92. Farnham: Ashgate.

Russell, R. 2007. 'Writing Traveling Cultures: Travel and Ethnography among the Yakha of East Nepal' *Ethnos* 72(3): 361–82.

Sadan, M. 2007. *A Guide to Colonial Sources on Burma: Ethnic and Minority Histories of Burma in the India Office Records, British Library*. Bangkok: Orchid.

Sagant, P. 1976. *Le paysan Limbu: Sa maison et ses champs*. Paris: Mouton.

Sagant, P. 1996. *The Dozing Shaman: The Limbus of Eastern Nepal*. Delhi: Oxford University Press.

Samuel, G. 1993. *Civilized Shamans: Buddhism in Tibetan Societies*. Washington DC: Smithsonian Insitution Press.

Sax, W.S. 2010. 'The Problem of Ritual Efficacy' in W.S. Sax, J. Quack, & J. Weinhold (eds) *The Problem of Ritual Efficacy*, pp. 3–16. Oxford: OUP.

Schrover, M. & F. Vermeulen 2005. 'Immigrant Organisations' *Journal of Ethnic and Migration Studies* 31(5): 823–32.

Seddon, D., J. Adhikari, & G. Gurung 2001. *The New Lahures: Foreign Employment and Remittance Economy of Nepal*. Kathmandu: Nepal Institute of Development Studies.

Seddon, D., J. Adhikari, & G. Gurung 2002. 'Foreign Labour Migration and the Remittance Economy of Nepal' *Critical Asian Studies* 34(1): 19–40.

Sharma, J. 2007. 'Mobility, Pathology and Livelihoods: An Ethnography of Forms of Mobility in/from Nepal'. Unpublished PhD dissertation, University of Edinburgh.

Sharma, P. 2008. *Unravelling the Mosaic: Spatial Aspects of Ethnicity in Nepal*. Kathmandu: Social Science Baha/Himal Books.

Shneiderman, S. 2009. 'Ethnic (P)reservations: Comparing Thangmi Ethnic Activism in Nepal and India' in Gellner (ed.), pp. 115–41.

Shneiderman, S. 2011. 'Synthesising Performance and Practice, Securing Recognition: Thangmi Cultural Heritage in Nepal and India' in C. Brosius & K.M. Polit (eds) *Ritual, Heritage and Identity: The Politics of Culture and Performance in a Globalized World*, pp. 202–45. New Delhi: Routledge.

Shneiderman, S. & M. Turin 2006. 'Seeking the Tribe: Ethno-Politics in Darjeeling and Sikkim' *Himal Southasian* 19(2): 54–8, March–April. (www.himalmag.com/2006).

Shrestha, B.G. & D.N. Gellner 2018. 'Invention and Tradition: Limbu Adaptations of Religion in the Diaspora' in Gellner & Hausner (eds), pp. 332–59.

Shrestha, N.R. 1990. *Landlessness and Migration in Nepal*. Boulder: Westview.

Sijapati, B. 2014. 'Being and Belonging: Mapping the Experiences of Nepali Immigrants in the United States' in Toffin & Pfaff-Czarnecka (eds), pp. 233–63.

Singh, P.M. 2006. 'Remittance Economy Nepal's Evolution towards Accepting and Incorporating the Labour of its Overseas Workers' *Himal Southasian* 18(5): 73–7.

Sinha, A.C. 2009. 'Introduction' in T.B. Subba, A.C. Sinha, G.S. Nepal, & D.R. Nepal (eds) *Indian Nepalis: Issues and Perspectives*, pp. 2–27. Delhi: Concept.

Sinha, A.C. & T. Subba (eds) 2003. *The Nepalis in Northeast India: A Community in Search of Indian Identity*. New Delhi: Indus.

Smart, N. 1989. *The World's Religions: Old Traditions and Modern Transformations*. Cambridge: CUP.

Southwold, M. 1978. 'Buddhism and the Definition of Religion' *Man* (N.S.) 13: 362–79.

Steinmann, B. 2003/04. 'National Hegemonies, Local Allegiances: Historiography and Ethnography of a Buddhist Kingdom' *European Bulletin of Himalayan Research* 25/26: 145–67.

Stiller, L.F. 1973. *The Rise of the House of Gorkha: A Study in the Unification of Nepal, 1768–1816*. New Delhi: Manjusri.

Streets, H. 2004. *Martial Races: The Military, Race and Masculinity in British Imperial Culture, 1857–1914*. Manchester: Manchester University Press.

Stroumsa, G. 2010. *A New Science: The Discovery of Religion in the Age of Reason*. Cambridge: Harvard University Press.

Subba, K. 2007. 'Drug Users of Dharan: Aspects of Marginalization' in H. Ishii, D.N. Gellner, & K. Nawa (eds) *Nepalis Inside and Outside Nepal*, pp. 283–306. New Delhi: Manohar.

Subba, T.B. 1992. *Caste, Ethnicity, State and Development: A Case Study of Gorkhaland Movement*. Delhi: Har-Anand & Vikas.

Subba, T.B. 1999. *Politics of Culture: A Study of Three Kirata Communities in the Eastern Himalaya*. Hyderabad: Orient Longman.

Subba, T.B. 2008. 'Living the Nepali Diaspora in India: An Autobiographical Essay' *Zeitschrift für Ethnologie* 133(2): 213–32.

Tamang, M.S., P.S. Chapagain, & P.K. Ghimire 2014. *Social Inclusion Atlas of Nepal: Ethnic and Caste Groups, Vol. 1*. Kathmandu: Central Department of Sociology/Anthropology, Tribhuvan University.

Taylor, C. 1994. 'The Politics of Recognition' in A. Gutmann (ed.) *Multiculturalism: Examining the Politics of Recognition*, pp. 25–73. Princeton: Princeton University Press.

Thapa, D. with B. Sijapati 2004. *A Kingdom under Siege: Nepal's Maoist Insurgency, 1996-2004*. London: Zed.

Thapa, D. 2012. 'In a State of Flux' *Economic and Political Weekly* (Aug 4) 47(31): 41–4.

Thieme, S. 2006. *Social Networks and Migration: Far West Nepalese Labour Migrants in Delhi*. Münster: LIT Publishing.

Thieme, S. & U. Müller-Böker 2004. 'Financial Self-help Associations among Far-west Nepalese Labor Migrants in Delhi, India' *Asian and Pacific Migration Journal* 13(3): 339–61.

Toffin, G. (ed.) 1991. *Man and his House in the Himalayas: Ecology of Nepal*. New Delhi & Bangalore: Sterling Publishers.

Toffin, G. & J. Pfaff-Czarnecka (eds) 2014. *Facing Globalization in the Himalayas: Belonging and the Politics of the Self* (Government, Conflict, and Civic Action, Vol. 5). Delhi: Sage.

Tölölyan, K. 2012. 'Diaspora Studies: Past, Present and Promise' (IMI Working Papers 55) (www.migration.ox.ac.uk/odp).

Uesugi, T. 2007. 'Re-examining Transnationalism from Below and Transnationalism from Above: British Gurkhas' Life Strategies and the Brigade of Gurkhas' Employment Policies' in H. Ishii, D.N. Gellner, & K. Nawa (eds) *Nepalis Inside and Outside Nepal*, pp. 383–410. Delhi: Manohar.

Vandenhelsken, M. 2011. 'The Enactment of Tribal Unity at the Periphery of India: The Political Role of a New Form of the Panglhabsol Buddhist Ritual in Sikkim' *European Bulletin of Himalayan Research* 38: 81–118.

Van der Veer, P. 1994. *Religious Nationalism: Hindus and Muslims in India*. Berkeley: University of California Press.

van Schendel, W. 2005. *The Bengal Borderland: Beyond State and Nation in South Asia.* London: Anthem.

van Spengen, W. 2000. *Tibetan Border Worlds: A Geohistorical Analysis of Trade and Traders.* London: Kegan Paul.

Vertovec, S. 2000a. *The Hindu Diaspora: Comparative Patterns.* London: Routledge.

Vertovec, S. 2000b. 'Religion and Diaspora' Transcomm Working Paper WPTC-01-01 (www.transcomm.ox.ac.uk).

Vertovec, S. 2011. 'The Cultural Politics of Nation and Migration' *Annual Review of Anthropology* 40: 241–56.

Von Stietencron, H. 1997. 'Hinduism: On the Proper Use of a Deceptive Term' in G.-D. Sontheimer & H. Kulke (eds) *Hinduism Reconsidered* (2nd ed.), pp. 32–53. Delhi: Manohar.

Watson, J.L. 1977. 'Introduction: Immigration, Ethnicity, and Class in Britain' in J.L. Watson (ed.) *Between Two Cultures: Migrants and Minorities in Britain,* pp. 1–20. Oxford: Blackwell.

Whelpton, J. 1991. *Kings, Soldiers and Priests: Nepalese Politics and the Rise of Jang Bahadur Rana, 1830–57.* New Delhi: Manohar.

Whelpton, J. 2005. *A History of Nepal.* Cambridge: CUP.

Whelpton, J. 2008 (1997). 'Political Identity in Nepal: State, Nation, and Community' in Gellner, Pfaff-Czarnecka, & Whelpton (eds), pp. 39–78.

Whelpton, J., D.N. Gellner, & J. Pfaff-Czarnecka 2008. 'New Nepal, New Ethnicities: Changes Since the mid 1990s' [new introduction] in Gellner, Pfaff-Czarnecka, & Whelpton (eds), pp. i – xxxii.

White, D.G. 1996. *The Alchemical Body: Siddha Traditions in Medieval India.* Chicago: University of Chicago Press.

Wimmer, A. & N. Glick Schiller 2003. 'Methodological Nationalism, the Social Sciences, and the Study of Migration: An Essay in Historical Epistemology' *International Migration Review* 37(3): 576–610.

Yamanaka, K. 2000. 'Nepalese Labour Migration to Japan: From Global Warriors to Global Workers' *Ethnic and Racial Studies* 23(1): 62–93.

Index